CNBC CREATING WEALTH

CNBC Profit From It Series

CNBC is the recognized global leader in business news, providing real-time financial market coverage and business information to more than 150 million homes and offices worldwide.

Now, bringing their expertise to a collaboration with Wiley, CNBC and Wiley are proud to launch the "Profit From It" book series—a publishing partnership dedicated to demystifying the markets for individual investors and active traders.

CNBC 24/7 Trading: Around the Clock, Around the World
 by Barbara Rockefeller

Money and Power: The History of Business
 by Howard Means

CNBC Creating Wealth: An Investor's Guide to Decoding the Market
 by Brian O'Connell

Available November 2001:
CNBC Profit Drivers: Proven Strategies from Market Leaders
 by Bob Andelman

Available December 2001:
CNBC Guide to the Markets
 by Jeff Wuorio

CNBC CREATING WEALTH

An Investor's Guide to Decoding the Market

BRIAN O'CONNELL

JOHN WILEY & SONS, INC.
New York • Chichester • Weinheim • Brisbane • Singapore • Toronto

Published by John Wiley & Sons, Inc.
Published simultaneously in Canada.

Library of Congress Cataloging-in-Publication Data:

O'Connell, Brian, 1959–
    CNBC creating wealth : an investor's guide to decoding the market / Brian O'Connell.
        p.   cm.
    Includes index.
    ISBN 0-471-39908-6 (alk. paper)
    1. Finance, Personal.   I. Title.

HG179.O2595 2001
332.024—dc21

                                                                            00-068490

10 9 8 7 6 5 4 3 2 1

In 1969, when I was 13 years old, my eighth-grade history teacher decided to teach us how the stock market worked. He rearranged the classroom to look like the New York Stock Exchange. Chairs and desks were turned into trading posts.

A handful of students took up positions at those posts and were assigned to watch over individual stocks. Other students were instructed to run from post to post with buy and sell orders. Our teacher stayed at the chalkboard and posted prices. It was all very exciting stuff for a bunch of California kids who had no idea what a stock was.

The teacher gave the signal, and trading began. I remember running around with my official-looking slips of paper that had company names typed on them—important-sounding names like U.S. Steel, General Motors, and American Telephone and Telegraph. Each slip indicated either a buy or a sell order, and a specific stock price. After we visited a trading post and executed a "trade," we were to run to the chalkboard and deliver the slip. The price was then posted.

Looking back, I marvel at how close we came to achieving the same kind of controlled chaos that I have since witnessed many times, first-hand, at the real New York Stock Exchange.

As trading progressed, our teacher yelled out bits of news about various companies:

"General Motors declares a dividend!"

"AT&T announces a stock split!"

This went on for a while. Then the teacher called out a shocking piece of news.

"Crash!" he yelled. "Stock prices are crashing!"

The activity in the room stopped. What did he say? Prices were crashing? What did that mean?

ACKNOWLEDGMENTS

The efforts of many people went into the making of this book. CNBC and Wiley would like to thank the author, Brian O'Connell. Thanks also to Claire Miller and Tracey Longo for editorial assistance.

The following individuals from CNBC provided input and feedback on the book: Bill Bolster, Bruno Cohen, Andrew Darrow, Patti Domm, Bill Griffeth, Mava Heffler, Howard Homonoff, Charles MacLachlan, and Pamela Thomas-Graham.

At Wiley, the following individuals contributed to the effort: Jeffrey Brown, Mary Daniello, Robin Factor, Greg Friedman, Peter Knapp, Joan O'Neil, David Pugh, and Debra Wishik Englander.

CONTENTS

INTRODUCTION

Now that you've decided you're serious about building personal wealth, you've come to the right place. Since its creation, CNBC has provided in-depth coverage and analysis of the markets, along with breaking news on the broad array of investment opportunities that await you. With this book, *CNBC Creating Wealth,* the goal is to go one step further, to give you the tools you need to understand and interpret critical investment information and make meaningful use of it for your own investment decisions. Whether your dream is to trade stocks from the comfort of your home office or to build a long-term portfolio of mutual funds, this is the definitive primer for understanding how to analyze and select investments that are right for you.

No one has to tell you that the markets today move with almost blinding speed. A splendid investment in the morning may suddenly decline in price by afternoon only to be resurrected by fickle investors early the next day. What's going on in a certain sector of the economy can impact the entire stock market, the bond market, and even money market rates, all the while creating both buying and selling opportunities for savvy investors who are able to act on the information in a timely manner.

How do you become one of those savvy investors? You have to know how to decipher the information. Basically, you have to know what you are looking for. Knowledge and know-how have always been significant factors to harnessing the best of the investment markets, but today, these skills are absolutely critical to success. The days of waiting for a broker to call with the next big investment idea are long gone. With each the World Wide Web. And millions of investors are flocking to investment industry Web sites like CNBC.com and TheStreet.com.

Today's financial junkies can gorge all day on financial news. Up-to-the-minute televised market coverage is carried live by CNBC, and online news services and chat rooms—CNBC.com, the Motley Fool, TheStreet.com, Microsoft Investor, SmartMoney Interactive, and dozens of others—can be visited on the Web. Personal finance magazines such as *Money, SmartMoney, Worth, Bloomberg Personal Finance, Mutual Funds, Kiplinger's Personal Finance, Individual Investor,* jam the newsstands with many offering their own online services.

Even general-interest business publications and, increasingly, mainstream media have embraced personal finance. *TIME* and *Newsweek* now offer regular investment and personal finance columns, and mutual fund and stock quotes are so commonplace they can be found on *Playboy*'s Web site and in your local newspaper.

The Web continues to change the face of investing. Investors turn to it to guide them through the uncertainties of a volatile stock market. Five years ago, a 2 percent one-day swing—in either direction—in the Standard & Poor's 500 was rare. Today, whether they are reacting to a speech by a Federal Reserve official or a bump in the price of pork belly futures, investors tune into CNBC as soon as possible to see how the world markets are reacting.

To keep up with a stock market that seems to move with the speed of a supernova, many investors are turning to the real-time, software-based information tools that are available on the Internet. Just a few years ago, most investors had to go to a library and leaf through copies of *The Wall Street Journal* or *The Economist* to figure out whether it was a good time to buy or sell their stocks. Today, an astounding number of sources on the Internet give much better information and deliver it 10 times faster.

The immediacy of electronic delivery channels meets the needs of today's time-strapped investment consumers. Television and the Internet have helped fuel that trend by removing some of the mystery that had surrounded the stock market. Anyone with a remote control or a Web browser now has access to the kind of information that used to be available only to big firms. Not everyone may want to check basis-point disparities in Portuguese debentures at 1:00 A.M. in their pajamas, but you can if you want to. The end result? A revolution in individual investing. After nearly two decades, more than half of all U.S. households own stocks directly or through mutual funds. The total worth tops the $10 trillion mark, compared to about $5 billion in 1929, $940 billion in 1980, and $2.3 trillion in 1999, according to the U.S. Census Bureau.

IN THE STREET'S SHADOW

But that wasn't always the way. For years, Wall Street insiders had the markets virtually to themselves. A lopsided playing field gave brokers, market makers, traders, and specialists a big advantage over small-account investors. Typically, insiders were in at the start of a stock's run-up and bowed out long before the stock tanked. Individual investors were left holding the bag.

That pattern began in 1792 when a handful of businessmen opened the New York Stock Exchange under a buttonwood tree near Wall Street. The exchange and "The Street" were known as hard-nosed places where great fortunes could be made—but at great risk. Small investors bore the greater brunt of the risk; most investments were for a very short term, and traders on the exchange tended to deal for themselves first, and for their clients if anything was left. According to historian Charles Geisst, the author of *Wall Street: A History* and *100 Years of Wall Street*, rules against predatory trading were in place but were usually drafted to protect the traders from each other. Information was peddled to the highest bidder, and investment advice was often provided by "tipsters," a breed of information merchants who delighted in spreading inside information. After many decades, the fastest form of information became the ticker tape. It reported only prices, not the fundamental information necessary for a good investment decision.

Without good information, Geisst points out, the investor was at the mercy of the market. After the Crash of 1929, financial reformers made substantial gains in cleaning up the markets, and investors eventually benefited. Vastly improved techniques for analyzing risk were developed, along with efforts to introduce what is now called "transparency." Finally, with the major newspapers translating difficult Wall Street jargon into language investors could grasp, investors could finally see what was going on inside; they no longer had to approach the stock market as though it were an impenetrable black box. While these improvements were substantial, small investors were still at a disadvantage to the big players.

For years, the term *investor* meant institutional investor. Pension funds, insurance companies, and mutual funds dominated the markets, acting on behalf of individuals but exercising their own special brand of institutional influence. Their collective financial muscle was both envied and courted by Wall Street. The stock market had become much more congenial for investors in general, but institutional investors were still in the driver's seat.

That began to change, inadvertently, when institutional investors began to advocate for lower commissions. The commissions charged by the New York Stock Exchange, they said, were too high; several threatened to buy their own seats on the exchange if they were not offered lower charges on their trades. As a result, the NYSE introduced negotiated commissions in 1975. The new scheme benefited mostly institutional investors, but it opened the door for individual investors by allowing discount brokers to begin offering bare-bones brokerage services to retail investors.

It was a step in the right direction, but no one could foresee the radical changes that discount brokers—using the World Wide Web—would later introduce. Another 20 years and unforeseen new advances in technology were needed before the full implications of this power shift would be felt. At first, the discounters offered bread-and-butter services, such as executing buy-and-sell orders at commissions lower than those charged by full-service brokers. The only catch was that investors had to know exactly what to do. Investor education was not part of the service. Even so, it became apparent at the dawn of the 1990s that individual investors were suddenly part of the Wall Street world.

EVENING THE SCORE

About the same time that Charles Schwab and Intel began meeting with average investors via online "live" chats in the late 1990s, corporations began responding to the growing numbers of individual investors, and their demands for information and services.

Continuing advances in technology were suddenly creating fast, comprehensive, and cheap information conduits between investors and corporations. More and more "Net freaks" were building stock portfolios, compiling information, manipulating data, and conducting transactions online. Hundreds of thousands of individuals were tapping the Web regularly, easily surfing their way to online resources and corporate Web sites. "We were seeing the democratization of information," says Richard C. Vancil, senior vice president and chief operating officer of Shareholder.com. "At the same time, individuals were feeling liberated and empowered as they did their own research and trading, no longer relying on the filters of brokers."

Information flowing to the investment community is now available equally to institutional *and* individual investors. The professionals retain a big advantage because of their direct access to corporate executives at meetings and through phone conversations. But the table has turned in favor of individual investors, thanks primarily to the Internet.

Audio and visual multimedia and real-time access feeds bring Webcast management presentations directly to investors. Analysts' research on individual companies (presented in video and, for high-profile firms such as Intel, audio format) is available to individuals over the Net. Investors can go to the Internet and access all of the information available from all online services on any given company.

The World Wide Web also offers advantages and benefits that were previously available only to professional investors. Foremost is the convenience of being able to access vast amounts of stock market data and information at any time. Anxious investors no longer have to wait until regular office hours to retrieve critical information from

REAL TIME, ALL THE TIME

Individual investors have significantly leveled the Wall Street professionals' playing field in recent years, but the biggest gains may be yet to come. So far, small investors, using information they couldn't have gotten a few years ago, are researching and trading stocks over the Internet. The cost of trading has plummeted. Some individuals are even prying open the previously cordoned-off world of initial public offerings (IPOs).

Now, through electronic communications networks (ECNs), NYSE Direct+™, and Level II computer trading screens, mainstream investors are slowly gaining access to dramatically advanced market data and to trading tools formerly reserved for institutional investors. Level II screens let investors monitor real-time trading patterns in Nasdaq stocks. ECNs allow them to execute Nasdaq trades directly with other investors rather than through brokers or market makers. Direct+™ provides a service similar to ECNs and the NYSE.

At the moment, these services are largely limited to Wall Street pros and to day traders. But already, experts say, ECNs and Level II screens are popping up on the desktops of average investors. Electronic Communication Networks (ECNs) provide stock trade execution services to market makers through computer networks. The introduction of the network concept to the financial industry in the mid-1990s introduced efficiency to market trading. The Nasdaq network requires market makers to post their customer's trading orders on a network for view by all network members. Legalized by the SEC in 1997, ECNs take the orders posted on their networks and actually execute the trades.

According to Steven Jessup, Tafari Smith, Jordan Bliss, Jonathan Herrmann, Jeffrey Spector, and Eleanny Pichardo Scope, students at The Wharton School of Business at the University of Pennsylvania and the authors of the online report Electronic Communications Networks, current (2000) trading volume on ECNs exceeds the AMEX and regional stock exchanges combined, with ECNs currently comprising up to 29.2 percent of current Nasdaq-Amex daily volume and 5 percent of the New York Stock Exchange (NYSE) daily volume.

Instinet (13 percent market share), Island (11.5 percent), and REDI-Book (1.2 percent) are the three top players in the ECN market, according to the Wharton report.

Previously, many day traders and other investors based their stock decisions on limited Level I data—stock quotes from their brokerage that showed only the market's best bid and ask prices. Most brokerages provided real-time quotes, either in single snapshots or in a stream that tracked each tick. But some quotes were still delayed at least 15 minutes.

Level II data have changed all of that for regular investors. Level II not only shows the market's best bid and offer, but also reports the bids and offers from every market maker and the number of shares available for each bid and offer.

For example, a trader might spot an order to buy 10,000 shares of a stock from one market maker when all of the market makers are offering a total of only 1,000 shares for sale. The trader might reason that the buying pressure will push prices higher. By moving quickly, the trader can ride the wave a bit.

Many investors may not realize that the quotes they see on many financial Web sites aren't real-time prices. They're delayed 15 to 20 minutes—an eternity when a hyperactive market's prices can gyrate wildly from one minute to the next.

In the past, anyone wanting real-time numbers had to pay hefty monthly fees, in part because the Web sites themselves had to buy the data from the New York Stock Exchange or from Nasdaq. Nowadays, however, the intense competition for eyeballs is causing a growing number of Web sites to offer real-time numbers at no charge. Most online brokers give free real-time quotes to their customers. Some firms, such as National Discount Brokers, TDWaterhouse, and E*Trade, give unlimited quotes. Others have monthly "quote banks" (the number of quotes available without additional charges is limited).

Basically, two types of real-time quotes are available on Web sites: (1) snapshot quotes and (2) dynamically updating quotes. A snapshot quote typically lists the last price at which a stock traded. (You must type in the ticker symbol and send in your request.) In addition to CNBC.com, other sites—for example, Microsoft's MSN Money Central (http://www.moneycentral.com) and Thomson Investors Network market itself. If the world markets have record-breaking advances in 2001, Datamonitor predicts that fierce competition will ensue and will drive commission levels down. Online stockbrokers who do not either specialize or diversify will face being swallowed up by retail banks or sunk by market forces. If the global markets suffer a correction and a prolonged bear market ensues, Datamonitor says the online trading enthusiasts lured into the markets by high returns will be scared off, and the remaining customers will pare down their trading activity.

as pension funds, mutual funds, and insurance companies have grown tremendously over the past two and a half decades," offers Jordan. "Today they own about half the publicly traded equities of American corporations. That's up from about 40 percent in 1980 and less than 20 percent in 1971. In 1998, institutions were managing equities valued at more than $4 trillion, or nearly eight times the amount they controlled in 1980."

Those are impressive figures, but Jordan adds that it's important to remember that individual investors still own equities of even greater value—about $10.2 trillion in 2000. That's up from $ 1.2 trillion in 1985. In fact, according to Federal Reserve data, Americans' stock holdings in 1998 surpassed the value of their home equity for the first time in decades.

That's good news for Wall Street, Jordan says. "I think there are some real dangers in an almost exclusively institutional focus," he explains. "Institutions controlling billions in assets and trading millions of shares at a time do provide needed liquidity, and they can move a company's stock price farther and faster than individuals alone. But this is a double-edged sword. Liquidity can quickly become volatility. Because of pressure to show consistently 'up' quarterly performance, some institutions tend to trade stocks frequently, particularly in a down market or when a company has a bad quarter (in other words, at precisely the time management would like to see price stability). They can drive a share price down just as quickly as they can drive it up. And, if most of a company's shares are held by institutions, that short-term

THE INTERNET AS EQUALIZER

Thanks again to the Internet, the barriers that separated professional and amateur investors are crashing down. These days, traders and analysts are apt to browse the same financial Web sites as average surfers.

Fortune magazine recently reported on a top financial analyst who used the World Wide Web to dig up some fresh news on Waste Management Incorporated (WMI), a company the analyst was tracking. By visiting various investment chat rooms, the analyst learned that Waste Management employees were venting about one snafu after another; many were attributable to incompatible computer systems at different units of the company. Some customers were getting multiple bills, others weren't getting any. Too often, the garbage wasn't getting picked up on time—if at all.

The analyst used the chat room postings as a springboard. He developed e-mail contacts with many of the employees and added to his trove of information. Armed with clear evidence suggesting inadequate firmwide systems, as well as other problems, the analyst advised his clients, in no uncertain terms, that something smelled rotten at WMI. Investors who paid heed and sold the stock, or stayed away from it, breathed a sigh of relief a few months later when WMI's share price collapsed. The massive problems came to light and wiped out two-thirds of the company's equity capitalization over a period of weeks. The company was forced to restate its earnings and sent several top executives packing. *Fortune* reported that "no other analyst" turned up what the Web-trawling analyst had uncovered. Welcome to the new world of financial research.

focus can sometimes spill over, creating pressure on management to sacrifice long-term goals for short-term results."

But if institutional investors are crying over the newly competitive investing landscape, they may well be shedding crocodile tears. For all its benefits, cyberspace hasn't completely eroded the biggest advantages that have set institutional investors apart in the bricks-and-mortar world: personal connections, portfolio size, and investing skill. Professional traders and analysts can still get the chief financial officer of any company in America on the phone when they need to, but a retail investor who has 500 or 1,000 shares can't.

Let's face it. The ability to pick up the phone and speak to a top executive is a huge advantage for the big trading houses. At the very least, it gives institutional investors more insight about a company. They may also have the opportunity to get a jump on news. Add to that equation the teams of analysts that professional money managers rely on when they are deciding how to use information.

Unlike most investors, fund managers know which Wall Street analysts are worth listening to. More importantly, they often receive voice-mail calls ahead of the research notes, or they can call the analysts and actually speak to them.

Few fund managers buy or sell stocks based on a recommendation from a securities brokerage firm. Instead, they rely on in-house analysts who are free of the conflicts of interest that many analysts from big brokerage houses face as their firms jockey for the next investment banking deal from the companies they cover.

In some ways, the glut of information now accessible through the Internet—for example, Securities and Exchange Commission filings, product information, and news reports—also puts individuals at a disadvantage. Institutions are in a better position to sift through the information and decide what's really important. However, a recent SEC regulation FD (Fair Disclosure) rule says that information about a company released to securities market professionals must be made public at the same time.

Consider a current trend: Publicly traded companies allow high-end individual traders into their initial public offering information sessions. These sessions, known as "roadshows," have been a staple of Wall Street for years. The CEO and his or her management team visit a brokerage house or a fund firm, lay out a blueprint for the company's future, and ideally walk away with a commitment from the money managers to buy hefty chunks of stock when the stock goes public—at favorable prices, of course. But the most important aspect of roadshows—attendance at the live event itself, rather than an Internet presentation—is still closed to individual investors. Consequently, the backslapping and wink-and-nod information sharing is missed by online observers.

Still, the trading turf today is significantly more user-friendly toward individual traders than at any other point in Wall Street's history.

There's no doubt that the Internet has become capitalism's great equalizer. Even individual investors of modest means can gain access—free, in most cases—to the kind of information that, until recently, was the province of Wall Street's financial elite. And it's not just about access. It's about speed. Real-time stock quotes are available at dozens of sites on the World Wide Web, as are financial calculators that give investors the power to make complicated projections quickly and then know how much money they will need for retirement a few decades hence. Add the interactive nature of many Web offerings—the latest versions of Quicken and Microsoft Money enable you to update your credit card balances and securities portfolios online—and the Web has provided investors with an incredibly powerful driving machine.

Whether you're an old hand at this stuff or just getting started, relax. We've designed this book so all of these tools—technology, analysis, selection, and monitoring—will become familiar aids as you read on and put your skills to the test.

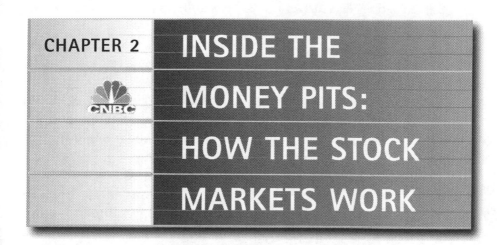

CHAPTER 2

INSIDE THE MONEY PITS: HOW THE STOCK MARKETS WORK

"The world affords no law to make thee rich."

—*William Shakespeare*

It's true there are no guarantees when it comes to investing. But with the creation of online investing, and an aggressive play for smaller investors by the two leading stock markets—the New York Stock Exchange (NYSE) and Nasdaq—buying and selling investments that interest you will only get easier and, as important, less expensive. The grab for company listings and investors by the host of U.S. and international exchanges, will only make it more so. Competition, both domestic and global, will continue to make stock transactions more transparent and more accessible for all investors. By understanding how the different stock markets work and compete for your business, you'll be better equipped to benefit your own investing.

A decade ago, Wall Street commentators likened the battle between the upstart Nasdaq stock market and the venerable, traditional, deeppocketed New York Stock Exchange to a David-and-Goliath affair.

But now the Nasdaq has grown in significance and represents an important indicator for market watchers. Gaining financial market supremacy has been the primary objective, but now a larger battle looms on the online trading front, an area fraught with peril but loaded with opportunity for both exchanges.

To get in condition for the showdown, which industry observers "predict will escalate into an intense fight for market share," both exchanges are cutting costs, shedding excess weight, and looking for new ways to capitalize on the burgeoning online markets.

These two U.S. exchanges are in the midst of a historic restructuring that will shape trading for years, if not generations, to come. As new electronic trading systems challenge the traditional order, Nasdaq has announced that it will go public to bolster its competitive position. Congress and the Securities and Exchange Commission (SEC) are trying to come up with a regulatory scheme to fit this changing environment.

NYSE TRADING COSTS

In this era of increased competition for small investors, the cost of trading stocks on the NYSE is declining. According to a study recently completed by Elkins/McSherry, a New York City consulting firm, the average cost of executing a trade on the NYSE fell by 25 percent in 1998. That tops the price decline of the Nasdaq stock market (23 percent) and makes the Big Board the cheapest exchange, worldwide, for executing a stock trade.

Those figures might surprise some Wall Street observers, many of whom maintain that the NYSE is hard-pressed to compete with Nasdaq and other strictly electronic trading floors. But it doesn't surprise the people paying closest attention. "The biggest single challenge to buyers and sellers is the feeling that a large percentage of trades come before specialists can be matched," says Dick McSherry, president of Elkins/McSherry. "The Nasdaq crowd says that bringing sellers and buyers together and matching them electronically is very doable, but how much of that is really true? In an electronic trading environment, you have anonymity and don't know who the third party is. On the Big Board, you always know who the intermediary is. There's a comfort level there for a lot of people."

McSherry adds that liquidity is another big factor in favor of using a NYSE specialist rather than an electronic trading environment. "Most of the big institutional desks still feel the best place to work an order is on the floor of the NYSE," he explains. "Looking at all the trading numbers we get, the NYSE comes out with the lowest overall trading costs, attributable to the fact that it is still the premier marketplace of the world to get orders executed at the best prices. So the order flow is there. I don't know if that can be matched electronically—at least nobody has done it yet."

For the big financial houses—Merrill Lynch, Goldman Sachs, J.P. Morgan, and other primary potential buyers and sellers of a company's stock—physical proximity to the trading floor is a big advantage. "We sit in the middle of the fund managers, so we're aware of what stocks they may be interested in buying or selling," says one NYSE trader. "So if an opportunity arises, we can say, 'Buy this now,' instead of waiting for a portfolio manager to recognize the situation and formally file an order with the trading desk. That often can minimize market impact costs."

Markets around the world are being forced to change just as rapidly. In Europe, the London Stock Exchange, German Deutsche Boerse, and the Stockholm Stock Exchange have all become public companies while other exchanges have discussed merging or creating common trading platforms. Nasdaq has joined the race by acquiring majority ownership of Easdaq, a pan-European stock exchange now called Nasdaq Europe.

The U.S. markets, prodded by competition and regulation, have taken some steps to drive their costs down. The move to quoting prices in decimals and Nasdaq's implementation of customer-friendly order-handling rules have continued to make trading cheaper in recent years.

A host of factors have contributed to the decline in execution costs: a growing shift toward index investing around the world; the increased use of such trading techniques as splitting large orders; and more intense scrutiny of trading costs by active money managers.

But the most intriguing factor influencing the financial markets may be the heightened competitive pressure from the new, exchange-like trading systems. The electronic communications networks (ECNs), which sprang up largely during 1998 and 1999 command roughly 30 percent of the Nasdaq's volume today. The NYSE has responded by launching Direct+™ to compete with the ECNs. The result? Investors now have more options and more power than ever before.

THE NEW YORK STOCK EXCHANGE

Viewers don't describe it that way the first time they watch it on CNBC, but the seemingly chaotic trading floor of the New York Stock Exchange is in reality a highly structured, regulated, and elegant marketplace.

The New York Stock Exchange is a 36,000-square-foot facility located in the heart of the city's financial district, which is wedged eastward between lower Broadway and the South Street Seaport and extends all the way down to the southern tip of Manhattan.

This oldest stock exchange in the United States uses an agency auction market system, which is designed to allow the public to experience the actual trading as much as possible. Open bids and offers are shouted out by NYSE members acting on behalf of institutions and individual investors. Buy and sell orders for each listed security meet directly on the trading floor in assigned locations. Every listed security is traded in a unique location, at one of the floor's 17 trading posts.

Critics say that as global equity markets restructure and realign, no other exchange has more to lose than the NYSE. Even though the NYSE boasts the biggest trading volumes, the bluest of blue-chip listings, and the greatest liquidity of any stock exchange anywhere, it is increasingly viewed as an anomaly among major world exchanges.

European bourses have switched to nearly all-electronic, dealer-run trading. But, the NYSE has remained committed to its floor-based, face-to-face, continuous-auction market system, which is run by specialists who have exclusive franchises. Increasingly, this has become a source of frustration among the exchange's biggest customers, many of whom face lower share and trading volume because of the competitiveness of online exchange markets.

INSIDE MACHINATIONS

What stocks can you buy on the NYSE? The exchange has guidelines for any companies that wish to list their shares on the exchange. Among the guides for an original listing of a domestic company are: There must be a national interest in the company, and a minimum of 1.1 million shares must be publicly held by 2,000 or more round-lot stockholders. The publicly held common shares must have a minimum aggregate market value of $18 million, and the company's net income in the most recent calendar year must exceed $2.5 million (before federal income tax) and $2 million in each of the preceding two years.

The NYSE also requires that domestic listed companies meet certain criteria with respect to outside directors, audit committee composition, voting rights, and related-party transactions. A company pays a significant initial fee, plus annual fees, to be listed on the NYSE. Initial fees are $36,800 plus a charge per million shares issued. Annual fees (also based on the number of shares issued) are subject to a minimum of $16,170 and a maximum of $500,000. For example, a company that issues 4 million shares of common stock would pay over $81,000 to be listed and over $16,000 annually to remain listed.

A listing on the New York Stock Exchange benefits a corporation in many ways. Because of its size, visibility, and liquidity, the NYSE provides excellent opportunities to raise equity capital. Because it inspires the confidence and broad participation of investors, the NYSE contributes to the fair valuation of a company's shares. And because spreads between the bid and offer prices on the NYSE are narrow, a

NYSE LISTING REQUIREMENTS FOR NON–U.S. COMPANIES

Over 350 non-U.S. companies have their shares traded on the NYSE. To be listed on the NYSE, a non-U.S. company must have:

Size and Earnings:

- Pretax income of $100 million cumulative for the latest three years, with a $25 million minimum for any one of those three years.
- Net tangible assets of $100 million.

Distribution:

- Publicly traded shares worth $100 million.
- 2.5 million publicly held shares.
- 5,000 shareholders who own 100 or more shares.

Listing Fees:

The initial listing fee is between $100,000 and $500,000, based on the number of shares outstanding. Annual fees range between $16,170 and $500,000.

Source: New York Stock Exchange.

listed company's shareholders can realize the best possible price whenever they buy or sell a stock. Figure 2.1 documents some record highs achieved on the NYSE in recent decades.

THE ROLE OF THE SPECIALIST

Although the majority of trading volume (approximately 88 percent) on the NYSE occurs with no intervention from the dealer, specialists play a significant—some say a diminishing—role on the NYSE. Specialists are members of the NYSE or the American Stock Exchange (AMEX)

SELECTED HISTORICAL RECORD HIGHS			
Item	Period	Record	Date/Period
NYSE reported volume	First Hour	581.4	December 15, 2000
(millions of shares)	Day	1,560.8	December 15, 2000
	Week	6,489.6	Week ended December 22, 2000
	Month	26,182.8	March 2000
	Monthly daily average	1,208.8	December 2000
	Quarter	71,848.0	Fourth quarter, 2000
	Quarterly daily average	1,140.4	Fourth quarter, 2000
	Year	262,477.7	2000
	Annual daily average	1,041.7	2000
NYSE reported dollar	Day	$74.5	April 4, 2000
value of trading	Week	$275.1	Week ended March 17, 2000
(billions of dollars)	Month	$1,172.5	March 2000
	Quarter	$3,009.1	First quarter, 2000
	Year	$11,060.0	2000
NYSE reported trades	Day	1,283.9	April 4, 2000
(thousands of trades)	Week	5,859.4	Week ended December 22, 2000
	Month	22,457.2	October 2000
	Monthly daily average	1,085.0	December 2000
	Quarterly	63,668.2	Fourth quarter, 2000
	Quarterly daily average	1,001.6	Fourth quarter, 2000
	Year	221,040.0	2000
	Annual daily average	877.1	2000
NYSE average shares	Day	4,924	June 17, 1988
per reported trade	Week	2,922	Week ended July 1, 1988
	Month	2,568	June 1988
	Year	2,303	1988
NYSE warrant volume	Day	12.6	May 15, 1975
(millions of units)	Week	23.3	Week ended May 16, 1975
	Month	35.9	August 1990
	Year	260.1	1990
NYSE Composite Index	Daily close	677.58	September 1, 2000
Industrial		851.94	August 28, 2000
Transportation		560.33	May 13, 1999
Utility		519.96	March 3, 2000
Finance		651.82	December 28, 2000
NYSE block transactions	Day	1,007.9	December 15, 2000
Volume (millions of shares)	Month	13,911.4	October 2000
	Monthly % of reported vol.	60.6%	June 1988
NYSE block transactions	Quarter	37,547.0	Fourth quarter, 2000
	Quarterly % of reported vol.	58.6%	First quarter, 1995
	Year	135,772.0	2000
	Yearly % of reported vol.	57.0%	1995
	Largest block	52.7	December 31, 1998

Figure 2.1   Stock Market Activity

Source: NYSE Fact Book 2000.

SELECTED HISTORICAL RECORD HIGHS			
Item	Period	Record	Date/Period
NYSE block transactions	Day	35.3	April 4, 2000
(thousands of trades)	Month	560.5	October 2000
	Quarter	1,518.3	Fourth quarter, 2000
	Year	5,529.2	2000
NYSE short interest	Mid-month	4,876.0	December 15, 2000
(millions of shares)			(Settlement date)
NYSE listed securities	Month-end		
Shares (billions)		318.0	November 2000
Market value (billions of dollars)		$12,880.4	August 2000
Securities market credit	Month-end		
Customer margin debt (billions of dollars)		$278.5	March 2000
Free credit balances in margin accounts			
(billions of dollars)		$100.7	December 2000
Free credit balancesin cash accounts			
(billions of dollars)		$85.5	March 2000
Member trading (purchases and sales)			
(millions of shares)			
Total member trading	Month	14,078.5	October 2000
	Year	140,937.0	2000
Specialist	Month	7,403.3	March 2000
	Year	72,290.0	2000
Off-floor	Month	7,054.4	October 2000
	Year	68,464.1	2000
Customers' odd-lot trading	Month	310.8	March 2000
(purchases and sales)	Year	3,021.0	2000
(millions of shares)			
Total round lot short sales			
(millions of shares)			
Total	Month	2,856.5	October 2000
	Year	28,776.6	2000
Specialist	Month	1,440.4	March 2000
	Year	13,129.4	2000
Off-floor	Month	356.6	October 2000
	Year	3,358.8	2000
NYSE membership sale	Cash transfer	$2,650,000	August 23, 1999

Figure 2.1   (Continued)

who perform a unique function by acting as the focal point for trading in the stocks assigned to them. Whether they specialize in the shares of blue chips or of small growth companies (specialist firms are assigned a diverse mix of large and small companies), the job of the specialist is to help maintain fair and orderly markets in those stocks. Specialists also serve as contacts between brokers who bring buy and sell orders to the NYSE's two-way auction market. Figure 2.2 shows the market results for the fifty most active stocks in 1999.

Let's look at how specialists work. Each stock listed on the NYSE is allocated to a specialist, who trades only in specific stocks at a designated location called a *trading post*. All buying and selling of a stock occurs at that location. Buyers and sellers—represented by the floor brokers—meet openly at the trading post to find the best price for a security. The people who gather around the specialist's post are referred to as the *trading crowd*. Bids to buy and offers to sell are made by open outcry. Interested parties are provided with an opportunity to participate, which enhances the competitive determination of prices. When the highest bid meets the lowest offer, a trade is executed.

To a large degree, the specialist is responsible for maintaining the market's fairness, competitiveness, and efficiency.

One of the specialist's key jobs is to act as an agent for the broker by executing orders for floor brokers in their assigned stocks. A floor broker may get an order from a customer who only wants to buy a stock at a price lower than the current market price—or sell a stock at a price higher than the current market price. Given those instructions, the broker may ask the specialist to hold the order and execute it only if and when the price of the stock reaches the level specified by the customer.

MAINTAINING AN ORDERLY MARKET

Each specialist may handle one or more of the stocks listed on the exchange. Specialists are found where the action is—on the floor, orchestrating the fair and capable execution of thousands of publicly traded stocks.

NYSE

Share volume	19,669,704	24,175,307
YTD share volume	203,850,173	262,477,705
Dollar volume	$ 794,547,000	$ 909,271,300
Market value (month end)	$12,296,000,000	$12,372,300,000
Number of companies (month end)	3,025	2,862
Number of issues (month end)	3,748	3,522
Number of initial public offerings	2	2
Average price per share traded	$40.39	$37.61

Amex

Share volume	905,533	1,477,231
YTD share volume	8,230,868	13,318,250
Dollar volume	$ 62,218,992	$ 82,473,867
Market value (month end)	$ 142,107,584	$ 124,926,634
Number of companies (month end)	769	765
Number of issues (month end)	902	894
Number of initial public offerings	0	0
Average price per share traded	$68.71	$55.83

are matched electronically through SuperDOT, the NYSE's Designated Order Turnaround system. (A similar system operates at the AMEX.) Specialists look at the unpaired orders to help determine the price at which a security will open. They may then issue pricing indications that signal imbalances. The traders then send in new orders, or they bridge the buy-and-sell gap by trading from their own account.

THE AMERICAN STOCK EXCHANGE

The American Stock Exchange (AMEX) lists over 700 companies and is the world's second largest auction marketplace. Like the NYSE (the

ANATOMY OF A TRADE

Most market orders for shares on the New York and American stock exchanges are now routed and executed through automated systems; however, many trades still follow this traditional path:

1. The customer sends a buy or sell order to a sales representative at a securities firm.
2. The sales representative sends the buy or sell order to his or her firm's trading department.
3. The order is transmitted to a floor broker on the floor of the New York Stock Exchange or the American Stock Exchange.
4. The floor broker takes the order to the specialist's trading post where the particular security is bought and sold.
5. At the post, the floor broker enters the order.
6. If the floor broker cannot find another floor broker who wants to match the trade, the specialist may fill the order from a limit order on his or her books or by acting as a dealer.
7. The trade is entered in the exchange's system for processing. Within seconds, the trade, including the name of the stock and its price, is recorded on an electronic ticker tape for public display. The data are later fed into other systems for clearance and trade settlement.
8. The floor broker notifies his or her trading desk of the completed trade.
9. The trading desk notifies the sales representative, who then notifies the client.
10. The client takes ownership of the stock.

Source: J.P. Morgan.

largest auction marketplace), the AMEX uses an agency auction market system that is designed to allow the public of investors to meet the sources of public shares as much as possible. (Visit AMEX's home page at www.amex.com.) Regular listing requirements for AMEX include pretax income of $750,000 in the latest fiscal year or in two of the most recent three years; a market value of public float of at least $3 million; a minimum price of $3 per share; and a minimum stockholder's equity of $4 million.

RUNNING WITH THE CYBERBULLS: THE NASDAQ AND HOW IT IMPACTS THE FINANCIAL MARKETS AND YOU

You can't walk down The Street these days without meeting someone who has traded on the Nasdaq.

The Nasdaq Stock Market began operating in February 1971, with 250 companies. It has since evolved into a full-fledged electronic stock

CONTACT INFORMATION

Here's how to contact the stock exchanges in North America:

- American Stock Exchange (AMEX): (212)306-1000; www.amex.com
- Canadian Venture Exchange (Result of the November, 1999 merger of the Alberta and Vancouver stock exchanges): (CVE): (403)974-7400: www.cdnx.ca
- Montreal Stock Exchange (MSE): (514)871-2424: www.me.org
- Nasdaq/OTC: (202)728-8333/8039; www.nasdaq.com
- New York Stock Exchange (NYSE): (212)656-3000; www.nyse.com
- Toronto Stock Exchange (TSE): (416)947-4700: www.tse.com

If you want to know the telephone number for a specific company that is listed on a stock exchange, call the exchange and request to be connected with its "listings" or "research" department.

market with over 5,000 companies listed. Trading volume broke the 500 million shares per day barrier in 1996. In the following year, the Composite Index broke 1,700 and was trading more shares per day than any other U.S. market—some 640 million, worth over $18 billion. On July 16, 1998, the Composite passed 2,000 for the first time in its 27-year history, closing at 2,000.56. On April 1, 1999, the Nasdaq Composite stood at 2560.06. By March 15, 2001, almost two years later, it closed at 1808.

The Nasdaq market is an interdealer market represented by over 600 securities dealers trading more than 15,000 different issues. These

SOME FACTS ABOUT NASDAQ

1. Nasdaq lists more companies than any other stock market in the world.
2. The Nasdaq outpaced all other U.S. markets in 2000, listing more than 88 percent of newly public companies.
3. The Nasdaq Stock Market is unique in that it openly displays competition between market makers.
4. The Nasdaq Stock Market was the world's first electronic stock market.
5. Nasdaq's computer network is capable of trading more than a billion shares per day, scalable to 4 billion by the end of 2001.
6. More initial public offerings (IPOs) are listed on Nasdaq than on any other U.S. stock market.
7. More international companies can be found on Nasdaq than on any other U.S. stock market.
8. More than half the shares that change hands in the United States each day do so on Nasdaq and Amex.
9. The Nasdaq-100 Index has outperformed all major domestic and international indexes during the past 10 years. It rose 86.3 percent in 1998, compared to the previous year, but like international markets spent most of 1999 and 2000 on the rocks, falling 50 percent from its market high in 2000 by year-end.

dealers are called market makers (MMs). Unlike the New York Stock Exchange, the Nasdaq market does not operate as an auction market. Instead, market makers are expected to compete against each other to post the best quotes (best bid/ask prices).

In contrast to traditional floor-based stock markets, Nasdaq has no single specialist through whom transactions pass. Nasdaq's market structure allows multiple market participants to trade stock through a sophisticated computer network linking buyers and sellers from around the world. Together, these participants help ensure transparency and liquidity for a company's stock while maintaining an orderly market and functioning under tight regulatory controls.

Two separate markets comprise the Nasdaq Stock Market: the Nasdaq National Market and the Nasdaq SmallCap Market.

THE NASDAQ NATIONAL MARKET

As the market for Nasdaq's largest and most actively traded securities, the Nasdaq National Market lists more than 4,400 securities. To be listed on the National Market, a company must satisfy stringent financial, capitalization, and corporate governance standards. Nasdaq National Market companies include some of the largest and best known companies in the world.

THE NASDAQ SMALLCAP MARKET

Nasdaq's market for emerging growth companies, the Nasdaq Small-Cap Market, lists nearly 1,800 individual securities. The financial criteria for listing on this smaller capitalization tier of Nasdaq are somewhat less stringent than on the Nasdaq National Market, but the corporate governance standards are now the same. As SmallCap companies become more established, they often move up to the Nasdaq National Market.

Nasdaq's dramatic expansion is proof that it is "both diverse and liquid, and it allows investors access to some of the world's major growth stocks" as it says on its Web site (www.nasdaq.com). The Nasdaq Stock Market's premier index is the Nasdaq 100. Similar to the FTSE 100, it contains 100 of the largest nonfinancial companies listed on the Nasdaq National Market. Each of the 100 components has a market capitalization of at least $500 million and an average daily trading volume of at least 100,000 shares. Nasdaq began trading on January 31, 1986, with a base of 250 companies. By the beginning of 2000, the average value of a Nasdaq company was $6 billion, although that figure is sure to slide after the carnage seen in Nasdaq in 2000. On one day alone—April 4, 2000—the Nasdaq lost 7.6 percent of its value.

The Nasdaq Stock Market is owned and operated by the National Association of Securities Dealers (NASD), a self-regulatory securities industry group to which every U.S. broker and dealer must belong. Completely independent from NASD is NASD Regulation, Inc. which ensures the fair and equal treatment of investors via multiple, highly sophisticated systems of continuous surveillance. For example, the Stock Watch and Automated Tracking (SWAT) System continually monitors the price and volume of each Nasdaq stock and immediately alerts market surveillance analysts when anything abnormal is detected.

NASDAQ IN BLOOM

In Wall Street circles, Nasdaq is known as the market for growth stocks rather than income stocks. Typically, young and fast-moving firms choose to reinvest the bulk of their profits in the business and support their investors by ensuring a steadily rising share price. Most Nasdaq companies are committed to this dynamic philosophy. Very few of the companies listed make dividend payments to shareholders.

So far, the strategy has paid Nasdaq dividends anyway. In recent years, the Nasdaq Stock Market has attracted some household names. Microsoft, Apple, Intel, and Northwest Airlines have chosen to list on Nasdaq.

Buying Stocks on Nasdaq

Executing a Nasdaq trade is easy. An investor who wants to buy or sell stock at the current market price places a *market order*. The multiple market makers in a Nasdaq stock continuously quote prices at which they will buy and sell the stock. The "bid" is the price at which a market maker will buy the stock; the "ask" (or "offer") is the price at which a market maker will sell the stock. The current market price reflects the best of the prices displayed by the multiple market makers—the highest bid and the lowest ask of all the market maker quotes. This is also known as the "inside market" or the "inside quotes." (An investor sells at the highest bid price and buys at the lowest ask price.)

Let's say an investor wants to buy 200 shares of ABCD stock at the best current market price—the lowest ask quotation displayed by any of the market makers in the stock. To do this, the investor calls a broker/dealer and places a market order for the 200 shares. The order is then executed by a market maker at the best (lowest) ask price. In this example, the current "inside" market is $10\frac{1}{4}$ Bid, $10\frac{3}{8}$ Ask. The investor receives the best ask price and buys 200 shares at $10\frac{3}{8}$. [An investor placing a market order to sell 200 shares of ABCD at the same time receives the best (highest) bid price and sells at $10\frac{1}{4}$.]

Orders can also be initiated online through the Internet. An investor uses an online trading account and places the order electronically with an online brokerage. (Schwab will open such an account for $5,000.) The trade order is then executed by a market maker or an ECN at the current best price.

How Is a Trade Executed (Limit Order)?

There are ways to limit your exposure to share price increases or decreases that may occur, particularly during days when there is heavy trading traffic in a stock you want to buy or sell. Investors who want to buy a certain number of shares at a specified price place what is called a *limit order*. Nasdaq's limit order visibility was enhanced with the implementation of SEC Order Handling Rules in 1997. Investors' limit orders, when priced better than the market maker's quote, can now set the inside spread.

Let's suppose an investor wants to buy 200 shares of ABCD stock, and the current best quotes in the market are $10\frac{1}{4}$ to buy, $10\frac{1}{2}$ to sell.

The investor wants to pay only $10\frac{3}{8}$, not the asking price of $10\frac{1}{2}$. The investor decides to place a limit order with a broker for 200 shares at $10\frac{3}{8}$. At $10\frac{3}{8}$ to buy, the limit order is now the most favorable bid price. Under this rule, the market maker must change the bid quote to display the new price and order size (200 shares at $10\frac{3}{8}$), immediately execute the order at the new price, or ship the order to an ECN. The displayed limit order participates directly in the market as the most favorable price to buy, and it appears on the trading screen for all market participants to see.

Exempt from display on trading screens are:

- *Odd lots*—orders of fewer than 100 shares. Odd-lot orders may be accepted and executed by individual firms' proprietary systems.

- *All-or-none limit orders*—limit orders to either buy or sell a security. The broker is directed to attempt to fill the entire amount of the order or none of it. Immediate execution is not required. Firms may accept and execute all-or-none limit orders internally.

Accepted for display are:

- *Round lots*—orders of 100 shares or multiples of 100.

- *Mixed lots*—orders not in 100-share increments (325 shares, for example). Mixed-lot orders are rounded to the next lowest 100-share increment.

- *Good-'til-canceled orders*—orders to either buy or sell a security. They remain in effect until canceled by the customer or until executed.

- *Day orders*—customer orders (to buy or sell a security) that expire automatically at the end of the trading day on which they are entered.

TRACKING THE WILD NASDAQ

In 29 short years, Nasdaq has become the second largest stock market in the world as measured by dollar volume. How did that happen so fast? Let's look at Nasdaq's time line.

1963: The SEC releases a completed study in which it characterizes the over-the-counter (OTC) securities market as fragmented and obscure. The SEC proposes a solution—automation—and charges the National Association of Securities Dealers, Inc. (NASD) with its implementation.

1968: Construction begins on the automated over-the-counter securities system—then known as the National Association of Securities Dealers Automated Quotation—or Nasdaq—System.

1971: Nasdaq celebrates its first official trading day on February 8—the first day of operation for the completed Nasdaq automated system, which displays median quotes for more than 2,500 over-the-counter securities.

1975: Nasdaq establishes new listing standards—which all listed companies are required to meet—that effectively separate Nasdaq-listed securities from other OTC securities.

1980: Nasdaq begins to display inside quotations—the market's best bid and offer prices—on-screen. As a result, both displayed and published spreads decline on more than 85 percent of Nasdaq stocks.

1982: The top Nasdaq companies split off to form the Nasdaq National Market, which requires higher listing standards and offers real-time trade reporting. The new unit will provide investors with broader access to market information.

1984: Nasdaq introduces the Small Order Execution System (SOES). Designed to automatically execute small orders against the best quotations, SOES enhances Nasdaq's trading capacity and efficiency.

1986: The Federal Reserve Board grants Nasdaq National Market stocks marginality. Customers can now purchase these securities on credit extended by a broker/dealer.

1990: Nasdaq formally changes its name to "The Nasdaq Stock Market." Creation of the OTC Bulletin Board (OTCBB) gives investors information on and access to securities not listed on Nasdaq.

1991: Nasdaq National Market securities attain virtual parity with the NYSE and AMEX on blue-sky laws—applicable state laws concerning the registration and sale of new securities. (Note: The National Securities Market Improvement Act of 1996 mandated that all states must exempt Nasdaq National Market securities from state blue-sky regulations.)

1992: Nasdaq International Service begins operation. This allows Nasdaq National Market securities to be traded during early morning hours, when the London financial markets are open. Real-time trade reporting is initiated for the Nasdaq SmallCap Market.

1994: A landmark year: The Nasdaq Stock Market surpasses the New York Stock Exchange in annual share volume.

1997: The SEC approves Nasdaq's request to begin quoting stocks trading above $10 in sixteenths of a dollar. Nasdaq implements new order-handling rules. In combination with Nasdaq's move to quoting in sixteenths, these rules produce better prices and an average spread reduction of 40 percent.

1998: A merger between the NASD and the AMEX creates the Nasdaq-Amex Market Group.

1999: The Nasdaq composite rose an astonishing 86 percent.

2000: Nasdaq falls 47 percent from February to the end of the year.

Source: Nasdaq (www.nasdaq.com).

The result, Nasdaq says, is better prices for investors. For more information on ECNs and global investing, read *CNBC 24/7 Trading Around the Clock, Around the World* by Barbara Rockefeller.

ORDER FLOW ON NASDAQ

Each market maker competes for order flow by displaying bid (buy) and ask (sell) quotations on screen. When an order is received, the market maker will immediately purchase for or sell from his or her own trading account, or will seek the other side of the trade until it is executed, often in a matter of seconds. Market makers can also interact with market orders brought to Nasdaq through ECNs and broker/dealers.

Because Nasdaq distributes trading in a stock among multiple market participants, fluctuations in volume can quickly be absorbed—even on particularly heavy trading days. Unlike the floor-based markets, no halts for order imbalances may occur on Nasdaq.

PRICING ON NASDAQ

A stock price is determined in much the same way as a company's products and services, and is influenced by the following factors:

- *Supply and demand.* The demand for a stock, relative to the number of shares currently available for trading "float," can greatly influence a stock's price. Just as demand for products or services can be influenced through a successful advertising or public relations program, demand for a stock can be escalated by increasing awareness of the stock among investors and analysts through a focused investor relations program.
- *Uncontrollable external influences.* Analysts' recommendations—regarding a company, its sector, or its industry—can influence a stock price. Other factors—the health of the economy,

interest rates, government regulations, the price of gold and other investment fundamentals, news reports, international events—can also have an effect on stock valuation.

NASDAQ TRADING ACTIVITY

Until recently, trading activity on the Nasdaq Stock Market was quotation-driven. Nasdaq market makers competed for investor orders by displaying their quotations—offers to buy and sell stock—on screen. On more traditional markets, trading activity is likely to be order-driven—that is, linked to the flow of incoming orders to buy and sell stock. In 1997, Nasdaq implemented new order-handling rules; certain customer limit orders must be displayed in both market makers' and ECN quotes. Nasdaq is now both quotation- and order-driven, and its evolution has incorporated features of what is sometimes referred to as a "hybrid" market.

BENEFITS OF LISTING

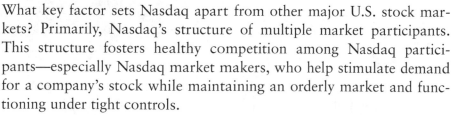

What key factor sets Nasdaq apart from other major U.S. stock markets? Primarily, Nasdaq's structure of multiple market participants. This structure fosters healthy competition among Nasdaq participants—especially Nasdaq market makers, who help stimulate demand for a company's stock while maintaining an orderly market and functioning under tight controls.

In much the same way that multiple distributors help meet increased demand for a company's product, Nasdaq market participants help create increased opportunities for a company's stock to be bought and sold in an orderly fashion. Through both market makers and ECNs, a company's stock is given greater access to available capital, increased visibility in the marketplace, and market qualities that are conducive to immediate and continuous trading.

Many investors became familiar with the Nasdaq Stock Market because of an extensive television advertising campaign that featured the slogan: "The Stock Market for the Next 100 Years."

FUTURE SHOCK

What is ahead for the New York Stock Exchange and the Nasdaq in the early years of this new century?

For starters, there is likely to be more automation and a further consolidation of specialists and market makers operating on both exchanges, as the cut rate costs of online trading continue to take a toll on professional traders and brokers.

For the NYSE, even a limited automated execution system would embrace a new theology and upend the exchange's historical premise: Shares are best traded through a continuous auction market, run by human beings on the floor.

A merger of the two exchanges someday may be the only way the two systems can be accommodated. Major brokerages such as Goldman Sachs, Merrill Lynch, and Morgan Stanley have already proposed the creation of linkages among all the exchanges and trading systems, which would, in effect, put the NYSE and Nasdaq on an equal footing with the leading ECNs. Essentially, that is a plan for a true national market system in which all stocks would trade on basically the same platform.

Under a new linked system, individual exchanges and venues could keep their own identities and offer different types of trading execution and services, but they would all be forced to compete directly with each other in a larger, centralized "virtual market." They would lose their historical trading advantages.

Then there's the question of what to do with the brokers, specialists, and market makers who have stepped up to the plate over the years and made markets in stocks at times when nobody else would. Supporters say that only an experienced market maker who is willing to risk his or her firm's capital can stabilize a tumultuous marketplace. Critics answer that, as technological advances raise questions about the future, there is, among some traders, no doubt that their talent and skill can still outsmart the best alternative trading systems.

With the evolution of electronic trading, the question remains: What will the two major global stock exchanges look like in 2005? Many believe the answer lies in cyberspace.

But whether that transformation takes two or ten years, knowing how the exchanges work, along with their particular advantages and disadvantages, makes you a better-informed investor. It also makes you more capable of buying and selling investments at the right time and price, to add profits, or the potential for them, to your portfolio.

HOW THE DOW JONES AVERAGE IS CALCULATED

It's not rocket science, but the Dow Jones Industrial Average ("the Dow") does have a special way of calculating its stock indexes.

When the Dow was first devised by the *Wall Street Journal* in 1896, its value was calculated by adding up the stock prices of 12 major companies and then simply dividing by 12. The resulting average was expressed in terms of points rather than dollars.

The formula remained the same in 1916 when the Dow was expanded to 20 companies.

After the Dow grew to 30 companies in 1928, the editors began using a new method. The calculation was based on divisors rather than on the number of stocks. This kept the average stable even if one stock was substituted for another or if a company split its stock.

Stock splits occur when a company cancels its shares and issues a larger number of new shares, but at a lower price. For instance, in a 2-for-1 split, the price would be cut in half, but the number of shares would double. Splits create a perception that a stock is cheaper to buy, which sometimes increases demand.

TRIVIAL PURSUITS

- The Dow Jones Industrial Average is named after Charles H. Dow, first editor of the *Wall Street Journal*.
- Of the original 12 stocks that were averaged, the only company that still exists today is General Electric.
- In 1792, a group of 24 men signed an agreement that initiated the New York Stock Exchange. They agreed to sell shares, or parts of companies, among themselves and charge would-be investors commissions, or fees, to buy and sell for them. They found a home at 40 Wall Street in New York City. Their enterprise grew, and they later moved into what is currently the New York Stock Exchange.
- The Nasdaq was created in 1971.
- Nasdaq stands for National Association of Securities Dealers Automated Quotation System.
- The American Stock Exchange (AMEX) merged with Nasdaq in 1998.
- When the American Stock Exchange first began operations, the transactions took place in an outdoor marketplace.
- On the television show *Jeopardy*, under the category of "Famous Ivans," the answer was: "This Ivan called arbitrage the best kept secret on Wall Street." The correct response was: "Who is Ivan Boesky?"
- Nasdaq is the world's largest stock market in dollar-volume terms.

DID YOU KNOW?????

- The NYSE represents 88 percent of the U.S. public equity market.
- Of all volume traded in stock markets, 83 percent takes place among individuals, institutions, and member firms interacting in the auction process.
- On an average day, to keep a fair and orderly market, specialists purchase and sell in excess of $2 billion of stock.
- Of all orders entered through the NYSE's electronic systems, 93.7 percent are executed, and the reports are sent, within one minute.
- During the last decade of the twentieth century, the NYSE spent $1.25 billion on technology for the trading floor.

THE PUBLIC COMES FIRST

The most critical role that a specialist plays is as an intermediary between a buyer and a seller of stock. Often, these buyers and sellers are ordinary people putting their hard-earned money to work in the stock market. Specialists know this and take special or extraordinary measures to ensure that the investing public gets a square deal.

One example of that dedication to the individual investor is known as "price improvement." Through price improvement, NYSE customers save hundreds of millions of dollars each year when their orders are executed at the Specialists' post. Price improvement is rarely offered in a dealer market because any saving by the customer is at the direct expense of the dealer.

Here's a glimpse at how price improvement works. Specialists often "guarantee" to protect a customer at the existing quote while they continue trying to do better. For example, if the quote of XYZ is 20.25 to 20.50, and a 1,000-share buy order comes to the post, the Specialist guarantees an execution of 20.50. The Specialist then attempts to execute the order at 20.375, thereby saving the customer $125 on this trade. Specialists' guarantees routinely result in orders executed at an improved price that saves the customer money.

CHAPTER 3

CNBC

MAXIMIZING YOUR STOCK INVESTMENTS

"There are only two emotions in the stock market—
hope and fear. The problem is, you hope when you
should fear, and you fear when you should hope."
— *Jesse Livermore, a famous Wall Street trader*

It's easy to get caught up in the angst or euphoria the markets can elicit from an even slightly emotional investor during a day of particular volatility in the markets. The purpose of smart investing, however, isn't to be propelled by knee-jerk emotions, but to have a calm, cool investment plan for buying and selling. It's the best way to avoid decisions based on the sheer adrenaline rush of fear or overconfidence and concentrate your resources and attention on staying the course.

As you read through the particular types of risks in this chapter, it's easy to see that any one of them could incite you to sell, or for that matter to buy. But by concentrating on the bigger picture, defining your most comfortable investing style, and taking proven steps to minimize your risk, you'll avoid the most common mistakes investors make. Instead, you'll reap the rewards of decisive investing and measured risk-taking.

That said, there's no reason not to try to achieve what knowledgeable investors call "an edge."

THE VALUE OF COMPANY RESEARCH

As the old adage goes, "To make money in the stock market, you must buy low and sell high." When you are looking for a stock to buy, try to find a company that you believe is undervalued now but will go up in value in the future. Find out all you can about any company whose stock you wish to purchase. These are some of the sources you can use to find out more about a company:

1. *Annual reports.* These reports contain basic information about the company's finances. You can obtain annual reports from a broker, the company's financial department, or the company's Web site.

2. *Form 10-K.* This form includes more detailed data: audited balance sheets, historical stock performance, earnings, and other information. You can get this form from the SEC at (800) 638-8241, at Yahoo!'s SEC filings, and at EDGAR—the Securities and Exchange Commission's Electronic Data Gathering, Analysis, and Retrieval system. The system is intended to benefit electronic filers, enhance the speed and efficiency of SEC processing, and make corporate and financial information available to investors, the financial community, and others, in a matter of minutes. Check it out at www.sec.gov/edgarhp.htm.

3. *Analysts' reports.* Many brokerages will provide financial information and advice on which companies to purchase. You can request analysts' reports from a broker.

4. *Value Line Investment Survey.* This survey contains analyses and detailed historical data on thousands of stocks. Ask for it at a library or order it from Value Line at (800) 633-2252.

5. *Standard & Poor's.* Data on over 5,000 companies are compiled by this source. You can get S&P reports at a library or order them at (800) 221-5277 or www.standardpoor.com.

6. *Moody's Investors Services.* Moody's keeps track of thousands of companies and hundreds of stocks. Their publications are available at libraries or call Moody's at (800) 342-5647, ext. 0546 or www.moodys.com.

7. *Financial Media.* The *Wall Street Journal, Barron's,* and *Investor's Business Daily* are reliable sources for information about stocks and investment markets. They are available at libraries and newsstands or through subscription. Don't be a one-issue jock. Be a reader for a week or two, at least, before you send your money out to increase and multiply. For broadcast programming, check out CNBC, CNNfn, the Bloomberg Network, and WebTV for straight-on business and financial news 24 hours a day.

8. *The Internet.* Many investing sites are available on the Internet. You can visit companies' Web sites and review their recent financial data, or explore some of the many sites that offer investment advice for subscribers. But before you ask for, or pay for, that advice, check out the reputation of the service that wants to advise you. A come-on-in Web page might be only a come-on.

Spend a few minutes in a commodities trading pit, or at an analyst's morning call session, or watching CNBC, and you'll hear the word "edge" a lot.

Investors like having an edge. Who doesn't? Everyone wants an edge. Pedro Martinez may have a 98-miles-per-hour fastball, but he spends hours poring over opposing batters' tendencies just the same. The CEO of a big beer company may have the bulk of the industry's market share, but that doesn't stop him from finding better ways to sell six-packs. Anything for an edge.

The same goes for trading stocks. Whether you're a Wall Street professional with 20 years on the trading floor, or a neophyte who just bought 50 shares of Disney, having an edge, perceived or real, is what stock trading is all about.

So how do you get an edge? There are plenty of obvious ways: Reading everything you can about a company, including press releases, annual reports, and analysts' commentaries; watching for industry trends; following quarterly earnings like a hawk; and so on.

The Wall Street crowd does all those things, but they also do a whole lot more. And now, with the clout provided to you by the Internet, you can too. Let's run down some of the things the experts in the crowd look at, and see how you can take advantage of them.

STOCK MARKET BASICS

A company sells some of its stock when it needs to raise capital for expansion. To raise money without borrowing from a bank, a company can offer shares to investors. An investor who buys stock in a company actually becomes a part-owner or a shareholder.

For example, let's say a company makes a net profit of $200,000. Its owner wants to raise $500,000 so that he can expand the company and increase his income. He decides to "go public"—to sell shares in his company to investors.

The benefit to an investor in this deal is the return on his or her investment—the profit that the company makes for each share of its stock. If the earnings are reinvested in the company, the stockholder may not get the earnings directly, but the growth of the stock will reflect the greater earnings. Let's assume that one investor desires a 10 percent return; for her investment of $500,000, she will expect to receive about $50,000. Of course, she hopes that the company will experience excellent growth after receiving the additional capital and will eventually return much more than 10 percent.

The owner knows that by giving up $50,000 of his income in return for the $500,000, he will relinquish 25 percent of his company ($50,000 divided by $200,000). He also knows that investors will normally pay about ten times the earnings for each portion of the income stream; that is, each investor would pay $50 for each $5 worth of earnings.

The owner then sells 25 percent of his company to investors. By offering (and selling) 10,000 shares at $50 per share, he realizes the $500,000 he needs to expand the company. He now has the capital he needs, and the investors are happy with the expected 10 percent return.

DON'T STICK WITH "BARGAINS"

While we're trained as consumers to find bargains, the stock market works differently than cars, houses, and clothing. It's a mistake to buy a stock simply because it's cheap in terms of absolute dollar value (say, $10.00). Instead, look for a stock that is considered undervalued, regardless of what it actually costs.

The price of a stock is often dependent on its earnings per share. Many other factors can affect the price of a stock: a company's product or service, operating costs, debt, and management, as well as overall market sentiment (general investor confidence). It may be better to own a few shares of a high-priced stock with good earnings growth than many shares in a low-priced stock with poor earnings growth.

WHAT COMPRISES A WINNING STOCK?

Wall Street analysts look for particular characteristics when they evaluate stocks. We have discussed several of those characteristics already in this chapter, but here, in a quick-read list, are four key traits that professional investors look for:

1. A price-to-book-value ratio less than 1.0. Book value is total assets less all debt. A price-to-book-value ratio below 1.0 indicates that the share price of the firm is below the net assets of the firm—an indication that it may be undervalued.
2. Accelerating earnings. This is an indication that the firm may be starting to turn around.
3. High and increasing relative strength. Relative strength is a technical indicator of the price change of a stock relative to the price changes of other stocks. Stocks with strong recent relative strength are considered likely to continue their performance—in other words, their momentum is greater than the market's movement.

(continued)

4. Fewer than 20 million common shares outstanding. This characteristic eliminates the very large firms. Stocks with fewer shares outstanding are considered more likely to have stronger price performance once the market "discovers" them and starts to bid up their share price. The reason? There is less liquidity.

An approach based on these characteristics points toward stocks that are out-of-favor and neglected (low price-to-book value), are starting to turn around financially (accelerating earnings), are just starting to be recognized by the market (high and increasing relative strength), and are likely to register strong price appreciation (lower number of shares outstanding).

For instance, Class A stock of Warren Buffett's Berkshire Hathaway sold for around $67,000 per share in the first quarter of 2001, but it earned $2,000. The actual cost of the stock is extremely high, but its earnings are proportionate to its cost.

REDUCING RISK

Some investors tend to focus only on the upside of putting money in the markets. But the truth is you have to be willing to accept risk in return for reward. In general, the greater the potential for reward, the greater the risk for loss. But as you'll see, understanding the different types of risk associated with stock investing and learning and abiding by investing discipline can go a long way toward mitigating most of the risk that is unnecessary.

Still, the old adage "Don't put all your eggs in one basket" is particularly appropriate advice for investors. If you are creating a portfolio, you want to buy not only a variety of stocks, but stocks from a variety of industries. Allocating some funds to other asset classes, such as bonds, affords additional safety.

In any time period, the financial performance of one industry or sector—pharmaceuticals, for example—may be quite different from the performance of other sectors. When a particular industry is doing well, even stocks without good earnings (in that sector) may appreciate. This happens because positive investor sentiment spills over to other companies, regardless of their performance. An opposite sequence may occur when stocks in a particular sector fall. As you can see in Figure 3.1, there can be dramatic up and down turns in the stock market each month.

When stocks go up, bonds usually go down, and vice versa. The value of gold often rises when currencies are in jeopardy or when stocks on the whole are performing badly. Because there's no way to predict these economic cycles, it's wise to practice risk-reduction strategies— for example, by diversifying your portfolio.

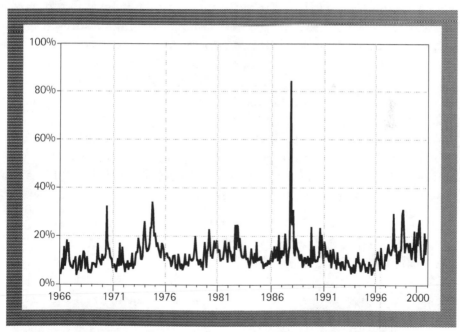

Figure 3.1   Stock Price Volatility of NYSE Composite Index by Month, 1966–2000

Source: New York Stock Exchange Web site (NYSE.com).

*Annualized standard deviation of daily close-to-close percentage price changes for each month.

SECTOR DIVERSIFICATION

The success of a given industry is cyclical, and different industries have different cycles. There's no way to predict these cycles, but you can spread your risk by investing in stocks in a variety of industries. By doing so, you protect your portfolio from being dependent on the fortunes of a single industry.

ASSET ALLOCATION

Asset allocation is the allotment of investment funds to various categories of assets, such as money market funds, stocks, bonds, and precious metals. As with sector diversification, buying different asset classes reduces your overall risk. Although investing in stocks is considered riskier than buying bonds, stocks have a higher return potential; bonds, on the other hand, have fewer and less dramatic price fluctuations. Money market funds, also called cash equivalents, carry even less risk than bonds. Generally, a younger person who expects to work for many years before retiring can take on more risk—in this case, allocate a greater percentage of assets to stocks than to bonds. Someone close to retirement might allocate a higher percentage of funds to bonds because a downturn in the stock market would have a greater effect on his or her resources.

DOLLAR COST AVERAGING

Dollar cost averaging is the practice of investing a fixed amount of money in securities at regular intervals. By doing so, the investor buys more shares of stock when prices are low, and fewer shares at higher prices. The overall cost is less than it would be if the investor were to buy a fixed number of shares at regular intervals.

GETTING TO KNOW RISK AND RETURN

Understanding the relationship between risk and reward is a cornerstone of sound investing. When weighing the risk in particular stocks, consider these factors:

- Returns are not known in advance. Instead, investors must make their decisions using reasonable return expectations, which should mesh with reality.
- All investments carry the possibility that the actual return won't meet expectations.
- The uncertainty surrounding the actual outcome of an investment creates risk; the greater the uncertainty, the greater the risk.
- For many reasons, investors' expectations may not materialize. All investments face each of these risks, but to varying degrees: business or industry risk, inflation risk, liquidity risk, and market risk.
- There is a trade-off between risk and potential returns. The higher the potential returns, the greater the risk; the lower the potential returns, the lower the risk. Be wary of any claims of high returns with low risk.
- In a portfolio, some risks can be reduced or eliminated—with little effect on return—through diversification. Always diversify among asset categories (stocks, bonds, cash), within each category, and among individual securities.
- Diversification is also important across market environments. The longer the holding period, the better. Don't invest in stocks or other volatile investments if you will remain invested for less than five years.
- Do not take on risks for which you will not be compensated.

When you build an investment portfolio, you are simply seeking answers to three questions:

1. What are the risks?
2. What risks can be eliminated or reduced through diversification, and what risks will remain?
3. What returns are associated with the risks I will be undertaking?

WHEN TO SELL

Buying stocks is easy to do; the important decision is when to sell them. Although many newsletters freely recommend good buys, they neglect to provide advice on when to sell. You don't want to sell a stock just as it is starting a spectacular growth spurt, but neither do you want to hold on to a loser, hoping that it will rebound.

There is no way to predict the direction of the overall market. It is also impossible to be sure that a particular stock will appreciate in value. But you can increase your chances of success by basing your buying and selling only on expectations of earnings growth—not on investor sentiment or economic predictions. It's more likely that you will correctly predict the next quarter or two of earnings, than the general market direction.

When it appears that earnings growth for a stock has stopped or slowed, it's time to replace it with a stock that has a better chance of gaining good earnings growth. However, if an earnings growth slowdown seems temporary, you may want to hold the stock. The bottom line is: Hold stock until the earnings growth slows or stops, or until a stock with even better earnings growth comes along. The main drawback to replacing a stock in a taxable portfolio is that you may have to pay [only if there have been significant gains] capital gains taxes.

WHAT DETERMINES STOCK PRICES?

The most important factors in determining stock prices are: the earnings of the company and the cost of those earnings. The value of a company (and the subsequent value of its stock) is proportional to its earnings per share. Generally, if the earnings grow and all other factors remain the same, the stock price will rise.

To make some sense of these countless factors affecting stocks, we ignore any factors that we cannot predict, and we concentrate on the factors that are more predictable. We cannot predict wars, weather, political factors, and similar happenings, so we just ignore them. We concentrate on the reasonably predictable factors—especially those that affect stocks the most.

Among the factors that indicate a good stock are:

- Expectations of high earnings growth during the next year.
- Past history of good earnings growth.
- History of good sales growth.
- Reasonable price-earnings growth relative to the stock's earnings growth.
- Leadership in its field.
- Low relative debt.
- Demand for product or service.

The idea is to find stocks that meet the factors listed above and hold those stocks until the fundamental parameters do not meet those expectations. When the fundamentals fail to meet the parameters desired, the stock should be sold.

PREPARING YOURSELF FOR RISK

Woody Allen once said that 90 percent of life is "just showing up." That's a great line, but don't apply it to your trading habits.

Getting ready to buy and sell stocks like a professional doesn't mean purchasing the best computer and the most sophisticated trade research and execution software. And it doesn't mean subscribing to and reading the most popular investment magazines and newsletters. These are important steps for investors who are just starting out, but they don't account for the human side of the trading experience.

A good stock trader knows that the best equipment and research will help only so much. Success comes from going in, every day, to set limits and boundaries that are not to be crossed, no matter what.

If you know (1) when to bail out of a bad stock, (2) how much you can afford to lose and still sleep at night, and (3) when to leap into a falling market, you possess traits that most new traders don't bring to the table when they log onto E*Trade or Ameritrade for the first time. They are making a big mistake.

If you know, going in, what your limits and expectations are, you're walking with the professionals on Wall Street. (See Figure 3.2.) What are your financial goals? What's your idea of a "safe" investment return? How much can you afford to lose in the market?

Investors have to ask themselves these questions before they can consider trading seriously on Wall Street. The key answer comes in response to one last, critical question: What is your personal tolerance for risk?

An investor's return consists of current income plus capital gains due to growth minus any losses from the investment. Sounds simple, and it is, except that most investors would prefer to know the return before making the investment.

Absent a crystal ball, investors can only make an educated guess as to what return can be expected. An investor whose actual return turns out to be different from the expected return could suffer an unexpected major loss.

Your expectations must be reasonable. Expecting a return of 25 percent just because a stockbroker said that's what a stock will earn is

Index	Compound Annual Return 1926–1997
S&P 500	12.4%
Long term government bonds index	5.3
U.S. Treasury bills index	3.8
Inflation (consumer price index)	3.1

Figure 3.2   Although bonds are a safer investment than stocks, you pay a price for opting for the conservative nature of bonds. As indicated in the chart above, stocks have historically performed significantly better than their fixed income brethren.

Source: Ameritrade.com.

not reasonable. Most expectations are based on what happened in the past, and, unfortunately, history doesn't always repeat itself. On the other hand, there is little else to go on. Reasonable conclusions about future returns can be reached by looking at the past, but those conclusions must be tempered with an understanding that these returns aren't guaranteed.

THE RISK/RETURN TRADE-OFF

According to financial expert and author Maria Crawford Scott, financial market uncertainty creates the potential for higher returns. How? Because of the risk/return trade-off.

"Every investor wants the highest assured return possible," says Scott. "But as we have seen, returns aren't certain, and different investors have varying degrees of uncertainty that they are willing to accept. In fact, each investor seeks the highest possible return at the level of uncertainty, or risk, that he is willing to accept."

In a competitive marketplace, this results in a trade-off: Low levels of uncertainty (low risk) are the most desirable and are therefore associated with low potential returns. High levels of uncertainty (high risk) are the most undesirable and are therefore associated with high potential returns. Over time, a long-term investment strategy such as dollar cost averaging (see Figure 3.3) often makes the most sense.

Over the past 55 years, stocks have produced returns that average 13 percent annually. Long-term bonds have averaged 5 percent annually, and short-term Treasury bills have averaged 4.5 percent annually. These returns reflect the risk/return trade-off.

The trade-off, however, exists on average, not in every single instance. Remember, the uncertainty is the degree of loss you might experience. As an investor, you must analyze each investment and compare the potential returns with the risks. On average, the potential returns from an investment should compensate you for the level of risk you undertake. If they do not—for instance, if low potential returns are associated with high risk—you should not make the investment.

An Easy Way to Minimize Risk

Developing a long-term plan is one of the smartest things an individual can do to become a successful investor.

It is very difficult to mitigate the short-term ups and downs of the market but, a long-term plan makes it easier to ride out these fluctuations. It also allows you to take advantage of some of the simple investment strategies that have proven to be successful over the years.

Dollar-Cost Averaging

Dollar-cost averaging is a classic strategy that actually allows you to benefit from market fluctuations. By consistently investing the same dollar amount at regular intervals you will purchase more shares when prices are low, and fewer shares when prices are high. Let's look at a simple example to illustrate:

Monthly Investment	Share Price	Shares Purchased
$ 600	$20	30
600	15	40
600	12	50
600	20	30
$2,400	$67	150

What is the result of this investing system? We invested $2,400 to purchase a total of 150 shares. But, we've achieved a significant advantage: our average share cost is $16 ($2,400/150), while the average share price over the four months is $16.75 (67/4). Our average cost is $0.75 less than the average price over the same period!

Of course, dollar-cost averaging is not a guaranteed system but it is effective in using market cycles to your advantage. Now let's consider how your plan would add up over the long-run.

Your Long-Term Plan and Compounding

If we assume that you have $10,000 invested today and that you will add $600 a month for the next 25 years (for a total of $180,000). If we assume an average return of 10 percent (and no taxes), your investment will add up to well over $850,000!

This simple example shows the power of compounding and the wisdom of a long-term investment strategy.

Figure 3.3   Time-Tested Strategies for Success

The trade-off also serves as a warning. High potential returns usually flag high risks, even when those risks are not obvious at first glance. Remember those higher-yielding certificates of deposit (CDs) issued by aggressive savings and loans several years ago? CD holders who were unaware of the savings and loans' financial situation and are now trying to collect their guaranteed deposits from the Federal Savings and Loan Insurance Corporation (FSLIC) would probably re-evaluate their decision if they could do it over again.

Not every trader views risk the same way. Dictionaries link risk to possible injury, damage, or loss. Relative to financial investments, risk is more than just an important word—it is a concept. There are different causes for different types of risk. Most people think of risk as a probable loss of principal, but other risk factors are just as important and must be understood and assimilated into any portfolio management strategy.

Risk refers to the volatility of a portfolio's value. The amount of risk investors are comfortable with is an extremely important factor because those who take on too much risk usually panic when they are confronted with unexpected losses. They abandon their investment plans midstream, at the worst possible time. Some investors do become more risk-averse as they get older, but risk tolerance is not necessarily a function of age; conservative *and* aggressive investors go through changes in asset allocation during their life cycle based on their goals and needs.

Which investments are more volatile? Stocks are much more volatile than bonds and cash. Among stocks, small stocks and international stocks are more volatile than large-cap stocks. However, stocks, on average, tend to produce higher total returns over the long term than do bonds or cash.

TYPES OF RISK

The total risk or total variability of return of an asset can be divided into two parts: systemic and nonsystemic. Some risk can be eliminated by diversification (nonsystemic risk) and some cannot (systemic risk). In addition, some risk can be avoided altogether.

So says Michael Leonetti, a Buffalo Grove, Illinois-based financial planner. According to Leonetti, systemic risk is that portion of total variability in return caused by factors that simultaneously affect the prices of all marketable securities. "Changes in the economic, political, and sociological environment that affect securities markets are sources of systemic risk," he says. "Systemic variability of return is found in nearly all securities in varying degrees because most securities move together in a systemic manner." For instance, the prices of nearly all individual common stocks tend to move together in the same manner, which is why nearly all stocks listed on the New York Stock Exchange are highly positively correlated with the rate of change in the New York Stock Exchange index. On average, 30 percent of the variation in a stock's price can be explained by variation in the market index. Interest rate, purchasing power, market, financial leverage, and operating leverage risks (the last two of which are cyclical) can all be described as types of systemic risk.

Nonsystemic risk is that portion of total risk that is unique to a firm or industry. Leonetti cites business changes such as labor strikes, management errors, inventions, advertising campaigns, shifts in consumer taste, and lawsuits as causes of nonsystematic variability of returns in a company. Nonsystemic variations are independent of factors that affect other industries and security markets in general. Nonsystemic risk is caused by factors that affect one firm—or, at most, a few firms—so it must be forecast separately for each firm.

Most investors equate risk with nonsystemic risk. For example, most investors are concerned with whether a bond they buy from a corporation will still be good in the future. The company may go bankrupt, or business may slow down so much that they may not be able to pay interest or fully fund the bond payments at maturity. This type of risk is also known as diversifiable risk; it can be significantly reduced by diversifying investments.

Most investors are aware of the systemic sources of risk (interest rate fluctuations, inflation, and general market risk), but they tend to associate risk with the volatility and price, or the performance results, of a particular investment (nonsystemic risk), and they discount systemic risk. This is a dangerous long-term course for investing. Some examples of nonsystemic risk are: financial leverage, operating leverage (both are noncyclical), management risk, and industry risk.

SOURCES OF SYSTEMIC RISK

Within the two main subdivisions of risk highlighted above—systemic and nonsystemic—there are narrower subcategories.

Interest Rate Risk

Interest rate risk is the variability in return caused by changes in the level of interest rates. All market interest rates tend to move up or down together. To some extent, changes in interest rates affect all securities in the same way. Securities prices move inversely to interest rates because, generally speaking, a security's value is the present value of the security's income. Because the market rate of interest is the discount rate used in calculating securities' present value, all securities prices tend to move inversely with changes in the level of interest rates.

Why does interest rate risk affect the prices of fixed-income securities, such as bonds, more than common stock? Because any change in the rate of return for a fixed-income security must be accomplished solely through capital gain or loss. The interest or dividend payment from a fixed-income security does not vary as long as the issuing firm is solvent. Fixed-income securities may have less business or financial risk than common stock, but they typically have more interest rate risk.

How can investors reduce the swings in value caused by interest rate risk? They can buy short-term bonds, which do not experience the wide swings in the market prices that characterize longer maturities. However, investors in short-term bonds face a series of short-term reinvestments at constantly changing market yields as their bonds mature. Thus, the variability of return from interest rate changes cannot be easily avoided.

Purchasing Power Risk or Inflation Risk

More conservative investors, especially those easily rattled by even short-term downturns in the market, probably believe their safest bet is a federally insured savings account or some Treasury bills, backed by the full faith and credit of the U.S. government. Even more aggressive investors can feel that way, too, when the overall stock market tumbles and it becomes difficult to absorb the losses, however short-term they may be. But there's a good deal of risk in this type of "safe" investing or savings. It's the risk that your money won't earn what you need it to earn to achieve your goals, whether it's the college education of a child or your own retirement. Safe investing is even more detrimental when you factor in inflation.

Because of inflation, there is a chance that the purchasing power of savings or invested wealth will decline. This risk is basically an uncertainty about the future purchasing power of invested funds. Figure 3.4 shows how inflation can erode your purchasing power.

Purchasing power risk is highest in savings accounts, whole life insurance, bonds, and other contracts that typically pay fixed interest rates. When the rate of inflation exceeds the fixed rates of return, the savings suffer a decline in purchasing power.

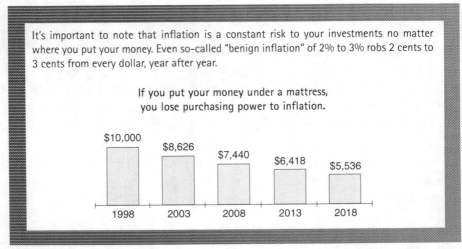

It's important to note that inflation is a constant risk to your investments no matter where you put your money. Even so-called "benign inflation" of 2% to 3% robs 2 cents to 3 cents from every dollar, year after year.

If you put your money under a mattress, you lose purchasing power to inflation.

1998	2003	2008	2013	2018
$10,000	$8,626	$7,440	$6,418	$5,536

Figure 3.4   Inflation as a Risk Factor

Source: Fidelity Investments, 1998.

Assumes inflation rate of 3%.

Business and Industry Risk

The risk here is the uncertainty of an investment's ability to pay investors income, principal, and any other returns, because of a significant fall-off in business (either firm-related or industry-wide) or bankruptcy. A stock, for instance, may fall in value because a firm's earnings have unexpectedly dropped due to bad management calls or an industry-wide slowdown.

Market Risk

Market risk is the chance of loss caused by market fluctuations. At summer's end in 1929, a share of US Steel was selling for over $260. Two and a half years later, the same share was selling for $22. By March of 1937, the share had climbed back to $126, only to fall to $38 a year later. The general market or the economic environment may cause an investment to lose value regardless of the strength of a particular security. When stock drops in value simply because the overall stock market has fallen; this is referred to as stock market risk. A bond doesn't face stock market risk, but it may drop in value because of a rise in interest rates. This is referred to as interest rate risk.

Liquidity Risk

This risk occurs when an investor is not able to get out of an investment conveniently at a reasonable price. If the market is volatile and the investor must sell immediately, he or she may be forced to sell at a significant loss. Another cause can be an inactive market. Selling a house may be difficult simply because there are no buyers.

All investments face each of these risks, but the degree of risk varies greatly. For instance, stocks face much less inflation risk than bonds. Over the past 50 years, bonds have barely kept pace with inflation, but stocks have outpaced inflation by about 8 percent annually. So while short-term bond and money markets are prone to purchasing power or inflation risk, they face little risk due to illiquidity. That's in contrast to stocks. Investors who are forced to sell stocks at an inopportune time suffer a large loss.

SOURCES OF NONSYSTEMIC RISK

Many of the sources of nonsystemic risk are familiar to individuals who invest in and analyze individual stocks and bonds.

Financial Leverage Risk

A company's financial leverage increases with its use of debt financing relative to equity financing. Financing leverage is usually measured with the debt-to-equity ratio or the debt-to-total-assets ratio. Holding all other things constant, shareholders' risk increases with the corporation's use of leverage or debt.

Operating leverage is measured by dividing the ratio of a company's fixed cost by its variable cost. Higher operating leverage results in increased variability of returns for the shareholder. This condition, called *operating leverage risk,* arises because the high fixed cost of maintaining fixed assets continues undiminished whether or not the firm's level of output increases or decreases.

Management Risk

Regardless of a firm's products or its financial position, its management can cause unique and nonsystemic variations in the returns to investors. Management risk is difficult to evaluate. Each firm's management team must be evaluated individually to determine its fitness. This appraisal is particularly important to common stockholders, whose investment returns are most sensitive to management actions.

Sometimes, all the firms in one industry or in a few related industries experience variability of returns because of some common force that does not significantly affect other industries. This is called *industry risk,* and it can stem from many sources. Production or delivery of material supplies may be disrupted. Entire industries can wither on the vine if their products become obsolete. Foreign competition, as represented by the Japanese steel and electronics industries, can quickly disrupt entire domestic industries if they are not competitive and have been unsuccessful in persuading Congress to erect international trade barriers to protect them.

Reducing Risk through Diversification

In a perfect world potential returns should compensate you for risk, but there are some risks that you will not be compensated for, and they should be avoided.

One risk to avoid, is the risk of overconcentration. If you invest in a single security, your return will depend solely on that security; if it flops, your entire return will be severely affected. If held by itself, the single security is highly risky.

If you add other unrelated securities to that single security, the possible outcome changes. If the original security flops, your entire return won't be as badly hurt. By diversifying your investments, you substantially reduce the risk represented by a single security. However, that security's return will be the same whether held in isolation or in a portfolio.

That's where diversification enters the mix. In *What Works on Wall Street,* author James P. O'Shaughnessy maintains that investors always use more than one investment strategy. "Unless you're near retirement and investing only in low-risk strategies, always diversify your portfolio by strategy," he writes. "How much you allocate to each is a function of risk tolerance, but you should always have some growth and value guarding you from the inevitable flow of fashion on Wall Street." The beauty of diversification is that it substantially reduces your risk with little impact on potential returns. The key is to invest in categories or securities that are dissimilar: Their returns are affected by different factors and they face different kinds of risks.

Diversification should occur at all levels of investing. Diversification among the major asset categories—stocks, fixed-income sources, and money market investments—can help reduce market risk, inflation risk, and liquidity risk because these categories are affected by different market and economic factors.

Diversification within the major asset categories—international or domestic stocks or fixed-income products—can further reduce market and inflation risk, and diversification among individual securities helps to shrink business risk.

Time Diversification

Why is it important to stay the course when investing, regardless of what markets are doing? For the same reason you don't want to buy high and sell low. One type of diversification is extremely important yet is often overlooked—time diversification, or remaining invested during different market cycles.

Time diversification helps reduce the risk that you may enter or leave a particular investment or category at a bad time in the economic cycle. Its impact is heaviest on investments that have a high degree of volatility, such as stocks for which prices can fluctuate over the short term. Longer time periods smooth those fluctuations. Conversely, if an investor cannot remain invested in a volatile investment over relatively long time periods, that type of investment should be avoided. Time diversification is less important for relatively stable investments, such as certificates of deposit, money market funds, and short-term bonds. But it grows increasingly more important with longer term stocks, bonds, and mutual funds.

The best example of the benefits of time diversification is in the stock market. During the infamous month of October 1987, the stock market suffered a loss of over 20 percent. But investors who came on board at the beginning of 1987 and remained invested through year-end earned 5.2 percent—not a king's ransom, but certainly better than a loss of 20 percent. Longer time periods illustrate the point even more dramatically. Over the five-year period from 1987 through 1991, which included the market crash, those who remained fully invested in the market earned an average of 15.4 percent annually. Actual annual returns varied between −3.2 percent in 1990 and 30.5 percent in 1991.

Time diversification also comes into play with investments or withdrawals of large sums of money. To reduce risk, it is better to do these transactions gradually rather than all at once.

Time is not often considered by investors, but you should make sure it's a fundamental factor you build into your own investing habits. It will give you an implicit advantage and ensure you don't shoot yourself in the foot when buying or selling assets. The more you can familiarize yourself with the history of the markets you're investing in, and the normal ups and downs they experience, the less prone you'll be to throw the timing of your investments to the wind.

Some risks do decrease as time lengthens. This is particularly true of stock market risk. The longer an investor's holding period, the greater the chance that total and average annualized returns will be positive and higher than those of straight "conservative" fixed-income investments.

Because of this, it can actually be riskier for an investor to become too concerned about whether the stock market is going up or down. "Instead of panicking during market declines," says Leonetti, "investors should expect periodic drops and make the most of them. The real key to making money in stocks is to wait out short-term stock declines." He adds that a decline in stocks is not a surprising event, it's a recurring event—as normal as frigid air in Canada. "If you live in a cold climate and your outdoor thermometer drops below zero, you don't think of it as the beginning of the next ice age. You put on your coat and hat, clean off the walkway, and remind yourself that by summertime it will be warm outside."

With experience, you can even begin to see changes in the markets' direction as buying opportunities for stocks or other investments you believe are suffering from a short-term drop in price. During the past 100 years, there have been 50 occasions when the market declined by 10 percent or more—roughly, once every two years. Of those 50 occasions, there were 15 declines of 25 percent or more—an average of every six years or so. The point is: Expect these declines and take advantage of them by accumulating stocks that you think will perform well in the future. On the other hand, don't put into the stock market any funds that you may need soon, or you will risk being forced to sell during a market decline.

Trying to time the market or attempting to forecast whether the market is at a peak or in a valley—and therefore whether to buy or unload stocks you wouldn't otherwise—seems to be a waste of time. Few people have been right more than once in a row, and the only thing we know for sure is that drops are inevitable. More important: Over time, the market will advance more than it will decline.

UNDERSTANDING GROWTH VERSUS VALUE

There are myriad ways to build a winning stock portfolio—including one's buy, sell, and hold strategies—but two investment styles are popular with Wall Street money managers: (1) growth and (2) value investing. First, the basics. Stocks that are considered to have above-average prospects for long-term growth, based on measures such as earnings, dividends, and book value, are called growth stocks. They may be high-priced, but investors believe they will be rewarded with prices that appreciate even further. Growth stocks generally produce little dividend income because the companies reinvest earnings in research and development.

Value stocks sell at relatively low prices in relation to their earnings, dividends, or book value. They're out of favor with the investment community, and value investors consider them undervalued or bargain-priced. Typically, value stocks produce above-average dividend income.

Although growth and value investors have the same goal—to see their stocks appreciate—they try to achieve that goal in very different ways:

Growth investors look for stocks that have:

- Consistently outperformed the growth rate of the overall market;
- The potential to continue to grow at an above-market rate.

In essence, growth investors believe a stock that performed strongly in the past may continue to do so in the future.

Value investors, meanwhile, seek stocks that:

- Are currently out of favor with investors;
- May have unrealized potential or a higher worth than the market indicates.

Value investors, in other words, are looking to buy valuable assets at sale prices.

Historically, growth and value stocks have gone through cycles of outperforming one another. Stocks that produce relatively high dividends (value stocks) have tended to lag the overall stock market during market upswings and to outperform it during market declines.

Growth stocks tend to be more volatile; they show a wider variation in returns, compared to value stocks. Total return includes both dividends and price appreciation or depreciation. Growth stocks focus on capital appreciation; value stock returns often include more dividend income. This makes value stocks more stable, in general, because many companies pay dividends even when stock prices are declining.

Stocks that appeal to investors who seek growth tend to have an established performance record that is expected to continue. However, a company's present earnings are not as important to growth investors as the expected growth of those earnings. Investors seeking growth theorize that earnings momentum will drive a stock's price higher. But they are not content to invest in profitable companies unless the companies' profits are growing.

In contrast, investors who seek value do not rely on projections of future company growth. They try to identify stocks that are trading at prices lower than those stocks' actual worth, as indicated by the company's fundamentals.

Investors seeking growth often find "diamonds in the rough" among stocks whose performances may be "off" for justifiable reasons, such as a recent restructuring or a temporary short-term trend. These investors are not afraid to pay a premium for stocks that show signs of rapidly increasing in value. Investors seeking value, however, consider buying a stock only if the price is a bargain.

Most growth investment returns come from capital gains, which currently receive preferred tax treatment. Therefore, individuals in high-tax brackets may favor this type of investment. Value investments tend to offer an investor's portfolio more "downside" protection.

Some investors adhere to a single type of investment; others blend value and growth investments in a single portfolio to help lessen its volatility. Such diversification can be accomplished by choosing individual growth and value stocks, by blending growth- and value-oriented mutual funds, or by selecting a fund that already combines the two types of investments.

THE CASE FOR GROWTH STOCKS

Growth stock investors use a balanced approach to determine their buy, hold, and sell strategies. *Fundamental analysis* focuses primarily on all aspects of the earnings of a company—past, present, and future—and helps in determining stocks that are appropriate for a growth portfolio. *Technical analysis* concentrates entirely on a stock's price and volume behavior to determine when to purchase it. Consequently, technical factors are essential in evaluating buy and sell points.

But other distinctions emerge that give credence to advocates for both investment strategies. Here's a look at why growth stocks should remain at the top of an investor's buy list.

Ideas That Pay Off

In today's economy, brains matter much more than brawn. Many prominent growth stocks base their success on technological, scientific, or marketing advances, which are less tangible but potentially far more profitable than capital-intensive assets such as mines and factories. Innovations such as new medicines and computer software can be patented, and powerful retail brands are copyrighted, allowing owners of these products and technologies to charge higher prices and keep profits growing.

Tax Advantage

Compared to value stocks, growth stocks tend to get a larger proportion of their total return from capital appreciation. This occurs because fast-growing companies typically pay low or no dividends; instead, they choose to reinvest their profits in research, marketing, or expansion. Dividends are ordinary income to the investor and are taxed at a top rate of 39.6 percent, but long-term capital gains are subject to a top tax rate of 20 percent. People who invest in taxable accounts are likely to continue to favor low-yielding growth stocks, which may be more tax-friendly than higher-yielding value stocks.

The Dependability Factor

Many top growth stocks have proven track records of solid earnings growth, year after year. Investors like this reliability; it's the reason they have been willing to pay higher price/earnings ratios to own these stocks. Low inflation and low interest rates make reliable growth stocks even more attractive, because they raise the current value that investors place on any given level of projected future earnings.

THE CASE FOR VALUE STOCKS

The key to value investing is being able to determine when a stock's current price does *not* reflect the value of its assets. For example, an investor might look for a stock in which current assets exceed liabilities, on a per-share basis, by more than the market price of the stock. More attention is paid to the financial statement, the brand names, patented technology, and the strength of the management team of the company than to earnings projections per se. The price-earnings (P/E) ratio of the stock is often a key yardstick in deciding whether a stock is under-valued, fairly valued, or overvalued. In a nutshell, value investors place more emphasis on the "fundamentals" of the company than on the stock itself. Their slogan is "Buy low and sell high."

Growth stocks have outperformed value stocks in recent years, but there are plenty of reasons for investors to camp out on the value side of the road. Here are a few of those better reasons.

Historic Cycles

Stock market returns tend to revert to long-term norms. Periods of un-usually high returns tend to be followed by periods of subpar returns, not only for the entire market, but for segments within it. History sug-gests that value stocks can be a good investment over the long haul. The king of all value investors, Warren Buffett, has seen his Berkshire Hath-away stock grow from $12 a share at its inception, to a high of $74,000 a share at the end of 2000—an annual growth rate of 27 percent.

Lower Expectations

Value stocks, as a group, generally trade at lower prices (in relation to earnings, dividends, and book value) because investors have relatively modest expectations for their future growth. Conversely, growth stocks typically carry high price tags because investors assume that past growth will continue indefinitely. Long-range forecasts of corporate earnings are notoriously poor. With expectations low, value stocks don't have to perform miracles to deliver pleasant earnings surprises and enjoy price appreciation.

Spectacular price increases during bull markets may make divi-dends seem irrelevant, but their role in long-term returns is anything but trivial. In a 10-year period from 1988 to 1998, dividends accounted for about 30 percent of the S&P 500 Index's cumulative return of 393 percent. If future returns decline toward long-term averages, dividends will matter even more. When stock prices are static or falling, dividends are the only positive source of returns.

MOMENTUM INVESTING

Before moving on to explain the different types of stocks that are available, a brief discussion of momentum investing, also known as *timing the market* as we've previously discussed, is worthwhile.

Momentum investing relates to the tendency of a stock's price to continue movement in a single direction, whether it is upward, downward, or sideways. Hence, direction—and, more importantly, the timing of the purchase or sale of the stock—is the essence of momentum investing. Substantial attention is given to the price and volume relationships of the stock, and their momentum is the underlying factor behind trend analysis of stock prices. Today's software analysis programs place tremendous importance on the "technical" analysis of a stock's price and volume trend; its aspirants are known as "trend followers." Momentum investing (the opposite of value investing) concentrates on the relative strength of the stock price and volume, and pays little attention to the company's fundamentals. Slogans such as "The trend is your friend" and "Buying high to go higher" are characteristic of this style of investing.

Momentum players like to think about the short term—maybe a few days, or a week. Consequently, they have little concern for earnings or for whether the company produces hula hoops, semiconductors, or steel pipes and tubes. They also have little appreciation for the need to understand the fundamentals of the stock, because the short span of their ownership reduces this to little importance in the decision-making process. As long as the stock "pops," they take the ride and are gone. However, momentum investors seldom ride a stock for long gains of 100 percent, 200 percent, and 400 percent. Instead, they hop on and off the same stock several times, making smaller gains in that stock over shorter bursts of time. They are usually content if they collect 25 to 30 percent profit in a very short period of time. They then move on to the next stock. The shortness of their engagement with a stock eliminates the need for them to do any fundamental analysis of the company itself. To be highly successful, they have to be glued to their screens and working with real-time computer tools. They seldom do well unless they have the best of online data on a real-time basis, plus good visibility of bid and asked spreads and volumes.

THE STOCK MARKET MENU

Stocks come in every shape and size. Some offer higher returns at greater risk; others yield little but provide more safety. The broad range of stocks can be broken down into these six categories:

1. *Growth stocks.* This general term applies to any stock that has a good chance of growing faster than the stock market in general. Investors buy growth stocks because they expect their value to go up in the future. Growth stocks include well-known companies such as Microsoft, Intel, Amgen, and Dell, and obscure ones such as Luby's Cafeterias.

2. *Blue-chip stocks.* Blue-chip companies are those that have had and will continue to have good records. People who invest in blue-chip stocks want some growth but primarily seek a safe investment. Some examples of stocks in this category are: GE, Coca-Cola, and Disney.

3. *Income stocks.* These stocks pay fairly high dividends, often providing stockholders with a decent income. Utility companies, real estate, and chemical corporations' stocks are in this category.

4. *Cyclical stocks.* Stocks in this category react sharply to turns in the business cycle. They do well in a strong economy but drop in a recession. The stock of automobile manufacturers, airlines, and steel companies can be considered cyclical stock.

5. *Defensive stocks.* People buy defensive stocks to protect themselves against a recession. The business cycle does not greatly affect industries such as food, beverage, and tobacco, which people use regardless of the economy.

6. *Speculative stocks.* As the name implies, these stocks are extremely risky investments. Investors who purchase speculative

stocks hope for a spectacular profit in a short period of time. Some examples of speculative stocks are penny stocks and extremely high P/E stocks.

CHOOSING STOCKS

Knowing which stock categories to choose from is important, but knowing what to look for when researching those categories is just as crucial. Here are the items investors should research on a company's profit-and-loss statement before they buy its stock.

1. *Earnings.* This number tells you the company's profit. By dividing the earnings by the number of shares outstanding, you can find the earnings per share. Check to make sure the earnings came from routine operations (e.g., sales) and not from a one-time occurrence (e.g., winning a lawsuit). Also, review the past earnings. Look for a company that has had strong earnings growth in the past several years and also has a low dividend payout ratio—an indication that the company reinvests most of its money back into the business.

2. *Price-earnings (P/E) ratio.* This number tells you how much investors are willing to pay for one dollar of the company's earnings. The Standard & Poor's 500 stock index usually has a P/E between 10 and 20. Stocks with a low P/E ratio trade at a discount; those with a high P/E trade at a premium. Stocks that trade at a premium can plummet during bad quarters, whereas discount stocks are not generally affected by bad news and can quickly rise in response to favorable earnings reports. When deciding which stocks to buy, look for those with a lower P/E ratio than others in its industry.

3. *Book value.* Also called shareholders' equity, book value equals the company's assets minus its liabilities. Usually, the stock price is higher than the book value per share (but not always). In general, the lower the stock price relative to the book

value per share, the better the value. Look for stocks trading for no more than 1.3 times book value.

4. *Return on equity.* Defined as net profit divided by the book value, return on equity shows how well the company has been doing. Look for companies with a high return on equity relative to others in its industry. Generally, you want a value of 15 percent or higher.

5. *Debt-equity ratio.* This is the company's debt divided by shareholders' equity. Choose companies with low debt-equity ratios—preferably, below 35 percent.

6. *Price volatility.* This quantity, usually measured by the beta, reflects the amount the stock moves in relation to the S&P 500. For example, a beta of 1.5 means it moves up or down 1.5 times as much as the S&P 500. Its volatility is related to risk. If a stock has a high beta, you have reason to expect a high return to justify its purchase.

INDICATORS THE PROS LOOK FOR

Knowing what to look for when choosing a stock is the cornerstone of investing. As shown above, there are some obvious signposts along the way, but other indicators are not so obvious. Money managers still have a few tricks up their sleeve when they are trying to figure out which way the market is headed. Some clues are more obvious than you think, but most aren't easily noticed. Here's a rundown of what the professionals check when their money's on the line.

HOW TO FIND OUT WHERE THE MARKET IS GOING

Want a quick and easy way to determine the stock market's general direction? Many Wall Street insiders like to see whether the discount rate is greater than the T-bill rate. If so, the outlook is bullish. Some other indicators: The federal funds rate is lower than it was a year ago, or the three-month T-bill rate is below 7 percent and lower than a year ago.

HOW MANY STOCKS SHOULD SOMEONE OWN?

According to Bill O'Neil, the founder of *Investor's Business Daily,* in his book *24 Essential Lessons for Investment Success,* the amount of stocks you own depends on your financial resources. If you have $5,000 or less, for example, you should own no more than two stocks. If you have $10,000, owning two or three stocks is appropriate. With $25,000, you should own perhaps three or four stocks; with $50,000, four or five; and with $100,000, five or six. Overall, says O'Neil, there's no reason to own 20 or 25 stocks. You simply can't know all you should know about that many companies. You'll also dilute your results.

"Real money is made, first, by buying stocks of the very best companies in their fields, and then by concentrating your portfolio on a limited number and watching them carefully," he says. "I don't believe in the principle of wide diversification, or trying to reduce risk by spreading your money in too many stocks."

WHAT ARE INVESTORS' WORST HABITS?

According to O'Neil, the almost "addictionlike" attraction to low-priced stocks is at the top of the list. O'Neil believes that the strategy of buying a large block of a $2, $5, or $10 stock and watching it double sounds wonderful. The only problem: Your odds of winning the lottery are better. "The fact is, investing in stocks is not the same thing as buying a dress or a car on sale," he explains. "The market is an auction marketplace: Stocks sell for what they're worth. And

THE PROS WATCH

- *Speculation index.* Divide the weekly trading volume on the American Stock Exchange (AMEX) by the number of issues traded (in thousands). Calculate the same ratio for trading on the New York Stock Exchange. Divide the AMEX ratio by the NYSE ratio to calculate what the pros call the "speculation index." Insiders think the market is bearish when the index is more than .38 and bullish when it is less than .20.
- *Members selling short.* Divide the number of shares NYSE members sell short every week by the total of NYSE short selling. The market is bearish above .87 and bullish below .75, experts say, especially if it lasts several weeks.
- *New highs and lows.* Some experts say the market is usually approaching an intermediate bottom when the number of new lows reaches 600. The probable sign of an intermediate top, they say, is 600 new highs in one week, followed by a decline the following week.
- *NYSE short interest ratio.* Divide the total number of outstanding shares sold short each month by the average daily trading volume for that month. A strong rally generally comes after the ratio reaches 1.75.
- *Ten-week moving NYSE average.* Compute the average NYSE index for the previous 10 weeks. Then measure the difference between last week's close and the average.

when you buy cheap stocks, you get what you pay for. Of the best-performing stocks of the last 45 years, the average per-share price, before they went on to double or triple or more, was $28 a share. That is fact."

O'Neil doesn't buy stocks under $15 a share. "Of my few really big winners over the years, I started buying two of them at $16 a share and five at $50 to $100 a share," he says. The best companies, the leaders in their fields, simply do not come at $5 or $10. Many people want to get rich overnight, and that simply does not happen. Success takes time *and* a willingness to objectively and honestly analyze your past mistakes in the market.

The analytical and risk reduction tools you learned about in this chapter should make choosing stocks and buying and selling them at the right time easier and less stressful. You should also be able to avoid some of the mistakes newer or sometimes less savvy investors make, like panicking because of a market downturn. Instead, with experience, you may come to see these types of market disruptions as buying opportunities for stocks you wanted to own but thought were a bit overpriced. As you learned, there is no crystal ball to success but there are proven techniques to help you develop a style of investing that fits your needs, goals, and timeline.

RECEIVE AN INVESTING NEWSLETTER

InvestorGuide, produced by InvestorGuide.com, is a well-regarded newsletter containing links to the most important stories of the past week, downloads of useful investing software, and forecasts of future trends. *Worldly Investor* (www.worldlyinvestor.com) offers many newsletters on a daily or weekly basis. Topics include high tech stocks, biotech stocks, mutual funds, and daily market updates.

Another good newsletter is ZDNet's *The Day Ahead* (www.zdnet .com). Get a pre-opening-bell newsletter every trading day, with commentary, warning signs from overnight markets, tips on stocks to watch, and much more.

THE LAST WORD FROM WARREN BUFFETT

Advice for investors of all stripes, from Wall Street legend Warren Buffett:

1. Avoid debt—perhaps not mortgage debt, but certainly credit-card debt: "It is idiocy, in my view, to be paying credit-card rates." *Chicago Sun Times,* June 6, 1999, reporting on Buffett's speech at Berkshire Hathaway's May, 1999, annual meeting.

2. Stay disciplined: "To get ahead of the game you have to do one of three things. You've got to hit the lottery . . . have somebody leave you a lot of money or spend less than you take in. The secret is getting a little ahead, and then a little more ahead. The first $100,000 is the hardest. After that, your disciplines are in place. Getting behind in the game and then incurring [credit card] debt at 18 percent— those people never get caught up. You feel terrible for them."

3. Buy index funds: Passive investors should accumulate stocks during a 20- or 30-year period, using an index stock mutual fund that simply buys all the stocks in, say, the Standard & Poor's 500 index or some other vehicle with low "frictional costs" (the costs of buying, maintaining, and ultimately selling an asset). For the typical person who saves some money month after month, Buffett says a stock index fund is "a perfectly intelligent thing." But watch the expenses. They are a much bigger percentage of investors' returns than most people think.

4. Do your homework: For aggressive investors, Buffett advises: "I suggest they do the same thing I did 50 years ago . . . and that is to simply start looking at all of the companies that they think might be within their field of competence, that they think they can understand. . . . And look for something where they think they are getting the right kind of business with the right kind of management at the right price. I think they will have a hard time finding that among big companies." As a start, he suggests devoting five to 10 hours a week to the task.

5. How to pick stocks: "The single principle of investment is laying out money today to get more money back sometime in the future. The equations are not complicated or hidden.... There's no Rosetta Stone to find or anything. They are very simple equations. You just have to plug in the right numbers."

Source: Chicago Sun Times, June 6, 1999.

CHAPTER 4

LEVERAGING THE BOND MARKET

"Money makes things happen."

—*Malcolm Forbes*

Since making things happen and accumulating assets to fund dreams and goals is a key driver of investing, there is a place in just about every smart portfolio for bonds. Why? Because the bond market typically zigs when the stock market zags. Buying individual bonds or bond mutual funds is a way to ensure that you have your bases covered when stocks stumble and fall.

That's why bonds function to minimize risk, not as a complete substitute for stocks, but as an enhancement that can be used to provide income to an investor, typically a retiree, who needs it. Because they often move in the opposite direction of the stock market, bonds can be a key component in both the risk-reducing diversification and asset allocation strategies you read about in Chapter 3.

There are a variety of types of bonds, as this chapter explains, ranging from government-issue to the more speculative and even foreign company and government bonds. They have different risk and investment characteristics, can create different tax situations, and may be used in a variety of ways to hedge stock exposure in a portfolio or to create an income stream for an investor who needs it. That's why it's important to understand the critical role that bonds can play in helping you to create wealth.

A FIXED-INCOME INVESTMENT PRIMER

Investing in bonds is a lot like exercising. Everybody knows it's good for them and many say they intend to do it, but not everyone gets around to taking the first step.

Why? Who knows; everyone has his or her reasons. Some investors have been so keyed into the stock market because of its spectacular rise during the 1990s that they've made little time for other investments. Others say they don't understand bonds and prefer the relative simplicity of stocks and stock mutual funds.

If you're in the first group, fine. Just don't be surprised when the stock market sputters (as it inevitably does) and you find yourself without the kind of diversity and asset allocation that can provide healthy yields as stock market returns begin to disappear. In short, bonds can minimize the downside of investing, while maximizing the upside. But if you're in the second group and just don't understand how bonds work, this chapter is for you.

BONDS DEFINED

Simply stated, bonds are securities that represent loans made to the U.S. Government, through the purchase of Treasury bonds (T-bonds); to state or local governments (municipal bonds); or to corporations (corporate bonds). These loans pay the investor a steady, fixed rate of interest annually. The bond market has been growing steadily. (See Figures 4.1 and 4.2.)

T-bonds are free of default risk. It is almost certain that the principal lent to the U.S. Government will be repaid and the interest payments (coupons) will be made on time. However, if the bonds are not held until maturity, their value can go up or down as interest rates fluctuate. Corporate bonds do have default risk, but the amount of risk depends heavily on the credit quality of the issuers.

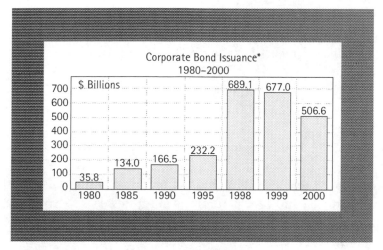

Figure 4.1   How Big Is the Market?

Source: Thomas Financial Securities Data.

*Includes all nonconvertible debt and medium-term note issues, but excludes all federal and agency debt.

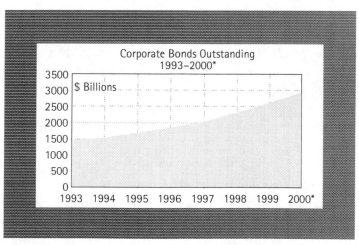

Figure 4.2   Corporate Bonds Outstanding, 1993–2000*

Source: The Bond Market Association estimates; Federal Reserve System.

*The Bond Market Association estimates.

Historically, the average return on bonds, particularly on T-bonds, is very low compared to the return on U.S. equities. According to figures from Pace University's Lubin School of Business, long-term T-bonds yielded an average of 5.35 percent from 1926 to 1993. Over the same period, the average return on the Standard & Poor's Composite Index was 12.31 percent. (Inflation during that period averaged 3.23 percent.) Long-term bonds barely provided a 2 percent return over inflation, while equities provided a return of about 9 percent more than inflation.

Stocks are subject to two kinds of market fluctuations: (1) fluctuations in earnings, and (2) fluctuations in interest rates—for example, in the value of money. Bonds (at least, T-bonds) are subject only to fluctuations in interest rates.

WHEN TO INVEST IN BONDS

A good time to purchase Treasury bills, bonds, and notes is during periods of high inflation, when interest rates are high. When the Federal Reserve decides to put the brakes on inflation by raising interest rates, you are holding high-yield, safe securities, and your yields are locked in until each security matures or you sell.

Another good time to purchase bonds is when the stock market is falling. Weak or negative stock returns can pale in comparison to the 6 or 7 percent you can gain on many Treasury bonds.

Above all, the decision to buy bonds should be part of a specific financial plan, rather than just an impulse response to various economic conditions.

Treasuries are available from banks, brokerage firms, and the Federal Reserve. Banks and brokers charge different rates for Treasuries, ranging from $2.50 to $1.25 per $1,000 of face value. Most brokers impose a $35 minimum commission. Discount brokers and full-service brokers usually charge a similar rate, but investors should shop around. A decision to buy directly from the U.S. government will allow investors to avoid commissions or sales charges. Call the Treasury direct line at 800-722-2678 for more information or log on to www.treasury.gov.

Among the types of bonds investors can choose from are: U.S. Government securities, municipal bonds, corporate bonds, mortgage and asset-backed securities, federal agency securities, and foreign government bonds. Among the many short-maturity options are Treasury bills, bank certificates of deposit (CDs), and commercial paper.

Because bonds normally have a predictable stream of interest payments and repayment of principal, investors use them to receive interest income or to preserve and accumulate capital. For example, investors who seek current income will most likely be interested in bonds that have a fixed interest rate until maturity and pay interest semiannually. But investors saving for retirement, or for a child's education or a similar capital accumulation goal, may want to invest in zero coupon

CLIMBING THE BOND LADDER

The Federal Reserve Board's penchant for adjusting interest rates to control the economy's growth can create havoc in the bond market. If you're a little nervous about which way the Fed will go in the coming months and years, but you still want to invest in the bond market, don't sweat it. All you have to do is create a "bond ladder."

You build a bond ladder by buying individual bonds with different maturities—the dates on which the bond issuer has agreed to pay back the principal on your bond. For example, you might buy roughly equal dollar amounts of two-, four-, six-, eight-, and 10-year Treasury or corporate bonds. Every two years, you cash in the bonds that have matured and reinvest the proceeds in the longest-term bonds on your ladder (in the case above, 10 years).

Bond ladders smooth out the risks of interest rate fluctuations, and, over time, you generally are earning the highest interest rates possible, given the type and quality of bonds you're buying. If rates rise in the future, you use the money from the maturing shorter-term bonds to buy new higher-interest-rate bonds. If interest rates fall, most of your ladder will remain invested in higher-earning bonds. You'll be forced to reinvest only a small portion (one-fifth, in our example) in the lower-interest-rate environment.

WHAT ARE THE KEY CONSIDERATIONS WHEN INVESTING IN BONDS?

There are a number of key variables to look at when investing in bonds: their maturity, redemption features, credit quality, interest rate, price, yield, and potential tax benefits. Together, these factors help determine the value of a bond investment and the degree to which it matches your financial objectives.

bonds, which do not have periodic interest payments. Instead, these bonds are sold at a substantial discount from their face amount, and the investor receives one payment—at maturity—that is equal to the purchase price (principal) plus the total interest earned, compounded semiannually at the original interest rate.

Investing in bonds can also be an important part of a strategy to minimize income taxes. Why? Some bonds offer special tax advantages. There is no state or local income tax on the interest from U.S. Treasury bonds. There is no federal income tax on the interest from most municipal bonds, and, in many jurisdictions, no state or local income tax, either. Deciding whether to invest in a taxable bond or a tax-exempt bond can also depend on whether the investor will be holding the securities in an account that is already tax-preferred or tax-deferred (a pension account, 401(k), or IRA). For example, a municipal bond will not yield the tax benefits it otherwise might if it is held in a tax-deferred account. In addition to the help you can get from your broker or financial or tax adviser for determining what bonds are best for you, many brokers and mutual fund companies offer bond investment calculators you can use yourself on the Internet to decide whether a bond will benefit your tax situation.

WHY SHOULD YOU INVEST IN BONDS?

Allocating some bonds or bond mutual funds to your investment portfolio is a good idea, especially if you have a lower tolerance for risk. For investors of every stripe, bonds offer a wide variety of benefits, including:

1. *Low volatility.* Diversification is one of the cornerstones of sound investment management, says Professor P.V. Viswanath, of Pace University's Lubin School of Business. Bonds stabilize a portfolio by helping to offset the investor's exposure to the volatility of the stock market. "Bonds have different risk and return characteristics than stocks, which means they will behave differently when the markets move," Viswanath explains.

2. *Better cash flow.* Bonds generally provide a scheduled stream of interest payments (except zero coupon bonds, which pay their interest at maturity). This attractive feature helps to meet expected current income needs or specific future expenditures

THE ADVANTAGES OF "INFLATION–PROTECTED" BONDS

The U.S. Treasury Department began selling inflation-protected bonds in 1997. However, their lack of historical performance made it difficult to determine whether investors needed to own them.

A new study by Ibbotson Associates, an investment analysis firm, has begun to fill in the gaps. Ibbotson created a model for adding Treasury Inflation Protected Securities (TIPS) to a portfolio.

Because TIPS are inflation indexed, "investors frequently underestimate their yield," the company said. For instance, bonds today yield about 6.6 percent, but TIPS yield 4.3 percent. Factor in a rate of inflation of 2.5 percent, however, and the real yield of long-term bonds falls below 4.1 percent and makes TIPS a better deal.

The Ibbotson study found that a portfolio with TIPS had a higher yield and less risk than one without TIPS. "TIPS possess unique characteristics that are not available directly through any other investment vehicles," said senior consultant Peng Chen. "They should be considered when constructing a long-term asset allocation policy."

Source: Deloitte & Touche OnLine.

such as college tuition or retirement income. Callable bonds and pass-through securities have less predictability, but investors are compensated for the uncertainty in the form of higher yields.

3. *Better security.* Unlike stocks, bonds are designed to return the original investment, or principal, to the investor at a future maturity date. This preservation of capital provides stability to a portfolio and balances the growth/risk aspect of stocks. Loss of principal can still occur in fixed-income investments if bonds are sold before maturity at a price lower than the purchase price, or if the borrower has a payment default. Investing in high-credit-quality bonds helps reduce the exposure to default risk.

BOND CLASSES

Bonds, like ice cream, come in a wide variety of flavors.

The type of bonds you buy depends on your investment objectives, risk tolerance, and tax situation. Here's a snapshot of the primary bond classes.

U.S. Treasury Securities

If the thought of watching a stock tumble in value makes you queasy or you have the need to invest in super-safe cash equivalents, consider U.S. Treasuries. Uncle Sam's gift to U.S. investors—the Treasury market—offers a safe haven to battered stock investors looking for short- or long-term relief.

Treasuries are predictable and lower-yielding (on average) than stocks, but they are also more secure. Generally, federal taxes must be paid on the interest, but the interest is free from state and local taxes.

Looking for a safe investment? Treasuries are backed by the "full faith and credit" of the U.S. Government.

Unfortunately for the bond market, sustained periods of low inflation and sizable stock maket gains in the United States during the 1990s resulted in a depressed appetite for Treasuries among investors. That is unfortunate because the Treasury market is an investor's ally.

There are three basic varieties of Treasuries:

1. Treasury bills (T-bills) offer the fastest rate of return: They are sold in 13- and 26-week maturities. Investors need a minimum of $1,000 to buy a T-bill.

2. Treasury notes mature in 2, 3, 5, and 10 years and can be purchased in $1,000 minimums.

3. Treasury bonds, which range between 10- and 30-year maturities, can be purchased in amounts as low as $1,000. Financial planners generally recommend Treasuries for people whose money can be parked for long periods.

What makes Treasuries so valuable? They are liquid investments and can be sold for cash. Treasuries are also easy to sell because of the enormous size of the government bond market. In fact, the Treasury market is the world's largest securities market. Its average trading volume exceeds $250 billion daily. Treasuries are also good hedges against interest rate fluctuations. Investors who buy them "lock in" a fixed, annual rate of return that holds firm even if rates change during the life of the Treasury.

For investors impacted by a volatile stock market, U.S. Treasury securities offer the highest degree of creditworthiness available. U.S. Treasury securities offer a combination of advantages that will not be found anywhere else—and certainly not in stocks.

- *Safety.* The timely payment of interest and principal at maturity is guaranteed by the full faith and credit of the United States Government.

- *No complications.* It's easy to understand Treasury securities, and their simplicity can be very reassuring in today's complex financial world.

- *Locked-in interest rates.* Most Treasury securities cannot be called or redeemed before their final stated maturity date. Their interest rate is locked in for the full term of the security.

- *Liquidity.* U.S. Treasuries are the most liquid fixed-income instruments in the world.

- *Selection.* With the wide range of Treasury maturities in the secondary market, it's easy to find the maturities and coupon rates that suit investors' precise needs.

- *Tax advantage.* Interest on U.S. Treasuries is exempt from state and local income taxes.

The U.S. Treasury issues its various securities at weekly, monthly, and quarterly auctions throughout the year. Small investors can submit tenders by mail to the Federal Reserve or online at the Treasury's Web site (www.uspublicdebt.gov). Information on upcoming bill, note, or bond auctions is available from Federal Reserve branches or from the Bureau of the Public Debt at 800-722-2678.

A special program called TreasuryDirect allows investors to open up an account via telephone over the Internet and buy Treasuries by transferring money from their bank account. Using this program you can also sell or reinvest your Treasury bills for up to two years, using the U.S. mail, a telephone, or an Internet connection.

The other big news from the Treasury market is a new auction schedule that cuts the number of Treasury offerings rolling into the markets and might also result in the elimination of the venerable 30-year Treasury Bond.

Starting in 2000, the U.S. Treasury cut, by more than half, the amount of 30-year debt it sold in 1999, and it is considering discontinuing the bonds altogether. As a result, 10-year notes are likely to become the new government benchmark as 30-year bonds gradually mature or are repurchased by the government. Auctions of one-year bills are cut to four times a year. At some point, they too may be eliminated. The frequency of auctions for two-year notes has not been reduced, but the average amount sold at each auction has been trimmed. The dollar amount of three- and six-month bills sold each week has been increased to offset the cutback in one-year bills.

Here's a snapshot of the new schedule:

- Thirty-year bonds will be auctioned once a year, in February, and their original-issue maturity may vary from 30 to 30¼ years. The Treasury will "reopen" its books in August to sell

WHAT'S THE BEST WAY TO BUY TREASURIES?

These days, Uncle Sam's TreasuryDirect program may be your best bet.

TreasuryDirect purchases are usually no-fee or low-fee transactions. You can buy Treasuries through a bank or broker, but you will usually have to pay a fee or commission and maintain an account.

If you wish, the Treasury can debit your bank account for the amount of a purchase *after* the price is set by the auction. You are no longer required to send in a check for the full face value and then wait for a refund. For a nominal fee, Treasury instruments can also be sold before maturity, using this same program.

To buy bonds through TreasuryDirect, contact any Federal Reserve Bank (in New York, the bank is at 33 Liberty Street, New York, NY 10045) and ask for forms to participate in the Treasury Direct program. The minimum for a Treasury Note (two years and up) is $1,000. Five-year notes require a $1,000 minimum. There are no fees for accounts below $100,000; accounts above that sum are charged a $25 annual fee. You may elect to have interest payments deposited directly to your account. TreasuryDirect allows you to roll over a matured Treasury instrument toward the purchase of a new one.

For brokering the sale of a Treasury instrument, the Treasury fee reportedly is less than the fee charged by most banks and brokerage houses. The instrument is sold via the Federal Reserve Bank of Chicago, which is responsible for getting a fair price. Holders of Treasury instruments can reinvest funds from maturing instruments simply by telephoning the "Reinvest Direct" service. Necessary information appears on a notice sent to holders of maturing instruments.

Investors can get more information about the TreasuryDirect program from the Bureau of the Public Debt's Web site: www .treasurydirect.gov smaller amounts of the February issue, but with a slightly shorter maturity.[1]

- Ten-year notes will be auctioned twice a year, in February and August. In May and November, they can be purchased again, but their maturities will be 9¾ years.

- Five-year notes will be sold in May and November and reopened in February and August. Their maturity will be 4¾ years.

- Two-year notes were eliminated in March 2001.

- Thirty-year inflation-indexed bonds will be auctioned once a year, in October; indexed 10-year notes will be sold twice a year, in January and July.

Economic Indicators That Count

It's common knowledge on Wall Street that prices in the financial markets often move in response to the monthly data produced by the U.S. Government and by the Federal Reserve. Traders also know that the data help create expectations for inflation and future Federal Reserve policy actions.

Following leading economic indicators is a tricky business. Hundreds of statistics about the economy are generated every month, each providing some information about the condition of the economy. However, none of these statistics alone is a reliable indicator of overall economic health. Many economic statistics (though certainly not all) can be assigned to one or another of three distinct groups, depending on the timing of their movements relative to changes in the national economy. Some tend to turn upward on a fairly regular basis in advance of the national economy and typically turn downward before the national economy begins to weaken. These are known as *leading indicators,* and they signal the advent of recessions and recoveries several months in advance. Others perform much in step with the economy as a whole and so are known as *coincident indicators.* Those whose turning points trail behind the national business cycle are known as *lagging indicators.*

---

[1] *Source:* Adapted from U.S. Treasury Department releases.

By and large, some indicators are released by the government; others are released by private entities and trade associations. In most cases, the reports are released monthly or quarterly. Let's look at the leading U.S. economic indicators:

- *Consumer Confidence Index.* Prepared monthly by the Conference Board, this index takes the pulse of 5,000 U.S. households to chart their take on the current and short-term economic outlook, including the direction of employment levels, salaries, and business conditions.

- *Consumer Price Index.* The granddaddy of all economic indicators, the CPI estimates the cost of goods bought and sold in the United States. That estimate helps economic gurus forecast the rate of inflation. The CPI is comprised of price changes at the consumer level for a "basket" of products and services. The CPI's "core rate" usually excludes two consumer goods categories—food and energy—because they fluctuate more than other consumer product categories.

- *Producer Price Index.* The PPI estimates how much it costs American businesses to produce the goods and services that the CPI addresses. The PPI measures prices charged at the producer level for finished goods from manufacturing plants, intermediate goods from suppliers, and raw materials sold to manufacturing companies. Most economists view the PPI as a long-range economic forecasting tool that tells whether any price pressures are present in the economy.

- *Housing Starts.* This indicator tells economists and the financial markets whether Americans are buying or building a lot of homes. Many factors influence housing starts, particularly weather. Housing starts don't simply estimate the number of new houses under construction; they also calculate how much home furnishings will cost new home buyers down the road.

- *The Index of Leading Economic Indicators.* The ILEI has gained a powerful following in recent years among investors who consider it a real bellwether of economic conditions. Produced by the

Conference Board, the ILEI is a composite of 10 or so economic reports that are meshed together to evaluate where the economy is headed in the next year. There are exceptions to the rule, but economists believe that three straight negative ILEI reports indicate a recession is at hand.

- *Employment Report.* This indicator, compiled by the U.S. Bureau of Labor Statistics, basically tells what its name implies: How many people are working in the United States? Using household and business surveys, Uncle Sam attempts to measure the level of employment.

- *Retail Sales.* A good indicator of how often Americans are opening their wallets and spending their money, retails sales account for about 70 percent of the consumer goods and services criteria used by the CPI calculations.

Even the government agencies that pull all of this economic data together admit that the process is hardly perfect. Like most forecasting formulas, variances apply. For example, the leading indicators may warn us about a change in the direction of the business cycle, but they do not provide us with very reliable information about the magnitude of that change. In addition, a magnitude of change in any one direction is not necessarily a measure of how good or bad the economy is likely to get. Only when an indicator clearly reverses direction is its value as a forecasting tool relevant. And rarely do all indicators signal a change in direction at the same time. Still, they're the best numbers we have as a society. Over time, they've proven to be reliable.

GOVERNMENT ECONOMIC INDICATORS

CNBC and other business networks and newssites, along with *The Wall Street Journal* and a growing number of local newspapers do a good job of providing a constant flow of stories on economic indicators, along with analysis from economists and business experts to put changes in perspective. Here's where to go on the Internet to find some of the economic indicators mentioned above—as well as a few others:[2]

Energy Prices [EIA]: www.eia.doe.gov/price.html

Employment [ESBR]: www.whitehouse.gov/fsbr/employment.html

Gross Domestic Product [BEA]: www.bea.doc.gov/briefrm/tables /ebr1.htm

Income and Expenditures [ESBR]: www.whitehouse.gov/fsbr/income .html

International Trade [Census]: www.census.gov/indicator/www/ustrade .html

Money, Interest Rates [ESBR]: www.whitehouse.gov/fsbr/money .html

Output [ESBR]: www.whitehouse.gov/fsbr/international.html

Per Capita Income [BEA]: www.bea.doc.gov/briefrm/tables/ebr5 .htm

Prices [ESBR]: www.whitehouse.gov/fsbr/prices.html

Production, Sales, Orders, and Inventories [ESBR]: www.whitehouse .gov/fsbr/production.html

Municipal Bonds

If you're looking for a tax-smart investment that will help you create a diversified portfolio, this may be it. Tax-exempt bonds, one of the few tax-advantaged securities available, are issued by states and municipalities in part to finance public projects such as schools, hospitals, and roads. The interest earned on municipal bonds is free from federal taxes and may be exempt from state taxes when issued in the bondholder's state of residence.

Lots of investors choose municipal bonds—and bond funds—because they provide a diversified portfolio that can generate tax-exempt

[2] *Sources:* U.S. Census Bureau (Census); Bureau of Labor Statistics (BLS); Bureau of Economic Taxing Power.

Under present federal income tax law, the interest income you receive from investing in municipal bonds is free from federal income taxes.* In most states, interest income received from securities issued by governmental units within the state is also exempt from state and local taxes. In addition, interest income from securities issued by U.S. territories and possessions is exempt from federal, state, and local income taxes in all 50 states.

One of the best ways to appreciate the tax-exempt advantage of a municipal security is to compare it to a comparable taxable investment. For example, assume you are in the 36 percent federal tax bracket, file a joint return, and you and your spouse claim $170,000 in taxable income.

Now assume you have $30,000 to invest and you are considering two investment alternatives: a tax-exempt municipal bond yielding 5%, and a taxable corporate bond yielding 7.5%. Which investment will prove most advantageous?

If you invested your money in the municipal bond, you'd earn $1,500 in interest (a 5% yield) and pay no federal income taxes. The taxable bond investment, however, would provide you only $1,440 in income after federal income taxes have been deducted (a 4.8% yield).

As you can see, the municipal bond would provide the best yield after taxes are taken into account. The tax-exempt security would be an even better investment if you accounted for state and local income taxes when calculating returns on the taxable bond investment.

Effect of Federal Income Taxes on Yield of Tax-Exempt and Taxable Instruments

	5% Tax-Exempt Bond	7.5% Taxable Investment
Cash investment	$30,000	$30,000
Interest	$ 1,500	$ 2,250
Federal income tax in the 36% marginal tax bracket	0	$ 810
Net return	$ 1,500	$ 1,440
Yield on investment after taxes	5.0%	4.8%

Figure 4.3   The Advantages of Tax Exemption

*If you are subject to the alternative minimum tax (AMT), you must include interest income from certain municipal securities in calculating the tax.

Source: The Bond Market Association.

income. They also may offer balance to an investor's portfolio because they have been relatively stable compared to riskier bonds and stocks. The tax advantages can be significant. (See Figure 4.3.)

Depending on your tax bracket, municipal bonds can also help you maximize your after-tax income. Municipal bonds are issued by local or state governments and pay interest that is exempt from federal taxes. You may further realize the benefit of paying no state or local tax if you invest in a bond issued by the state in which you reside.

As more states increase their taxes, the advantages of investing in fully tax-free municipal bonds become obvious.

Normally, there are two types of municipal bonds: (1) General Obligation Bonds and (2) Revenue Bonds.

A General Obligation Bond, the most common type of municipal bond, is considered one of the more secure investments available today. It is backed by "the full faith and credit" of the issuing municipality. The municipality may be authorized to use virtually any means, including its taxing powers, to pay both the interest and principal, on time and in full, to investors.

A Revenue Bond is issued by a municipality or by a special authority to fund specific types of projects, such as hospitals, turnpikes, and water and sewer systems. The income realized from the sale of the services provided by the completed project is used to pay the interest and principal of this type of bond.

FREE MUNI BOND INFORMATION

Bondtrac, which provides bond information to professional traders and brokers, also has free services for individual investors. You won't get prices, but you can search for things like muni bonds of a particular state, coupon rates, maturities, and S&P or Moody's ratings (www.bondtrac.com).

Source: SmartMoney.

Mortgage-Backed Bonds

A popular bond category since the 1980s, mortgage bonds can be a profitable, if somewhat complicated, investment option. Of the several types of mortgage-related securities available today, one of the most common is the pass-through "Ginnie Mae," issued by the Government National Mortgage Association (GNMA), an agency of the federal government. GNMA guarantees that investors will receive timely interest and principal payments. Investors receive potentially high interest payments, consisting of both principal and interest. The rate of principal repayment will vary with current interest rates.

Corporate Bonds

Issued by large corporations, corporate debt represents different industries and credit qualities. By paying close attention to a bond's credit rating, you can select a bond to match your own risk tolerance.

Corporate and municipal bonds are evaluated by independent rating services. The best known are Standard & Poor's and Moody's Investors Service Inc. Each service measures the financial stability of the issuer and assigns a rating from AAA to D. Any bond rated Baa or higher by Moody's, or BBB or higher by Standard & Poor's, is considered investment quality. Usually, the higher a bond's rating, the lower the interest it must pay to attract buyers.

Zero-Coupon Bonds

"Zeros" are issued by corporations, the federal government, or municipalities, at a deep discount to their maturity (face) value. Investors receive no interest income until maturity, but, each year, they must pay taxes on that year's increment of accrued interest (unless they purchase taxable zeros for a tax-deferred retirement account, or municipal bonds). At maturity, investors get all interest that has accrued, plus principal.

Convertible Bonds

Investors can enjoy the security of receiving fixed income from a bond plus the growth potential of stocks by investing in convertible bonds.

CREDIT RATINGS			
Credit Risk	Moody's	Standard & Poor's	Fitch
INVESTMENT GRADE			
Highest quality	Aaa	AAA	AAA
High quality (very strong)	Aa	AA	AA
Upper medium grade (strong)	A	A	A
Medium grade	Baa	BBB	BBB
NOT INVESTMENT GRADE			
Somewhat speculative	Ba	BB	BB
Speculative	B	B	B
Highly speculative	Caa	CCC	CCC
Most speculative	Ca	CC	CC
Imminent default	C	C	C
Default	C	D	D

Source: www.investinginbonds.com.

These securities can be converted into common stock at a later date and at a prestated price.

U.S. Savings Bonds

You can buy up to $15,000 of U.S. Savings Bonds each year, from banks or through payroll deductions. They're inexpensive; you can invest as little as $25 and get a guaranteed rate of interest if you hold them until they mature (or for five years). More good news: there's no commission and no state or local tax on the interest. Plus, you don't owe federal taxes until you redeem the bonds. You may be able to avoid taxes entirely if you use the bonds to pay for your child's education, though you'll have to check the conditions that apply.

WHAT TO LOOK FOR IN A BOND

The first item to check on a bond is its rating by Standard & Poor's or by Moody's. You'll find these rating guides at libraries, or you can ask your broker for them. Standard & Poor's highest rating is AAA. Moody's uses "Aaa." Both sources use C for the poorest rating. If an S&P rating is lower than "A," pass it up. Investors who buy high-yield, low-quality bonds because they yield 13 percent or more will be sorry during a recession.

Some bonds are insured against the issuer's default. Everything else being equal, the return from an insured bond is somewhat lower than from a same-rated noninsured one. However, the bondholder is insured against loss of principal and interest if the bond issuer defaults.

It's important to read the fine print and ask questions about any bond issue. Although a noncallable bond will have a lower yield than a callable bond, you usually lose your gain if the bonds are called early. The following fictitious example is based on numerous real-life outcomes:.

- Company XYZ issued a 30-year callable bond yielding 11 percent. In three years, interest rates dropped and the company decided to call the bonds. Just before the call, the bonds were trading at an 8 percent premium ($1,080 per $1,000 of par value). Then the company redeemed the bonds at par ($1,000). Bondholders took an 8-point loss; if they held 10 bonds, they lost $800.

Source: Investor's Alliance.

HOW TO INVEST IN BONDS

Bond investors have two avenues to choose from when investing in fixed-income securities: (1) purchasing individual bond offerings or (2) investing in bond funds. For Treasury bonds, the first method is best. As noted above, it's cheaper to buy individual Treasuries directly from the U.S. Government. For other types of bonds, weigh the pluses and minuses.

Whether you buy bonds or invest in bond funds, certain fundamentals apply. Much depends on: (1) the amount of money you will have to invest in order to achieve diversification, (2) the degree to which you want professional management of your portfolio, and (3) your willingness to pay for professional selection and portfolio management (bond funds). Generally, investing in individual bonds is best for preserving your capital, assuming the bonds closely match your other objectives (like the desired amount at maturity). However, bond funds offer convenience and diversification even at minimum investment levels. The minimum investment for bond funds and UITs is typically between $1,000 and $2,500, or $500 for retirement accounts. Individual bonds are usually sold in $5,000 denominations, and some dealers require a minimum investment of $20,000.

Another factor to consider when investing in bonds is the interest rate. Interest rates move in the opposite direction of bonds. When rates go up, bond prices go down. With bonds, you always risk tying up your money at a lower interest rate. When rates go up, new bonds with their higher interest rates, will bring you better returns. Older bonds that you already own become less attractive because they have a lower interest rate. Using bond mutual funds, which buy and sell bonds frequently, allows you to avoid locking in as interest rates rise, as you would if you bought individual bonds.

Another key issue, inflation, can be a concern for bond investors. When things cost more, your dollars are worth less, and the money you get back from your bonds is worth less. Here are some more issues to consider before investing in bonds:

- *Call risk.* Check the bond agreement's fine print. A company may have the right to pay you back early, which means the interest and regular income you receive will stop before the original date.
- *Market volatility.* Demand can have an effect on bond prices, just as it does on stocks. High demand might force you to pay $1,200 for a $1,000 bond. On the other hand, low demand might force you to sell your $1,000 bond for $800.

USING THE BOND MARKET TO READ THE STOCK MARKET

The bond market acts as an indicator of the direction of the stock market. Listed below are three ways you can use the bond market to predict the stock market:

1. In a down or bear market, watch for rising bond prices; they may signal the start of a bull market or rally.
2. A drop in high-grade bond prices is the same as an increase in bond yields. In the market declines of 1974 and 1987, AAA bond yields increased before the market dropped.
3. A decline in high-yield, junk, or second-grade bond prices may signal that speculators are moving out of the bond market.

- *Dependability.* Government bonds are pretty secure; governments don't usually go out of business. Corporate bonds can be riskier. Shaky companies may go out of business, leaving you out in the cold.

- *Average returns.* As noted above, the average return for bonds is about 6 percent. That's about half of the stock market's average return of 10 to 12 percent.

- *Security.* Unlike stocks or mutual funds, bonds guarantee to pay your money back with interest. Treasury and municipal bonds are backed by the issuing government, so there is almost no risk involved.

- *Steady income.* Most bonds pay you back regularly. That means you can get a steady monthly payment, with interest.

- *Tax benefits.* Many government bonds pay tax-free interest. Their returns are usually a little lower, but if you account for the tax savings, they can be good investments.

- *Discounts.* Depending on demand, you can buy bonds for less than their face value. For example, a bond promising to pay you

$1,000 might sell for only $800. And that's before the interest rate is applied.

ARE BOND MUTUAL FUNDS FOR YOU?

Many investors choose to bypass individual bonds and opt for the perceived security of bond mutual funds. There, savvy bond fund managers do the investing for investors.

Bond mutual funds are suitable for investors seeking to earn maximum interest income or relatively stable long-term growth through reinvestment of income. Bond mutual funds' unit values fluctuate but, historically, they have been less volatile than equity mutual funds.

It's important to remember that the market value of bonds will fluctuate daily as interest rates change. Consequently, investors should recognize that daily fluctuations in the market value of bonds will affect the value of the bond fund units as well. Investing in bond mutual funds is therefore a little riskier than investing in bonds directly.

The good news on the funds' side is that bond funds are fairly basic and you get instant diversification and professional management. Even a $1,000 initial investment can get you into a fund. Subsequent deposits can be as low as $100. Bond fund dividends are reinvested automatically; your account gets monthly interest payments. Some bond funds are no-load (commission-free). Others charge a commission.

Commissions tend to be higher for funds purchased through a broker than for funds purchased directly from the fund manager, but then you lose the convenience of having all your investments held in one place. All bond funds charge what's called an annual expense ratio. The average bond fund expense ratio is .75 percent, according to the Charles Schwab Center for Investment Research in San Francisco, but it can be as low as .20 percent.

Whether you invest in individual bonds or in bond mutual funds, you'll pay a bid/ask spread, which, as with stock, is what the market maker gets for creating a market for the security. The less you're investing, the higher bid/ask spread you'll pay. Small lots of individual bonds—less than $10,000—can be expensive. If you're buying individual bonds, ask your broker what you're paying for each bond.

Fortunately, some criteria are available to help you decide whether to invest in bonds or bond mutual funds. According to the Charles Schwab Center for Investment Research, which has published a study on the issue, you should consider investing in individual bonds if you:

- Have $50,000 or more to invest in fixed-income products.
- Desire a fixed level of income or are saving for a specific future goal.
- Want to be actively involved in managing your own money.

You should consider investing in bond mutual funds if you:

- Have less than $50,000 to invest in fixed-income products.
- Can tolerate fluctuations in your level of income and in the value of your principal.
- Are seeking professional management and additional diversification.

But, as the Schwab Center's study says, choosing between individual bonds and bond mutual funds does not have to be an "either-or" decision. Some investors may want to choose a combination of individual bonds and bond mutual funds to meet their investment objectives. For more information on the subject, check out the Schwab Investment Center's Web site, at www.schwab.com/funds.

BOND INVESTING IN FOREIGN LANDS

Are foreign bonds a good bet? Some might be—if you value diversification and can stomach a little risk.

The factors for evaluating global bonds and U.S. bonds are the same. Interest rate levels, credit market conditions, actual and expected inflation, and the pace of economic growth top the list. In addition, a bond's price reflects its particular characteristics, such as credit quality, maturity, and supply and demand.

Still, important differences between domestic and foreign bond investing can increase your overall risk. Many countries have less political stability and a less diverse economy than the United States. Political or economic upheaval in those countries could jeopardize local bond markets, so investors must continually monitor and interpret the internal developments of the countries they invest in. However, this risk can be greatly reduced by investing in government bonds of developed nations.

The aspect of foreign investing that probably generates the greatest day-to-day concern is the impact of currency translation. Initially, to purchase a foreign bond, dollars must be converted to the local currency. Subsequently, price quotations, interest, and any sale or redemption proceeds received in the foreign currency must be converted back into U.S. dollars. Because foreign exchange rates fluctuate constantly, reflecting changes in each currency's supply-and-demand situation,

TABLE 4.1
THE IMPACT OF CURRENCY FLUCTUATIONS ON
GERMAN BOND RETURNS FOR U.S. INVESTORS

Year	Local Market Return	Local Currency vs. U.S. Dollar	Return to U.S. Investors
1994	−1.8%	11.8%	10.0%
1995	16.3	9.6	25.9
1996	7.3	−7.7	−0.4
1997	6.2	−15.2	−9.0
1998	10.9	8.9	19.8
1999	−2.1	−14.3	−16.4
2000	7.31	−6.34	0.51

Source: Salomon Smith Barney.

currency movements can increase or decrease a bond's dollar value (and investment return) even if its price remains unchanged.

One tactic is to compare, for a particular security, the returns to local investors and to U.S. investors during identical time periods. As Table 4.1 shows, German bonds lost 1.8 percent for all of 1994, but a U.S. investor would have realized a solid 10 percent return on the same bonds because the deutschemark rose nearly 12 percent against the dollar. In 1996 and 1997, however, the deutschemark fell in value against the dollar, so returns to U.S. investors were reduced. In contrast, a weak dollar and strong German bond market performance in 1998 resulted in a gain of nearly 20 percent for U.S. investors.

To combat portfolio fluctuations, portfolio managers may use sophisticated hedging techniques involving forward exchange contracts or options to cushion the impact of potentially negative currency movements.

A GREAT BOND INVESTING WEB SITE

While bonds can be beneficial to a diversified investment portfolio, mastering their different characteristics or attempting to build a bond ladder can be a bit trickier to master than, say, buying shares of IBM or Microsoft. For a great source of information on the basics of bond investing, check out the Bond Market Association (BMA) Web site: www.investinginbonds.com.

This is a genuine retail-oriented Web site that focuses on bond-investing education. The site, which was launched in 1998, includes an investor's guide to bond basics, an overview of the bond markets, and guides for investing in bonds, including municipal bonds and corporate bonds.

The site also offers information on BMA member firms and includes an informational section on investing in high-yield bonds later in the present quarter. Don't confuse this site with the organization's other site (www.bondmarkets.com), which mainly delves into the Bond Market Association's legislative and regulatory lobbying agenda.

BOND GLOSSARY

Asset allocation   The strategy of dividing investment dollars among various types of investments, such as stocks, bonds, and money markets.

Average maturity   The average length of time until the principal must be repaid for all bonds in a mutual fund portfolio.

Basis point   A unit of measure of the value of a bond. Basis points are calculated as 1/100 of 1 percent. Thus, if bank interest rates fall 25 basis points, that is the same as 25/100 = ¼ of 1 percent.

Bond   An IOU issued by federal, state, and municipal governments and their agencies, or by corporations.

Bond maturity   The lifetime of a bond; it concludes when the final payment of that obligation is due.

Credit risk   The possibility that an issuing organization could default on an interest payment or repayment of principal (when the bond matures).

Default   The failure of an issuing organization to make interest payments or to repay principal upon maturity.

Diversification   The act of spreading money across a wide range of investments and a variety of markets.

Duration   The average life of fixed-income investments. For instance, a 10-year bond is not technically a 10-year bond because interest payments shorten the average term. The bigger the interest payments, the shorter the duration. For a zero coupon bond, maturity and duration are the same because there are no cash flows. This term is used by bond traders as a way of measuring risk.

Face value   The stated nominal value of a fixed-income investment. For example, you invest $98,000 in a bond that matures to $100,000. That is the face value of the bond. The market price may go higher or lower, but the face value is the amount that will be returned to you.

Par   Par refers to a price of 100. Bonds mature at par or 100 percent of their face value.

Risk tolerance   The ability to endure declines in the value of investments.

Spread   The difference between the bid side and the offered side of a bond quotation. The shorter the bond and the higher the quality of the bond, the closer or "tighter" the bid-ask spread. The spread usually indicates a trader's feel for how quickly a bond may be sold.

Total return   The percentage of increase or decrease for a given period. The return reflects reinvested income and any change in share price.

Yield   A bond fund's net income per share, expressed as a percentage of share price.

CHAPTER 5
MAKING MUTUAL FUNDS WORK FOR YOU

"Behold the turtle. He makes progress only when he sticks his neck out."

—*James B. Conant*

With investing you have to stick your neck out, at least a little. But there are ways to diligently reduce your risk and one of them is by investing in mutual funds. By their very nature—as a pool of securities—their risk is tied to a number of companies or entities, so even if one or two have stocks that slip in value, there is still the performance of any number of other stocks or bonds to shore up the performance of the overall mutual fund.

Of course some funds are riskier than others—for instance, those that invest solely in one type of industry or asset, say biotechnology, gold or speculative low-grade company bonds. But at the other end of the spectrum are funds that spread their risk out among entire stock markets, such as S&P 500 index funds. That doesn't mean that a fund won't perform poorly if its investments do poorly, as we've seen. But pools of securities can have poor performance offset by individual investments in its portfolios. That can be particularly important for investors who are just getting started, those with a smaller pot of money to invest (in contrast to a mutual fund it's more difficult to achieve diversification by buying just one or two individual stocks) and those who are simply not interested in doing the company research needed determine which company stocks to buy, hold, and sell.

In fact, outside of mutual funds it's hard to think of another vehicle so perfect for accessing professional money management services designed to provide long-term prosperity at a reasonable price.

That's why this chapter is designed to give you both an understanding of and a strategy for purchasing mutual funds to benefit your plan to create wealth. And since mutual funds are the vehicle of choice in so many investors' 401(k) plans and other retirement vehicles, it becomes doubly important to understand how you can put them to work in your long-term strategy.

Unfortunately, the rising tide of the stock market throughout most of the 1990s, and the belief by investors that they could trade funds like some people trade stocks, has created a bit of havoc even in the realm of mutual funds.

Remember "irrational exuberance?"

That was the phrase Federal Reserve Chairman Alan Greenspan used to describe investors who, in his learned opinion, were overestimating the stock market.

Perhaps a more accurate term would have been "unrealistic expectations." Indeed, figures of no less stature than Vanguard Group Chairman John Brennan and former Securities and Exchange Commission Chairman Arthur Levitt have become fond of the phrase in recent years. It seems that, in an era of double- and triple-digit annual returns, investors have grown increasingly impatient with anything less.

That's a big problem in the mutual funds world, where, in order to capture those extraordinary returns, investors have been shifting their money arbitrarily to whatever funds promise the highest returns, and are giving little thought to a long-term plan.

This dynamic has frightened Wall Street observers because it placed too much emphasis on one area of the market—technology stocks. Wary analysts feared, in hindsight correctly, that if the technology bubble burst, it would take much of the market down with it. It would also underscore the importance of a long-term, diversified approach to investing again.

"Investors need to step back from the frenzy and invest for the long term," said Vanguard's Brennan in a speech to a New York audience on December 31, 1999, and reported by Associated Press. "It sounds stodgy, but it's the best way to make money. It's not a dash; it's a marathon when you're creating wealth for your retirement."

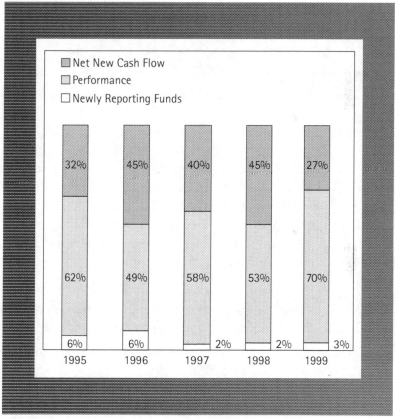

Figure 5.1   Components of Mutual Fund Asset Growth*

Source: Mutual Fund Factbook, 2000.

Note: The data contain a series break beginning in 1996. Data for funds that invest in other mutual funds were excluded from the series. Data prior to 1996 have been restated to create a consistent series back to 1995.

*Newly reporting funds are excluded from the calculation of fund performance and net new cash flow during the month in which they are introduced to be the Institute's database.

But with much of the industry's advertising geared toward U.S. investors, and with new trading technologies that make it easier to buy and sell stock, the idea of investing for the long term is becoming old-fashioned to some investors.

Other observers believe the shift in investors' attitudes is merely a symptom of a larger philosophical movement that is emerging from within the mutual fund industry—a movement that emphasizes short-term performance rather than the achievement of long-term goals. Figure 5.1 shows the growth areas of the mutual fund industry.

FUND FRIENDLY

With some of the so-called irrational exuberance drained out of the market, it seems to be a good time to return to basics that mutual fund investing can exemplify. At their most fundamental, mutual funds are professionally-managed baskets of stocks and bonds that allow investors to own multiple investments at a low price.

Everyone has his or her own investment style, strategies, and programs when it comes to mutual funds, but certain common denominators do exist. Establishing a successful mutual fund portfolio is a three-step process:

1. Identify investment objectives and preferences, including portfolio amount, return objectives, time horizon, and risk tolerance;
2. Formulate a detailed asset allocation strategy by fund type category, to reflect chosen objectives;
3. Select suitable funds to match each category.

The second step is the most challenging because of the abundance of asset allocation theories and strategies. Most asset allocation strategies fall into two groups: one primarily treats risk as a stock-bond allocation, with risk tolerance changing the percentage of stock and bond funds; the other is primarily a fund category allocation, with risk tolerance affecting the type of fund categories and their allocation percentages within a basic stock-bond allocation (see Figure 5.2).

How to Read Newspaper Fund Quotes

	NAV	Offer	Chg
Apzbc:			
Axyte	9.95	10.73	...
Bxy Xer	10.37	11.33	−.01
Dar Rppe	7.38	8.07	+.09
Income	3.16	3.45	+.01
Tbq Ratl	9.97	10.47	+.01
Tbqr Dt	10.19	10.70	−.02
Xypr Ap r	10.05	10.98	−.01
Brlkd:			
Blgr Dfr	15.64	16.46	−.03
Bmo Pnc	8.54	N.L.	−.06
Bto Bmd	7.27	7.65	...
Cmyog:			
MIA p	11.86	12.79	+.01
MIX	11.44	12.33	+.03
MIY p	9.70	10.46	−.01
MBF	11.58	12.49	+.04
MBI	14.18	15.92	+.20
MBR	11.99	12.93	+.03
MRI	10.01	10.79	−.02
MII	7.66	8.26	+.02
MDX	10.00	10.50	...
DMX r	9.74	10.23	...
GYI	6.93	7.47	−.03
JAM	13.47	14.18	−.04
JEL	10.09	10.59	−.06
MTNC	10.25	10.76	−.02
MPRS r	10.12	10.62	+.02
Jellies	20.33	N.L.	+.01
Sulter	23.81	N.L.	+.13
Drxpg:			
Bakc Jau	8.19	8.53	−.01
Cryl Ba	20.68	22.12	+.05
Gryd 3	12.10	12.60	−.04
Frp Dur p	9.80	10.45	−.11
Fye Pm p	12.61	N.L.	...
Hy Finc	15.45	16.52	+.06
Hx Papie	10.96	11.42	−.06
Lerl Eiy t	10.02	10.95	+.02
Jxt RP	10.90	11.12	−.04
Lante	12.01	13.14	−.02
Mina Si	7.36	7.67	−.01
Msall p	9.56	9.96	+.01
Nuz Bai	9.85	9.95	...
Oceana	16.49	17.64	+.12
Grxya	15.30	N.L.	+.04
Gsrxab r	12.96	N.L.	−.04
Hilt ltd	10.54	N.L.	−.02
Holpre r	8.40	N.L.	−.02
Hprl Rd	13.58	N.L.	+.07
Nev Sra	16.65	N.L.	−.01
Ow Nort r	13.53	N.L.	+.17
Sys Run	5.08	N.L.	+.01
Tqr Hyd	8.73	N.L.	+.02
Tuir IS	10.26	N.L.	−.03
Tvsa Ei	5.11	N.L.	+.01
Veersl Yr	9.49	9.87	+.07
Fdrlk:			
Uhd Eec	10.18	N.L.	+.03
Rho Qnd p	10.77	N.L.	+.02
Iro Nico t	8.54	N.L.	−.06
Gpprl:			
Allist B	24.00	N.L.	+.01
Cuy Nini t	10.76	N.L.	−.03
Eqryti	15.87	16.71	+.02
Ginta Ir	12.00	N.L.	+.01
Gvrt Lis	10.18	N.L.	+.03
Heal lec f	10.40	10.51	−.02
Jbd Hld	10.23	10.77	−.04

The following is an example of how mutual fund tables appear in many newspapers.

The first column is the abbreviated fund's name. Several funds listed under a single heading indicate a family of funds.

The second column is the Net Asset Value (NAV) per share as of the close of the preceding business day. In some newspapers, the NAV is identified as the sell or the bid price—the amount per share you would receive if you sold your shares (less the deferred sales charge, if any). Each mutual fund determines its net asset value every business day by dividing the market value of its total net assets, less liabilities, by the number of shares outstanding. On any given day, you can determine the value of your holdings by multiplying the NAV by the number of shares you own.

The third column is the offering price or, in some papers, the buy price or the asked price—the price you would pay if you purchased shares. The buy price is the NAV plus any sales charges. If there are no initial sales charges, an "N.L." for no-load appears in this column, and the buy price is the same as the NAV. To figure the sales charge percentage, divide the difference between the NAV and the offering price by the offering price. Here, for instance, the sales charge is 5 percent ($14.18 − $13.47 = $0.71; $0.71 ÷ $14.18 = 0.050).

The fourth column shows the change, if any, in net asset value from the preceding day's quotation—in other words, the change over the most recent one-day trading period. This fund, for example, gained six cents per share.

A "p" following the abbreviated name of the fund denotes a fund that charges an annual fee from assets for marketing and distribution costs, also known as a 12b-1 plan (named after the 1980 Securities and Exchange Commission rule that permits them).

If the fund name is followed by an "r," the fund has either a contingent deferred sales charge (CDSC) or a redemption fee. A CDSC is a charge if shares are sold within a certain period; a redemption charge is a fee applied whenever shares are sold.

A "t" designates a fund that has both a CDSC or a redemption fee and a 12b-1 fee.

An "f" indicates a fund that habitually enters the previous day's prices, instead of the current day's.

Other footnotes may also apply to a fund listing. Please see the explanatory notes that accompany mutual fund tables in your newspaper.

Figure 5.2   How to Read Newspaper Fund Quotes

Source: *Mutual Fund Factbook*, 2000.

THREE COMMON MISTAKES IN MUTUAL FUND INVESTING

Mutual fund investing isn't an exact science, so you'll probably make some mistakes along the way. To avoid as many missteps as possible, take note of fund investors' more common errors:

1. *No strategy.* This is probably the most frequent mistake among mutual fund investors. "I never cease to be surprised by the vast number of individuals who select specific mutual funds without giving any thought to an asset allocation strategy," says Jack L. Piazza, managing principal of Sensible Investment Strategies. "Many investors may actually define and identify their investment objectives, but then skip the next vital step in establishing a successful mutual fund portfolio: creating a detailed asset allocation strategy." Without a well-defined, appropriate asset allocation strategy that accurately reflects individual investment objectives and preferences (time horizon, return objectives, risk tolerance, and so on), the selection of mutual funds is haphazard instead of logical.

2. *Overweighting in high-risk, nondiversified funds.* This mistake is a specific example of portfolio imbalance: a very large percentage of total portfolio assets becomes concentrated in funds with very high risk-reward characteristics, even though the fund types may actually reflect chosen investment objectives. The result is excessive volatility in the price movement of these funds, which, in many instances, can cause disappointing portfolio performance because the very large percentage of risk does not justify the potential reward. In other words, the risk is highly disproportionate to overall profit potential. Overweighting can occur with any type of risk tolerance, although this specific type of overweighting is more likely to be a problem in portfolios with aggressive risk tolerances.

3. *Buying at the wrong time.* One of the biggest tax faux pas an individual investor can make is to invest in a mutual fund before it makes its annual capital gains distribution. Most funds declare their distributions in December, but some do so as early as October. Even if you buy the fund just one day before gains are distributed, you'll owe taxes as if

you owned the fund all year. Before you invest, call the fund to find out when it declares its distribution.

It's not uncommon for high-turnover growth funds to realize gains equal to 10 percent of net asset value. If you invest $10,000 before that distribution, you will owe taxes on an extra $1,000. If you're investing in a tax-deferred retirement account or buying a low-turnover fund, you don't need to concern yourself with these year-end tax issues.

Regardless of which asset allocation method an investor prefers, the important message is clear: To avoid the pitfalls of haphazard fund selection, develop a detailed asset allocation strategy that accurately represents your investment objectives and preferences.

WHERE TO START

Given the old axiom about the longest journey beginning with a single step, it's a good idea to understand why you want to invest in a particular fund. The fund's investment objectives—stated in the fund's prospectus—should be compatible with your financial goals. Thankfully, SEC regulations now demand that investment prospectuses must be user-friendly—not stated in the financial mumbo-jumbo that only a Wall Street lawyer could love.

The prospectus will describe the fund's objectives (for example, long-term capital growth; income) and the strategies used to achieve them. The discussion of investment strategies may describe risks (market risk, manager risk, country risk) faced by investors in the fund. The prospectus will also note the types of securities (common stocks, preferred stocks, bonds, options) the fund purchases, and will identify any investment advisers employed by the fund. The document may set forth investment parameters that the fund follows (for example, limits on the use or purchase of derivatives, foreign stocks, short sales). The parameters may also indicate the maximum and minimum percentages for specific types of securities and/or holdings in any one company.

Remember that stock mutual funds are either "actively" managed by a fund manager or "passively" managed to match the performance of an index (for example, the Standard & Poor's 500). For actively managed funds, it is important to know the manager's tenure and track record. Changes in a fund's management can have a significant impact on the fund's performance.

To track your fund's performance, or those on your wishlist, you can use the fund tables in your daily newspaper, which will show how much fund shares were trading for at the close of yesterday's business, along with historical performance. For more up-to-date pricing and analysis, try Web sites like www.morningstar.com.

BENEFITS OF FUND OWNERSHIP

The good news with mutual funds has always been that you can have your cake and eat it too.

By their diversified nature, mutual funds allow you to invest in myriad companies at the same time. Best yet, your fund is handled by an accomplished fund manager who knows what he or she is doing. By owning shares in a mutual fund instead of buying individual stocks or bonds directly, your investment risk is spread out. And because your mutual fund buys and sells large amounts of securities at a time, its costs are often lower than those you would pay as an individual investor. Here are some other benefits of owning mutual funds:

- *Professional money management.* Mutual funds give individual investors the benefit of experienced and skilled professional investment managers who have the knowledge and information necessary to make informed investment decisions. Fund managers devote themselves exclusively to monitoring market and economic trends, analyzing securities, and implementing a consistent investment strategy that reflects the goals of the fund.

- *Diversification.* Funds can reduce risk by spreading it among a large number of investments. If one stock performs badly, its impact on the overall portfolio can be mitigated. Funds can also reduce risk by investing in a number of different asset classes: stocks (in international as well as U.S. enterprises), bonds, cash, and other securities.

- *Cost.* Many mutual funds can be purchased commission-free. This reduces the impact of commissions and expenses on an investor's portfolio. Also, by pooling money accepted from many investors, mutual funds can reduce the percentage of expenses. Many investors strive to keep commissions as low as possible, but commissions can still swallow 3 to 5 percent of an investor's portfolio. Funds typically have expenses of about 1 to 2 percent. The minimum initial investment for most mutual funds is quite low. Many mutual fund companies will accept an initial investment as low as $500. You can also set up a purchase plan that will automatically debit your checking account each month (or each quarter) for an amount as low as $50 per month, and you have the option of increasing your investment level any time.

- *"Targeted" investments.* Funds provide ways of targeting sectors and specific goals. As an example, international funds offer a way of investing globally without worrying about currency or political risks. Fund companies hire experts who understand the complicated capital markets outside the United States and can follow and react quickly to news in those markets. Fixed-income and tax-free mutual funds fulfill very distinct purposes, and an index fund can ensure that an investor matches the performance of the overall market (or sector) year after year.

- *Liquidity.* Mutual funds are a very liquid investment for individuals. If cash is needed in a hurry, an investor can always sell fund shares and get that day's closing redemption price. There is no need to worry about finding a buyer or knowing the price at which the shares might sell. Investors can sell their mutual fund units on any business day and receive current market value on their investments. Current unit values are usually calculated daily, based on the market value of the underlying securities.

- *Easy management.* Mutual fund companies often offer an array of attractive free services for shareholders: reinvestment of dividends and distributions, the ability to transfer between funds in a family, systematic investment or withdrawal plans to allow you to invest or sell on a monthly basis, and detailed recordkeeping and tax reports.

- *Reports and statements.* Mutual funds provide you with detailed reports and statements that make record-keeping simple. You can monitor the performance of your mutual funds simply by reviewing the business pages of most newspapers. Most mutual funds will also provide you with the convenience of periodic purchase plans, automatic withdrawal plans, and the automatic reinvestment of interest and dividends.

DISADVANTAGES OF MUTUAL FUNDS

The most significant downside to owning shares of mutual funds is that it can be hard, even in a bull market, to pick an outstanding fund. According to Investor Alliance, a mutual fund industry group, about 80 percent of all mutual funds perform worse than average. Here are some more downsides to fund ownership:

- *Hidden fees.* One of the reasons for lower returns is that funds have a variety of fees and expenses. All funds have fees for management and operating expenses, which typically range from 1 to 2 percent. But some funds also charge a sales fee (known as a "load") of 3 to 5 percent, and in some cases up to 8½ percent. Some funds charge their investors "distribution fees" or "12b-1 fees." Marketing and advertising costs are passed right along to the fundholders. These expenses can severely impact an investor's return and must be carefully considered (and usually avoided).

- *Hard to keep score.* It's nearly impossible to tell whether a fund is a good value at any particular point in time. Compared to stocks, it is much harder to determine whether a mutual fund's net asset value (NAV) really represents good value. A fund may show a solid rate of return for a particular period, but that could have resulted from holdings having reached peaks and then declined.

- *Revolving doors.* A fund is only as good as its management, and fund managers may move to greener or wealthier opportunities. The Magellan Fund survived Peter Lynch's departure, but other funds have not done so well after dynamic and talented managers have left. There are some exceptions. Funds in the Twentieth Century family have no individual manager. They are guided by committee.

HOW FUNDS CAN EARN YOU MONEY

In a good overview on mutual funds, entitled "Introduction to Mutual Funds," the Securities and Exchange Commission (SEC) points out that you can earn money in three ways:

1. A fund may receive income in the form of dividends and interest on the securities it owns. "A fund will pay its shareholders dividends that represent nearly all of the income it has earned," says the SEC.

2. The price of the securities a fund owns may increase. When a fund sells a security that has increased in price, the fund has a capital gain. At the end of the year, most funds distribute these capital gains (minus any capital losses) to their investors.

3. If a fund does not sell but holds onto securities that have increased in price, the net asset value (NAV) of its shares

increases. A higher NAV reflects a higher value of an investment. If you sell your shares, you make a profit (this also is a capital gain). Usually, funds will give you a choice: The fund can send you payment for distributions and dividends, or you can have them reinvested and instruct the fund to buy more shares—often, without paying an additional sales load.

TAX ISSUES

In some ways, mutual funds are an accountant's dream. A host of tax issues are associated with fund ownership.

Right off the bat, you will owe taxes on any distributions and dividends in the year you receive them (or reinvest them). You will also owe taxes on any capital gains you receive when you sell your shares. Keep your account statements in order; you'll need them to figure out your taxes at the end of the year. If you invest in a tax-exempt fund (such as a municipal bond fund), some or all of your dividends will be exempt from federal (and perhaps state and local) income tax. You will, however, owe taxes on any capital gains.

If you sell mutual fund shares, you realize a capital gain or loss. Mutual funds also distribute their dividends received and their own realized capital gains—usually, at the end of the year. These distributions, whether taken in cash or reinvested, are taxable. (Note that the nontaxability of municipal bond funds applies only to dividend distributions. Capital gains distributions are always taxable.)

Often, it's a bad idea to buy a mutual fund just before the distribution date. Part of your investment will be immediately returned to you as a taxable distribution, so you will be paying taxes much earlier than if you had waited until after the distribution. The distribution lowers the NAV of your shares and allows you to "deduct" it when you sell the shares, but paying taxes sooner rather than later prevents you from gaining investment income on the amount that is taxed. Reinvesting is considered identical to taking a distribution in cash and sending the same amount into the fund as a new investment. Keep that in mind when you are calculating the basis in your account. When selling, it is best to know ahead of time the different methods for calculating the basis of shares sold. Some methods require that you designate which shares are to be sold.

TYPES OF MUTUAL FUNDS

Like the ice cream menu at Baskin-Robbins, the choices that await you in the mutual fund world are bountiful. Most mutual fund company Web sites will provide a good description of the different kinds of funds.

The three main categories of mutual funds are: (1) money market funds, (2) bond funds, and (3) stock funds.

1. *Money market funds.* These funds try to maintain a constant NAV (usually, $1) per share, while yielding dividends from their investments in short-term debt securities. They offer very low risk but usually have low long-term return. Most restrict investments to the top two (out of four) Moody's and Standard & Poor's ratings for short-term debt; some, like national-government-only funds, restrict themselves to only the top rating, which provides a bit of extra credit safety, usually at a slightly lower yield. Most also invest in repurchase agreements (a.k.a. repos) collateralized by short-term debt securities; these are subject to the credit or fraud risk of the other party in the repo deal. It's important to remember that money market fund values are not insured by the FDIC or any other government agency. Heavy defaults in a fund's securities can cause it to be unable to maintain its constant NAV.

2. *Bond funds.* As we saw in Chapter 5, bond funds invest in longer-term debt securities. Thus, the short-term risk is greater than the infinitesimal risk of the money market. But returns are usually higher. The NAVs may fluctuate due to both interest rate risk and defaults. Unlike individual bonds, most bond funds do not mature; they trade to maintain their stated future maturity. The types of debt of bond funds are similar to those of money funds (but longer-term); however, futures and options are sometimes used for hedging purposes.

3. *Stock funds*. The most common and popular types of fund class, stock funds invest in common and/or preferred stocks. Stocks usually have higher short-term risk than bonds, but have historically produced the best long-term returns. Stock funds often hold small amounts of money market investments to meet redemptions; some hold larger amounts of money market investments when they cannot find any stock worth investing in, or when they believe the market is about to head downward. Some of the possible investment goals (they are not necessarily mutually exclusive) are:

- *Growth*. These funds usually tend to be volatile. They seek maximum growth of earnings and share price, with little regard for dividends.

- *Aggressive growth*. Similar to growth funds, but even more aggressive; they tend to be the most volatile.

- *Equity income*. These funds are more conservative and seek maximum dividends.

- *Growth and income*. In between growth funds and income funds; they seek both growth and a reasonable amount of income.

- *Small company*. Their focus is on smaller companies, usually of the growth or aggressive growth variety, since smaller companies usually don't pay much in dividends.

- *International*. The focus here is on stocks outside the United States. Generally, investments include many nations' companies.

- *Country or regional funds*. These funds buy stocks primarily in the designated country or region.

- *Index funds*. These funds do no management; they just buy some index, like the Standard & Poor's 500. Some index funds, particularly those emulating indexes with large numbers of stocks, such as the Wilshire 4500 or Russell 2000, emulate the index by buying a subset with similar industry mix, capitalization, price/earnings ratio, and so on. Expenses are usually very low.

- *Sector funds*. These funds buy stocks only in one industry. They usually are considered to be among the riskiest stock funds, though different sectors tend to have different levels and types of risk.

- *Balanced funds.* By mixing stocks and bonds (and sometimes other types of assets), a balanced fund is likely to yield a return that is between the return of stocks and bonds—usually, at a lower risk than investing in either alone, since different types of assets rise and fall at different times. An investor can create his or her own balanced fund by buying shares of a personal-favorite stock fund(s) and a personal-favorite bond fund(s) (and other funds, if desired) in the desired allocation.

- *Regular balanced funds.* These funds usually hold a fixed or rarely changed allocation between stocks and bonds.

- *Asset allocation funds.* These funds may switch to any allocation. To some degree, they are usually based on market timing.

DUE DILIGENCE: WHAT MATTERS WHEN SHOPPING FOR A FUND

Shopping for the right mutual fund is no less important than shopping for the right car or home, or a college for your son or daughter. The ramifications from choosing the wrong fund may last for years. Correspondingly, choose the right fund and watch your investment portfolio grow by leaps and bounds. Here are some issues to consider when you are studying a mutual fund.

- *The fund's reputation and past performance.* The Investors Alliance's Mutual Fund report and Mutual Fund Database provide this information as do other business or investment publications such as *The Wall Street Journal, Barron's, Forbes,* and *Money* magazine. Past performance does not predict the future but it probably is a good indicator of management quality. See whether the fund has been around for the past 10 to 15 years. How well has the fund done in the past? How has its performance compared to the S&P 500 and other market indexes in up years and down years? How long has the fund manager been running the fund?

VIEWING PAST PERFORMANCE

A fund's past performance is not as important as you might think. Advertisements, rankings, and ratings tell you how well a fund has performed in the past. But studies show that the future is often different. This year's "number one" fund can easily become next year's below-average fund. (*Note:* Although past performance is not a reliable indicator of future performance, volatility of past returns is a good indicator of a fund's future volatility.)

- *Your personal investment goals and risk tolerance.* Some growth stock funds deliver high returns in bull markets but tend to do poorly in bear markets. If the possibility of capital loss disturbs you, consider a more conservative growth-and-income fund or an "all-weather" fund. Check the fund's beta—the same volatility measure used for stocks. Funds with a beta higher than 1.0 are more price-volatile than the market; funds with a beta below 1.0 are less volatile.

- *The fund's risk.* Funds with high risk ratings usually have higher betas and are more price-volatile. Funds with low risk ratings usually have lower betas. Remember, neither beta nor the risk level predicts your long-term return. Funds with high risk ratings have good *and* bad long-term records, and this also holds true for lower-risk funds. Check the funds' long-term records.

- *The fund's investment objectives and goals.* Read the fund prospectus to learn about the objectives of the mutual fund. Some funds buy and hold stocks, a strategy that lowers the funds' expenses. Others turn their portfolio over very often, in large blocks of shares, to profit from a $1 or more increase in a stock's share price. Others try to time the market so that they can buy more stocks during market lows and sell when they think the market is overvalued. The Investors Alliance prefers funds that purchase undervalued companies and hold the stocks until they reach the desired target price.

- *Information about the fund manager.* Most funds have a fund manager who is in charge of picking the stocks or bonds that the fund holds. Fund managers are in a competitive business; if they do a good job, the fund will want to reward and keep them. Find out how long the manager has been managing the fund. Be wary of selecting a fund based on its excellent track record if the portfolio manager who created those excellent returns has left the fund.

- *The fund's expenses.* If the expenses are too high (over $1.50 per $100), you may want to consider another fund. (See Figure 5.3.)

- *Commissions and fees.* No matter what a commission or fee is used for, sales fees, redemption fees, or 12b-1 fees all have the same effect: They reduce the investment return. Information on fees and loads is listed in the "fee table" on the inside front page of a fund's prospectus. Other ancillary information is often disguised or buried in the fine print. If you are not sure about a dollar amount, call the fund and ask for specifics.

- *The dollar value of the fund's assets.* Some experts believe that when a fund gets larger than $1 billion to $2 billion in assets, it will not do as well as the smaller funds ($50 million to $300 million). Often, when funds get large, the mutual fund company stops accepting new members. Some fund companies spin off clone funds, but the new funds may not have the same fund manager as the original fund. Funds typically stop accepting new shareholders because the fund manager believes that he or she cannot handle additional money without lowering the quality of performance anticipated by the current shareholders.

- *The high performance of smaller funds.* Smaller funds have a greater probability of outperforming larger funds and the market.

Annual Fund Operating Expenses reflect the normal costs of operating a fund. Unlike transaction fees, these expenses are not charged directly to an investor but are deducted from fund assets before earnings are distributed to shareholders.

Management Fees	0.47%
Distribution (12b-1) Fees	0.21%
Other Expenses	0.36%
Total Annual Fund Operating Expenses (Expense Ratio)	1.04%

Example

This example is intended to help an investor compare the cost of investing in different funds. The example assumes a $10,000 investment in the fund for one, three, five, and ten years and then a redemption of all fund shares at the end of those periods. The example also assumes that an investment returns 5 percent each year and that the fund's operating expenses remain the same. Although actual costs may be higher or lower, based on these assumptions an investor's costs would be:

1 year	$ 552
3 years	$ 771
5 years	$1,013
10 years	$1,730

Management Fees—This is a fee charged by a fund's investment adviser for managing the fund's portfolio of securities and providing related services.

Distribution (12b-1) Fees—This fee, if charged, is deducted from fund assets to pay marketing and advertising expenses or, more commonly, to compensate sales professionals. By law, 12b-1 fees cannot exceed 1 percent of a fund's average net assets per year. The 12b-1 fee may include a service fee of up to 0.25 percent of average net assets per year to compensate sales professionals for providing services or maintaining shareholder accounts.

Other Expenses—These expenses include, for example, fees paid to a fund's transfer agent for providing fund shareholder services, such as toll-free phone communications, computerized account services, Web site services, recordkeeping, printing, and mailing.

Total Annual Fund Operating Expenses (Expense Ratio)—This represents the sum of all of a fund's annual operating costs, expressed as a percentage of average net assets. Total annual fund operating expenses are also known as the fund's expense ratio.

Example of the effect of expenses on a $10,000 investment is a hypothetical illustration required by the SEC to be included in every fund's fee table. It is presented in a standardized format and based on specified assumptions (5 percent annual return, expenses unchanged) in order to make it easier for investors to compare different funds' fees.

Figure 5.3   Annual Fund Operating Expenses

Source: Mutual Fund Factbook, 2000.

It is easier for a fund manager to get high returns when managing a $50-million or a $200-million fund than when managing a $1-billion to $4-billion fund. Even the legendary Peter Lynch, former portfolio manager of the $20-billion Fidelity Magellan fund, says it is easier to manage a smaller fund. Still, be sure the manager of *any* fund that you choose for investment has a good track record. A huge fund with an excellent manager is far better than a small fund with a mediocre manager.

- A *two- or three-fund portfolio*. One fund could be for growth and income; another could be a growth fund. *Forbes* and other investment magazines have a listing of funds that do well in bull markets and bear markets. If you cannot find a fund that does well in both, you may want to buy one that does well in an up market and another that does well in a down market.

COMPARING COSTS

While high fees and expenses can be hidden by a rising Bull market, it's less true when returns fall back down to earth. That's why experts are beginning to stress that over the long-term, fees will be a deciding factor in how well your investments perform. As noted above, funds charge investors fees and expenses. A fund with high costs must perform better than a low-cost fund or it will not generate the same returns. Over time, even small differences in fees can translate into large differences in returns. For example, if you invested $10,000 in a fund that produced a 10 percent annual return before expenses and had annual operating expenses of 1.5 percent, then after 20 years you would have roughly $49,725. But if the fund had expenses of only 0.5 percent, you would end up with $60,858—an 18 percent difference. To calculate your own fund costs, the Securities and Exchange Commission offers a Mutual Fund Cost Calculator for computing how the costs of different mutual funds add up over time and eat into your returns. Look for it at www.sec.gov. Or, call

MUTUAL FUND FEES AND TIPS FOR COMPARING COSTS

Understanding the types of fees you may pay to invest in a fund is critical to managing your costs and to deciding which funds to invest in. Here's a rundown of the more important ones.

- *Front-end load.* A front-end load is a sales charge you pay when you buy shares. "This type of load, which by law cannot be higher than 8.5 percent of your investment, reduces the amount of your investment in the fund."

Example. If you have $1,000 to invest in a mutual fund with a 5 percent front-end load, $50 will go to pay the sales charge, and $950 will be invested in the fund.

- *Back-end load.* A back-end load (also called a deferred load) is a sales charge you pay when you sell your shares. "It usually starts out at 5 percent or 6 percent for the first year, and gets smaller each year until it reaches zero (say, in year 6 or year 7 of your investment)."

Example. You invest $1,000 in a mutual fund with a 6 percent back-end load that decreases to zero in the seventh year. Let's assume, for the purpose of this example, that the value of your investment remains at $1,000 for seven years. If you sell your shares during the first year, you will get back only $940 (ignoring any gains or losses); $60 will go to pay the sales charge. If you sell your shares during the seventh year, you will get back $1,000.

- *Rule 12b-1 fee.* One ongoing fee that is taken out of fund assets has come to be known as a Rule 12b-1 fee. It is most often used to pay commissions to brokers and other salespersons, and occasionally to pay for advertising and other costs of promoting the fund to investors. It usually is between 0.25 percent and 1.00 percent of assets annually. Funds with back-end loads usually have higher Rule 12b-1 fees. If you are considering whether to pay a front-end load or a back-end load, think about how long you plan to stay in a fund. If you expect to stay in for six years or more, a front-end load may cost less than a back-end load. Even if your back-end load has fallen to zero, you could, over time, pay more in Rule 12b-1 fees than if you paid a front-end load.

- Beware of a salesperson who tells you, "This is just like a no-load fund." Even if there is no front-end load, check the fee table in the prospectus to see what other loads or fees you may have to pay.
- Check the fee table to see whether any part of a fund's fees or expenses has been waived. If so, the fees and expenses may increase suddenly when the waiver ends (the part of the prospectus that appears after the fee table will tell you by how much).
- Many funds allow an exchange of shares for the shares of another fund managed by the same adviser. The first part of the fee table will tell you whether there is any exchange fee.

Source: Securities and Exchange Commission, "Introduction to Mutual Funds."

the agency directly and ask for its informative handbook: "Invest Wisely: An Introduction to Mutual Funds." You can also get other SEC publications by calling the SEC's toll-free publications line at 1-(800) SEC-0330.

Costs are important because they lower your returns. A fund that has a sales load and high expenses will have to perform better than a low-cost fund, just to stay even with the low-cost fund. Find the fee table near the front of the fund's prospectus. Review the fund's costs. You can use the fee table to compare the costs of different funds.

The fee table breaks costs into two main categories:*

1. Sales loads and transaction fees (paid when you buy, sell, or exchange your shares).
2. Ongoing expenses (paid while you remain invested in the fund).

* *Source:* Securities and Exchange Commission.

SALES LOADS

The first part of the fee table will tell you whether the fund charges any sales loads.

No-load funds do not charge sales loads. When you buy no-load funds, you make your own choices, without the assistance of a financial professional. There are no-load funds in every major fund category. However, even no-load funds have ongoing expenses such as management fees.

When a mutual fund charges a sales load, it usually pays for commissions to people who sell the fund's shares, and for other marketing costs. Sales loads buy you a broker's services and advice; they do not ensure superior performance. In fact, funds that charge sales loads have not performed better on average (ignoring the loads) than those that do not charge sales loads.

TIPS FROM THE SEC FOR COMPARING PERFORMANCE

The SEC's Web site (www.sec.gov) has a wealth of information on choosing the right mutual fund. It also offers tips on fund performance comparisons. Among the tips are:

- *Check the fund's total return.* You will find it in the Financial Highlights, near the front of the prospectus. Total return measures increases and decreases in the value of your investment over time, after subtracting costs.

- *See how total return has varied over the years.* The Financial Highlights in the prospectus show yearly total return for the most recent 10-year period. An impressive 10-year total return may be based on one spectacular year followed by many average years. Looking at year-to-year changes in total return is a good way to see how stable the fund's returns have been.

Past performance, especially the short-term performance of relatively new or small funds, is not as important as you may think. As with any investment, a fund's past performance is no guarantee of its future success. Over the long term, the success (or failure) of your investment in a fund also will depend on factors such as:

1. The fund's sales charges, fees, and expenses.
2. The taxes you may have to pay when you receive a distribution.
3. The age and size of the fund.
4. The fund's risks and volatility.
5. Recent changes in the fund's operations.

- *Consider the age and size of the fund.* Before investing in a fund, read the prospectus to find out how long the fund has been operating and the size of the fund. Newly created or small funds sometimes have excellent short-term performance records. Because these funds may invest in only a small number of stocks, a few successful stocks can have a large impact on their performance. But as these funds grow larger and increase the number of stocks they own, each stock has less impact on performance. This may make it more difficult to sustain initial results. You can get a better picture of a fund's performance by looking at the fund's results over longer periods and noting how it has weathered the ups and downs of the market. Think about the volatility of the fund.

- *Consider fund or sector volatility.* Past performance does not necessarily predict future returns, but it can tell you how volatile a fund has been. Generally, the more volatile a fund, the higher the investment risk. If you'll need your money a year from now to meet a financial goal, you probably can't risk investing in a fund with a volatile history because you will not have enough time to ride out any declines in the stock market. Read the fund's prospectus and annual report, and compare its year-to-year performance figures. These figures can help tell you whether the fund earned most of its returns in a few small bursts or in a steadier stream. For example, over 10 years, two funds may have gained 12 percent per year *on average,* but they may have taken drastically different routes. One might have had a few years of spectacular performance and a few years of low (or negative) returns, while the performance of the other may have been much steadier from year to year. Be sure to factor in the risks the fund takes to achieve its returns.

- *Know the fund's strategy.* Read the fund's prospectus and shareholder reports to learn about its investment strategy. Funds with higher rates of return may take risks that are beyond your comfort level and are inconsistent with your financial goals. For example, a fund that invests primarily in stocks that are subject to quick changes in price—like initial public offerings or high-tech stocks—will usually be riskier than other types of funds. But remember that all funds carry some level of risk. Just because a fund invests in government or corporate bonds does not mean it has no significant risk. The fund's investments could be very sensitive to interest rate changes. Thinking about your long-term investment strategies and your tolerance for risk can help you decide what type of fund is best suited for you.

- *Ask about recent changes in the fund's operations.* Has the fund's investment adviser or investment strategy changed recently? Has the fund merged with another fund? Operational changes such as these can affect future fund performance. For instance, the investment adviser or portfolio manager who generated the fund's successful performance may no longer be managing the fund.

- *Check the types of services offered and the fees charged by the fund.* Read the fund's prospectus to learn what services it provides to shareholders. Some funds offer special services, such as toll-free telephone numbers, check-writing privileges, and automatic investment programs. Find out how easily you can buy and sell shares, and whether the fund charges a fee for buying and selling shares. International funds require extra work by their managers and usually have higher costs.

- *Assess how the fund will impact the diversification of your portfolio.* Generally, the success of your investments over time will depend largely on how much money you have invested in each of the major asset classes—stocks, bonds, and cash—rather than on the particular securities you hold. When choosing a mutual fund, you should consider how your interest in that fund affects the overall diversification of your investment portfolio. Maintaining a diversified and balanced portfolio is key to maintaining an acceptable level of risk.

THE ADVANTAGE OF NO-LOAD MUTUAL FUNDS

Since how much you spend determines how much you make, it's important to choose your poison, so to speak, right up front. Do you want to invest in load or no-load funds? Advocates of each type of fund give the following arguments: load funds are necessary to compensate for research and advice; no-load funds save you money by eliminating unneeded expenses.

Let's first review the different types of mutual fund structures. Load funds charge a commission; no-load funds are commission-free. According to Jack Piazza, the structure of load funds can be (1) front-end, with the commission varying from 3 percent to 6.25 percent of the investment, or (2) back-end (also known as redemption) with the commission usually at 3 percent of asset value when sold. In addition, the vast majority of all load funds charge annual distribution fees (12b-1 fees), which are used to pay for promotional costs. These costs vary from 0.25 percent to 0.75 percent of annual asset value. Some no-load funds also charge 12b-1 fees. No-load funds that do not charge 12b-1 fees are known as 100 percent no-load or true no-load funds.

Is there really that much of a worthwhile difference between load and no-load funds? Piazza compares mutual fund structures to a

100-yard race. "If the race competitors have equal ability," he says, "but one has a five- to six-yard head start, you obviously know who would win the contest. In fact, the one with the head start would only lose to a competitor with far superior ability." The mutual fund illustration below assumes that all "competitors" have equal ability. This allows an accurate demonstration of the differences in performance.

Illustration

A $10,000 investment has a very conservative 9 percent annual net return rate (after annual fund operating expenses of 1.0 percent) over three years. Following are the differences in total return and return on investment (ROI) among three different types of mutual fund sales structures:

1. 100 percent no-load (no 12b-1 fees).
2. 5 percent front-end load with 0.5 percent per year 12b-1 fees.
3. 3 percent back-end load with 0.5 percent per year 12b-1 fees (redemption in year 3).

FUND STRUCTURE: TOTAL RETURN COMPARISON

	Start	Year 1	Year 2	Year 3
100% No-load	$10,000	$10,900	$11,881	$12,950
5% Front-end load	9,500	10,303	11,174	12,119
3% Back-end load	10,000	10,845	11,762	12,374

FUND STRUCTURE COMPARISON: CUMULATIVE ROI

	Year 1	Year 2	Year 3
100% No-load	9.0%	18.8%	29.5%
5% Front-end load	3.0	11.7	21.2
3% Back-end load	8.4	17.6	23.7

Source: Sensible Investment Strategies (seninvest.com).

In cumulative ROI after three years, the 100 percent no-load fund outperforms the 5 percent front-end load fund by 39.3 percent and the back-end load fund by 24.4 percent, even though a conservative 9 percent annual return rate is identical for all three funds. The ROI advantage of the 100 percent no-load fund is due entirely to the absence of sales load and annual 12b-1 distribution fees. The advantage of the 100 percent no-load fund in this illustration is very apparent. Comparative ROI differences would be more dramatic as the annual return rate parameter falls below 9 percent, and less dramatic as the annual return rate parameter rises above 9 percent.

Does this imply that all no-load funds are superior to all load funds? Of course not, says Piazza. "Obviously, a 5 percent front-end load fund with a 15 percent annual return will outperform a no-load fund with a 9 percent annual return," he adds. "However, no-load funds that carry above-average rankings (from Morningstar or Lipper) will most likely outperform load funds, provided that the funds are in the identical fund category (i.e., growth, growth and income, global, corporate bond, and so on) with a time frame of at least three years."

Finally, you should be aware of asset-based fees. Recently, major brokerage firms have announced that they will offer no-load funds from many fund families without charging commissions or 12b-1 fees. However, these firms will compensate salespeople by charging clients up to 1.5 percent of their assets on an annual basis. Over a relatively short time, these fees would be substantially greater than even a 5 percent front-end load! It is best to avoid these types of fees and maintain the no-load advantage.

THE ROLE OF RISK IN MUTUAL FUND STRATEGIES

Call it the sleep-at-night factor. Identifying individual risk tolerance is one of the basic factors in determining an optimum investment strategy for a mutual fund portfolio. Regardless of whether a strategy applies to a total portfolio, a portion of a portfolio, or a qualified retirement plan, risk tolerance can affect both asset allocation and the selection of fund categories (i.e., small company growth, global, growth and income, corporate bond, government bond, and so on).

Let's first define risk. According to Piazza, risk generally refers to the tendency for investments to change in value from time to time. "Many different types of specific risk exist which can affect investment value: bonds generally have various degrees of credit risk, inflation risk, interest rate risk, and principal risk; stocks can have dividend risk, market risk, and, in foreign stocks, currency and political risks," he explains. "However, risk in mutual funds usually refers to the fluctuations in the price of a fund. These fluctuations, known also as price volatility, can range from stable to very volatile."

As risk increases, both price volatility and total return potential proportionately increase; conversely, as risk decreases, price volatility and total return potential proportionately decrease. This "risk/reward" rule is often illustrated with risk and reward both escalating over a broad spectrum that begins with cash reserves, changes to bonds, and then ends with stocks.

In mutual funds, risk tolerance is normally associated with the degree of fluctuation in the price of bond or stock funds. Investors typically fall into one of three categories of risk tolerance: (1) conservative, (2) moderate, or (3) aggressive. Conservative risk tolerances will accept lower returns to minimize price volatility. Moderate (or average) risk tolerances will accept increased price volatility to pursue higher returns. Aggressive risk tolerances seek the highest returns and will accept large swings in price volatility. Note that these risk tolerances can apply to one broad risk/reward spectrum or to separate bond and stock spectra.

There are two contrasting viewpoints regarding the application of risk tolerances. One treats risk tolerance primarily as an asset allocation adjustment covering only one risk/reward spectrum (cash, bond, and stock funds). Examples include aggressive growth (100 percent stock), growth (80 percent stock, 20 percent bond), moderate growth (60 percent stock, 40 percent bond), conservative growth (40 percent stock, 40 percent bond, 20 percent cash), and income (20 percent stock, 40 percent bond, 40 percent cash). The other viewpoint treats risk tolerance primarily as a fund category adjustment, starting with a selected asset allocation (based on time horizon, return objective, and portfolio size) and then denoting the types of fund categories to match with the desired risk tolerance. Compared to the asset allocation method, this method allows more precision and customization in designing an investment plan.

Using the fund category allocation method, conservative, moderate, or aggressive risk tolerances can combine with a variety of return objectives, subject to certain time horizon restrictions. For example, any one of these risk tolerances can match with a growth, balanced, or income-oriented return objective, provided that the time horizon is a long term. With short-term or intermediate time horizons, any one of these three risk tolerances can match with an income-oriented return objective (growth-oriented return objectives require long-term time horizons). Even with specific return objectives (i.e., low growth-high income, high growth-low income), and subject to time horizon restrictions, any one of these risk tolerances can be used in most instances. One exception is a very high growth-no income objective, which requires an aggressive risk tolerance along with a long-term time horizon.

Let's look at two hypothetical situations that use the fund category allocation method. In the first scenario, Eileen and Danny share nearly identical investment objectives. Each will retire in 10 years and wants to reallocate $100,000 in a long-term, balance-oriented plan (equal emphasis on growth potential and income). Eileen prefers an aggressive risk tolerance; Danny wants a conservative risk tolerance. A fundamental allocation consisting of 50 percent stock funds and 50 percent bond funds applies to both portfolios. In this scenario, one example of the application of risk tolerances could produce the following fund categories and their allocation percentages:

	Stock Funds	Bond Funds
EILEEN	20 percent growth	25 percent multisector bond
	20 percent global	15 percent high-yield bond
	10 percent mid-cap growth	10 percent international bond

DANNY	20 percent growth and income	25 percent government bond
	20 percent equity	15 percent corporate bond income
	10 percent global	10 percent GNMA ("Ginnie Mae")

These two portfolios, while reflecting the investment objectives of Eileen and Danny, are very different in fund type selections and allocations, even though risk tolerance is the only investment characteristic difference between them.

In another scenario, Tom and Janice have each inherited $10,000. Each wants to add one fund to an existing portfolio. Both have the same high growth-low income return objective over a long-term time horizon. However, Tom seeks maximum returns in this category and will accept large swings in price volatility; Janice will accept lower returns to minimize price volatility in this category. Tom could select a mid-cap growth fund to match with an aggressive risk tolerance; a growth and income fund would be appropriate for Janice's conservative risk tolerance. As in the first scenario, the application of risk tolerance created distinct fund type selections even though all of the other investment objectives and characteristics were identical.

When combined with investment objectives of time horizon, return objective, and portfolio size, risk tolerance can be used to design an optimum investment strategy by customizing fund type selections. However, the key is to define all of the objectives so that the strategy has a clear and precise focus—the foundation for an effective investment plan.

HOW MANY FUNDS SHOULD YOU OWN?

Diversification in an investment portfolio is universally recommended by financial planners. It is not only desirable, it is necessary to achieve an effective "well-rounded" investment strategy. Yet, the optimum number of funds in one's mutual fund portfolio is an issue subject to differing opinion. There is no standardized formula to determine the quantity of funds in any given portfolio. (See Figure 5.4.)

Let's first review what mutual fund diversification is and what it accomplishes for an investor. Ideally, diversification spreads an investment portfolio among different fund categories to achieve not only a

It's a simple approach that uses just three mutual funds. Each of the funds is a special kind of fund called a market fund (also known as an "index fund") that is designed to be representative of a particular sector of the market. The three funds are:

- Any mutual fund that mimics the Standard & Poor's Index (also known as the S&P 500).
- Any mutual fund that mimics the Russell 2000 Index small-cap stocks.
- Any mutual fund that mimics the Morgan Stanley EAFE Index, an index of stocks in Europe, Australia, and the Far East.

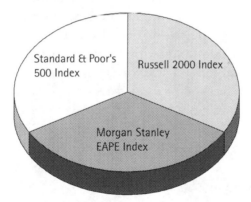

Why is the strategy good for long-term investors? A few reasons, really. The investment is completely in the stock market. As we've already learned, the market has done better over time than any other kind of investment—so nothing protects you better against the wealth-corroding effects of inflation.

It's also broadly diversified—this means that if a particular stock or sector that the funds invest in drops in value, there are plenty of other stocks and sectors to help counterbalance the effect.

Figure 5.4   The Three-Fund Mutual Strategy

Source: ArmchairMillionaire.com.

variety of objectives, but also a reduction in overall risk. Different fund types (i.e., growth, growth and income, corporate bond, and so on) offer distinct risk/return objectives; diversification increases as the combination of different risk/return objectives increases. The following fund categories depict different risk/reward objectives on an escalating risk basis:

- *Stock funds:* Equity income < growth and income < growth < global/international < small company growth < aggressive < sector.

- *Bond funds:* Short-term corporate/treasury < government mortgage < corporate < multisector < high-yield corporate < international.

The emergence of specialty fund categories and style classifications has increased the number of funds now available. For example, international stock funds can concentrate on a particular continent or region (Europe, Latin America, and so on); in fact, it is even possible to obtain a regional fund that excludes particular markets. *Style* in stock funds refers to the capitalization and the method of stock selection; a stock fund can have a large, mid-size, or small capitalization and a growth, value, or blended method of stock selection. *Style* in bond funds refers to the length of maturity (short term, intermediate, or long term) and to the measure of volatility (low, moderate, or high). The point of all this? An investor has more fund choices than ever; consequently, the pursuit of diversification can sometimes be complex or overwhelming.

The following guidelines are intended to simplify the diversification process:

- *Define your investment objectives.* Time horizon, return objectives, risk tolerance, and portfolio amount—all of these objectives contribute to a clear and precise focus for your investment strategy. This should be your number-one priority. If your selected funds accurately represent your objectives, you have an effective investment plan.

- *Choose quality over quantity.* What is important is how distinct your funds are and how they fit your investment strategy, not how many funds you own. Many investors, rather than dealing with diversification to reflect their investment objectives, sometimes view diversification as a container to be filled with as many different objects as possible. A significant portion of their portfolio could then be inappropriate for their strategy.

- *Choose fund category before fund style.* Style, while important, is really a subcategory. A fund category defines the objectives; the corresponding style states the method used to pursue those objectives.

- *Avoid duplication.* It is unnecessary to have multiple funds that have identical objectives. For example, owning two growth and income funds and two small-cap growth funds in a four-fund portfolio is inefficient diversification. In general, represent a particular fund category with just one fund.

- *Less is best.* Use the fewest funds possible to accomplish your goals. Most funds are comprised of 50 to 150 separate stock or bonds, you do not need a huge number of funds in a portfolio to achieve effective diversification.

   Normally, portfolio amount determines the number of funds in a portfolio; as portfolio size increases, more funds can be added to enhance diversification. But because individual circumstances and preferences vary, one investor may be satisfied with four or five funds in a $100,000 portfolio, and another may prefer seven or eight funds for the same portfolio amount. Regardless of the quantity of funds in your portfolio, the key to effective diversification is to always verify that each fund fulfills a separate and distinct purpose for your investment strategy.

WHEN TO SELL A FUND

A market on the upswing is good news on a lot of fronts. First, you're making money. Second, you're making money. But a rising market also offers a good opportunity to thin out some of your less-than-stellar mutual funds.

Several factors can make selling a fund appropriate: a fund's unsuitability for your present portfolio; a deteriorating performance; a change in the style or allocation of a fund; a change in management; or inefficient service. (These factors are not listed in any order of importance.)

According to financial planner Dhirendra Kumar, the most important reason for selling a fund is an echo of the reason for buying it—your investment goal. "You should buy or sell funds solely on the basis of how they contribute to your long-term financial goal," says Kumar. "Is your fund helping you achieving it?"

Kumar adds that even the best performing fund can qualify as a "sell" if it does not suit your requirement. "Your changing needs and feelings can drive a *sell* decision. Someone approaching retirement may wish to sell aggressive funds and put the money into more conservative investments. Sometimes it's time to sell a fund simply because you need the cash."

Taxes can provide another motive for selling a fund. Taking a loss on a fund and switching to another fund may allow the government to share in the loss via an income tax deduction. Or, occasionally, it may be appropriate to correct for past overzealousness.

Having a good night's sleep is a factor as well. Many investors simply sell when they just can't take it anymore. The point of investing is meeting financial goals, not developing ulcers. If your fund is so volatile that not even the vision of your brand new house calms you down, then by all means sell—as long as you're sure you would never buy the fund back again. One should sell a fund that is doing badly because it is not sticking to any discernible style. Investors who buy a fund because of the way it claims to invest should first consider whether the fund is doing what it said it was going to do. If the fund is not following its charter, the investor must approach the sell decision from a different angle—one that questions the viability of the investment concept itself.

Investors who purchase a fund for a specific purpose should always sell when the fund is no longer satisfying that aim. "Investors should always sell a fund when their own goals have changed," concludes Kumar. "This is easy to overlook, especially if a fund is performing well."

In this chapter you learned the fundamentals of fund investing, including how to identify funds that meet your needs and shop wisely for those that have the best potential for performance and the lowest volatility. If you take little else away from this chapter, remember the impact that fees and expenses can have on your returns, annually and especially over the long run. Shopping smart can pay off when your looking for mutual funds that will help you create wealth. And remember not to get caught up in any futures bouts of irrational exuberance. The only way to avoid the impact of the down markets is to be comfortable with the funds you're buying in the first place and stay invested.

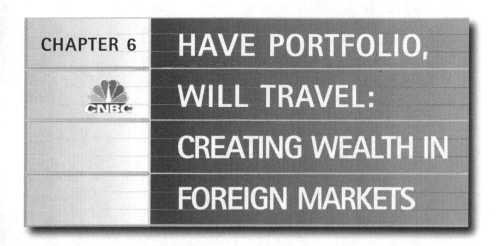

CHAPTER 6

HAVE PORTFOLIO, WILL TRAVEL: CREATING WEALTH IN FOREIGN MARKETS

"Opportunity is where you find it."

—*Old Proverb*

Investing in countries and companies that are outside of our realm of experience and outside our country's borders can feel like a stretch, but as you'll soon find out, a worldwide perspective is integral to creating wealth. Not only do the broader markets of the globe allow us to diversify and minimize risk, large slices of the global market have been known to outperform the U.S. markets, repeatedly, over a long period of time.

In fact, opportunity is always there and always rewards those who get there first. As you'll discover in this chapter, there are a growing number of reasons for going global and a growing number of tools to help you take the guesswork out of choosing the right investments to enhance your investment strategy.

Think of Alexander Graham Bell, inventor of the telephone, who beat another inventor to the U.S. Patent Office by ten minutes. Or astronaut and former U.S. Senator John Glenn, who increased his chances of becoming the first American in space by making a coast-to-coast flight at an average speed of mach 1. "Everybody knew it could be done, but nobody bothered to do it until I did," said Glenn.

The best reason to go global is, unsurprisingly, geographic opportunity: Why limit yourself to one area of the world, even if it is the United States? As in every other individual country, the U.S market represents a fraction of the world's opportunities. Individuals who strictly limit the scope of their investments to the U.S. market are missing out on some of the world's largest and best managed companies. Many foreign countries are home to some truly world-class industries. Says one report issued by investment banking giant Morgan Stanley, "Investing globally literally offers a world of opportunity. The evidence in favor of taking a global approach to investing is so abundant that only the imprudent would ignore it."

A look at the numbers reinforces that sentiment:

- Over 25 years, foreign stocks returned 990 percent and U.S. stocks returned 270 percent.

- Not once in 25 years has the United States been the top performing stock market in the world.

- In 25 years, the U.S. stock market beat the average of all major foreign markets only once every six years.

- In a recent 10-year period, foreign investments quadrupled while U.S. stocks doubled.

- In the 1980s bull market, foreign stocks returned 525 percent and U.S. stocks returned 280 percent.

- Although the United States is the world's largest market by far, it accounts for only 47 percent of the total market value, or capitalization, of the world's stocks.

- The MSCI (Morgan Stanley Capital International) EAFE (Europe, Australia, and the Far East) Index, a widely recognized international benchmark composed of 22 major markets in Europe, Australasia, and the Far East, equaled or outperformed the S&P 500 Stock Index in 16 of the past 20 10-year periods.

Historically, returns from foreign stocks have exceeded those achieved by U.S. stocks over the long term. Among the 10 major foreign markets from 1980 to 2000, the U.S. market was the best performing in only one year: 1982. (See Table 6.1.)

International equities are attractive for a number of reasons. Firstly, globalization and the spread of information technology have caused many economies around the world to mature at an ever-faster pace. The United States is no longer the only source of fast-growing high-technology industries. In addition, because of changing global demographics, many overseas countries are experiencing enormous changes within their social systems and infrastructure. It makes sense, therefore, to identify the regions and sectors around the world that will benefit most from structural changes in the global economy. Once this has been done, the next step is to find the companies, whether based overseas or in the United States, that stand to gain the most. An international long/short investment strategy can capitalize on such structural changes by investing in fast growing sectors while simultaneously shorting declining industries, companies, and markets.

Secondly, assets from pension funds and mutual funds are increasingly flowing into international equity markets as the baby boom population prepares for retirement. The amazing increase in the liquid capital being pumped into U.S. stock exchanges has fueled an incredible bull market since 1993. It is unlikely that this effect can continue. More and more money is being diverted into international equities in the hope of realizing greater risk-adjusted returns. This is possible because investors can benefit from diversification and low correlation when they allocate part of their portfolio to overseas markets. International long/short managers are able to profit the most because of their innate knowledge of local markets and their ability to hedge out risks related to structural conditions on local exchanges.

Finally, as markets have become more closely integrated, nearly every investor seems to have some international exposure, regardless of whether his or her portfolio consists entirely of U.S. companies. Few firms have escaped the global marketplace, and many U.S. companies now conduct more business overseas than at home. Therefore, investors must have some way to hedge international exposures. This

TABLE 6.1
PERFORMANCE OF THE WORLD'S STOCK MARKETS

Year	Best Market	U.S. Rank, Out of 10 Major Markets
2000	Switzerland	6
1999	Japan	5
1998	France	3
1997	Switzerland	2
1996	Hong Kong	5
1995	Switzerland	2
1994	Japan	6
1993	Hong Kong	10
1992	Hong Kong	3
1991	Hong Kong	3
1990	United Kingdom	4
1989	Germany	4
1988	France	7
1987	Japan	6
1986	Japan	9
1985	Germany	8
1984	Hong Kong	4
1983	Australia	7
1982	United States	1
1981	Japan	2
1980	Hong Kong	5

Sources: MSCI; FAME Information Services, Inc.

is best achieved with a long/short equity strategy that can isolate specific market exposures while hedging out potential currency risks.

By investing in international securities, investors can open their portfolios to more than half the value of the world's stock markets. Leading companies in many major industries—from automobiles and electronics to chemicals and construction—are based outside the United States. What's more, some promising economic trends lie abroad, such as the rebuilding of Eastern Europe and the expansion of consumer markets in Asia and Latin America.

GREATER DIVERSIFICATION

Everyone likes the thought of increasing reward while reducing overall risk. Adding foreign stocks to a well-rounded portfolio has been shown to reduce overall volatility, according to studies. By moderating downward swings, a modest allocation to international stocks may also improve overall portfolio returns and make it easier for investors to ride out downturns in domestic markets.

There is no question that businesses have become increasingly global (witness the recent wave of corporate mergers that have crossed international borders) and that economic ties between nations have become much stronger during the past decade. But, interestingly, the longer-term correlation between markets—the degree to which markets move in the same direction and in similar magnitudes—has not increased significantly.

The reasons are simple. Economic policies, growth rates, inflation, interest rates, currency values, and investor perceptions differ markedly from one country to another. Consequently, market returns, which are affected by all of these factors, differ as well. Economic expansions are not perfectly synchronized around the globe, nor are recessions. Thus, when the U.S. economy slows down, foreign economies may continue to grow. As U.S. stock prices rise or fall, foreign stocks may shift in different increments—or even move in the opposite direction—and may possibly cushion the fluctuations in the United States.

FIRST IN WAR, FIRST IN PEACE . . . BUT NOT FIRST IN MARKET GAINS

If you believe investing in your own backyard or country is all the strategy you'll ever need, think again. Remarkably, in the last 21 years, the U.S. market was the world's number-one performing market only once! In contrast, during that same period, Hong Kong was the world's top performing market six times, Japan was in first place five times, while Switzerland and Germany were number one twice.

Historically, investing in certain foreign markets would have helped to increase overall returns during some periods. But it's important to resist the temptation to concentrate assets in a particular region or country that looks promising. Logically, each individual market—or region—cannot be expected to outperform the broader average over the long term.

As Table 6.2 shows, the best-performing market usually differs from year to year. For example, returns from emerging markets trounced those of U.S. stocks during the early 1990s, but they fell far behind during the second half of the decade. These variations highlight an important lesson. It is as imprudent to market time foreign investments as it is U.S. stocks and bonds. Because it is extremely difficult—if not impossible—to predict which market will lead in any given year, switching from market to market in pursuit of the best return is an expensive, and probably fruitless, investment approach.

History has shown that investing by looking in a rearview mirror simply does not work. Past returns are not accurate indicators of future returns. For example, in 1995, an investor might have concluded that foreign stocks were superior to U.S. stocks because, during the previous 10 years (1985 through 1994), the MSCI EAFE Index provided an annualized return of 17.9 percent, versus 13.9 percent for the Wilshire 5000® Total Market Index, a measure of the entire U.S. stock market. But since then, U.S. stocks have outshone international stocks by 24.8

TABLE 6.2
INTERNATIONAL MARKETS VERSUS U.S. MARKET
ANNUAL RETURNS, 1984–1999

Year	Wilshire 5000 Index (%)	MSCI EAFE Index (%)*	MSCI Emerging-Markets Free Index (%)*
1984	3.0	**7.9**	n/a
1985	32.6	**56.7**	n/a
1986	16.0	**69.9**	n/a
1987	2.3	**24.9**	n/a
1988	18.0	28.6	**40.4**
1989	29.1	10.8	**65.0**
1990	**−6.2**	−23.2	−10.6
1991	34.3	12.5	**59.9**
1992	9.0	−11.8	**11.4**
1993	11.2	32.9	**74.8**
1994	−0.1	**8.1**	−7.3
1995	**36.4**	11.6	−5.2
1996	**21.3**	6.4	6.0
1997	**31.3**	2.1	−11.6
1998	**23.4**	20.3	−25.3
1999	23.8	27.3	**66.4**
2000	-10.89	-13.96	-30.61

Sources: Wilshire Associates Inc.; Morgan Stanley Capital International, Inc.
Note: Bold entries indicate the highest return among the three indexes for that year.
*Total Gross Return in USD.

percent in 1995, 14.9 percent in 1996, 29.2 percent in 1997, and 3.1 percent in 1998. In 1999, international stocks once again outperformed U.S. stocks, by 3.5 percent, but in 2000, the trend once again reversed.

DIVERSIFICATION CAN DISAPPEAR IN CRISES

One benefit of diversifying your domestic portfolio with some international holdings is that, historically, you reduce the risk of your overall investment program.

Unfortunately, the benefits of diversification often disappear when investors need them most. In times of financial market crisis, worldwide markets tend to move in tandem, at least temporarily. For example, very few exchanges sidestepped the stock market collapse in late 1987; markets around the world declined in 1990; and international exchanges dove in unison during the summer of 1998 and the sell off of 2000 and 2001. Therefore, it is unreasonable to expect that foreign markets will head in the opposite direction when the U.S. stock market drops sharply.

However, over longer periods—years and decades—the benefits of diversification become evident. When you are considering international investing, think of the advantage of diversification as coming through *over* time, not *all the time*.

TYPES OF INTERNATIONAL STOCK FUNDS*

One of the challenges associated with foreign investing is that it is hard to figure out where to start. As always, mutual funds offer the best introduction. Here are some brief descriptions of the different types of international stock funds.

* *Source:* Vanguard Funds.

International Funds

The most popular and widely held international equity funds are those that invest in the stocks of "established" markets: prominent European countries (such as the United Kingdom, Germany, and France) and some major Pacific Rim nations (such as Japan and Australia).

In general, international funds are broadly diversified; they hold stocks from many companies in different countries. The investment strategies of international funds vary widely. Some funds try to identify the best countries in which to own stocks, rather than trying to select the best individual stocks. Such funds seek to emphasize the markets or regions that the fund's adviser believes will rise the most. Other funds focus on trying to identify the most promising companies, using a fundamental investment approach that analyzes a company's finances and competitive position.

Another approach employed by international stock funds is indexing. Index funds seek to match the performance of a recognized market measure, known as an index, that is made up of a group of securities representing a given market. The most prominent index of established international markets, the MSCI EAFE Index, includes stocks of companies located in more than a dozen countries, including Japan, Germany, the United Kingdom, and France. There are also indexes—and index funds—that track regional stocks and stocks of emerging markets.

Regional Funds

International funds that invest in stocks in a particular geographic region, such as Europe or the Pacific Basin, are known as regional funds. Because these funds concentrate investments in a specific area, their share prices typically fluctuate more than the share prices of broadly diversified international funds.

Single-Country Funds

International stock funds that limit their investments to a particular country (for example, investing only in German companies or only in Japanese companies) are called single-country funds. These funds are considered highly risky because of their narrow focus.

Emerging-Markets Funds

Some mutual funds invest in the financial markets of countries that are evolving from an agricultural to an industrialized economy, or from a government-controlled economy to a free market. Argentina, Indonesia, Hungary, and Turkey are examples. These mutual funds are generally called emerging-markets funds.

Evolving countries generally offer the potential for higher rates of economic growth than the more mature markets of the United States,

---

ARE ADRs FOR YOU?

For investors that are more interested in individual foreign stocks, American Depository Receipts or ADRs may be an option. ADRs offer investors the opportunity to invest in foreign markets without actually working through foreign brokers or foreign exchanges.

Many foreign stocks are listed directly on the exchanges in the United States. Most are found on the Nasdaq, but the NYSE and American Stock Exchange list ADRs as well.

An ADR is a negotiable U.S. certificate that represents ownership of shares in a non-U.S.-based corporation. They are quoted and traded in U.S. dollars. Their dividends are also paid to investors in U.S. dollars. ADRs were designed to allow non-U.S. companies to broaden their shareholder base and raise capital in the United States.

You can research ADRs the same way you would any U.S. stock. In fact, many ADRs are rather closely followed because, in most cases, the foreign companies are important in their home countries. Some firms, such as Sony or Nokia, are known worldwide.

Unlike standard shares, each ADR can represent a single foreign share, a portion of a share, or a bundle of shares. Many ADRs have a 1:1 ratio (one underlying share equals one depository share), but ratios can also range from 100,000:1 to 1:100.

For a more detailed account of ADRs, consult *CNBC 24/7 Trading*.

Source: Barbara Rockefeller, *CNBC 24/7 Trading*, John Wiley & Sons, 2000.

Western Europe, and Japan. However, these funds are generally riskier than those that emphasize stocks of companies in developed countries.

Small Capitalization (Cap) International Funds

The funds select holdings from global economies by buying shares in companies with a market capitalization under $1 billion. Diversification can be a challenge for small cap fund managers because the market for small caps can contract in countries during times of declining investor interest or market conditions. But the possibility for greater reward usually exists in tandem with greater risks in these funds.

Global Funds

Mutual funds that invest in a mix of U.S. and foreign stocks are known as global, or world, funds. Like international funds, global funds typically seek long-term growth. Keep in mind that global funds may duplicate some U.S. stocks already owned by investors who have broadly diversified holdings.

FACTORS TO CONSIDER WHEN INVESTING ABROAD

The key to developing a long-term strategy is to find one that you will be comfortable following and will not abandon prematurely. You will need to think about your willingness to accept day-to-day fluctuations in the value of your portfolio. Adding foreign investments may enhance your return potential and reduce your risk over the long run, but your portfolio may suffer some losses along the way.

In addition, investors who participate in global markets must brace themselves for changes—if not surprises. Different cultures, different languages, different currencies, and different rules and regulations ensure that your experience overseas may be as educational as it is profitable. Fortunately, investment principles are universal, and the tools to implement an effective portfolio for citizens of almost all countries are widely available. Naturally, the techniques will have to be adapted to local conditions and respond to the individual's concerns.

"All investors have a strong local bias," notes Frank Armstrong III, Chief Financial Partner and president of Managed Account Services Inc., a Miami-based financial planning firm. "We tend to be more comfortable with the devil we know than one we don't know. Still, there is much to be gained by overcoming local prejudice. No matter where you are in the world, international diversification will benefit your portfolio. Even if you live in a country blessed with a large, liquid, "safe," efficient, convenient, and economical market, the benefits of cross-border investing are immense."

Chief among those benefits, Armstrong says, is that the world's markets offer lots of opportunities not available to local investors. "Raw materials are not evenly distributed," he adds. "As an American, I have few opportunities to invest in coffee, tea, diamonds, rubber, or many other natural resources in my local markets. Many products and services are unique to limited geographical areas and cultures."

Cross-border diversification is also a strong tool for investors who wish to reduce local market risk. Foreign markets are not highly correlated, so international investing will both increase the returns and reduce the risk over time.

In addition, investing in foreign securities is a great way to hedge against a devaluation of our own currency. "While we almost always buy our groceries in local currency, the cost of everything we import varies directly with the strength of our local currency," says Armstrong. "After WW II, Americans endured more than forty years of sliding dollar values, making everything they bought overseas more costly, but everything they owned overseas more valuable."

There are some very strong benefits to international investing, but there are also risks to consider, although most are relatively small in consequence and are generally outweighed by the benefits mentioned above.

Market Risk

Just as U.S. stock prices fluctuate widely from month to month and year to year, prices of foreign stocks are subject to substantial gains and declines. Indeed, past returns from international stocks have fluctuated even more widely than returns from U.S. stocks.

INTERNATIONAL MARKET VOLATILITY

Table 6.3 shows the extremes in foreign stock market returns (denominated in U.S. dollars) for 1-, 5-, and 10-year periods, as measured by the MSCI EAFE Index. Returns in a single year ranged from a 69.9 percent gain to a 23.2 percent decline. Over longer time periods, however, the average fluctuations became smaller; returns ranged from 5.9 percent to 22.8 percent over 10-year time horizons. The lesson here is that although time tends to dampen volatility, international investments have the potential for significant short-term declines.

If history serves as a guide, even higher volatility should be expected in emerging markets. Consider that emerging markets achieved a 66.4 percent gain in 1999, after posting a negative return of −25.3 percent in 1998—a swing of more than 90 percentage points over a two-year period. The market followed this performance by falling nearly 31 percent in 2000. (See Table 6.2.) Prudent investors should plan on holding international stock investments for much longer

TABLE 6.3 AVERAGE ANNUAL TOTAL RETURNS FOR THE PERIOD ENDED DECEMBER 31, 1999			
	1 Year (%)	5 Years (%)	10 Years (%)
Best	69.9	36.5	22.8
Worst	−23.2	1.5	5.9

Source: Morgan Stanley Capital International, Inc.

periods—a minimum of five years—to decrease the risk of loss from selling in down markets. Over long periods, the benefits of diversification are more likely to take hold, and stocks to rebound from the inevitable fluctuations of various markets.

ADVANTAGES OF INVESTING ABROAD

For much of the post-World War II period, the United States dominated the world economy. In 1970, America's gross national product represented nearly one-half of the world's output. By 1999, however, the U.S. share was only one-third. Similarly, in 1970, U.S. stocks represented two-thirds of the world's equity market capitalization. Today, they account for about one-half.

Source: Morgan Stanley Capital International, Inc.

Overseas you will find:

9 of the 10 largest steel companies.
8 of the 10 largest electronics companies.
8 of the 10 largest automobile companies.
6 of the 10 largest appliance/household companies.
5 of the 10 largest banks.

Sources: MSCI; FAME Information Services, Inc.

Currency Risks

When you invest in another country, your investment bears currency risk. You make the investment in U.S. dollars, which must be converted to the foreign currency. The fluctuations in the foreign currency's value can affect your return because, at some point in the future, you will have to convert this foreign investment back into U.S. dollars. When you invest in a mutual fund that invests in foreign securities, your risk may be reduced if the fund uses currency-hedging instruments.

Political Risks

Investing in foreign markets can involve political risks that most U.S. investors do not face. A government coup, a national labor dispute—these are examples of possible political risk. Emerging markets (e.g., Russia) face greater risks than more established markets like Germany or the United Kingdom. Diversification among countries in a mutual-fund type of investment product (where investments are made in many countries) may significantly *reduce* this risk, but it's important to understand that the risk will still exist.

A stronger dollar diminishes the value of foreign assets owned by U.S. investors; a weaker dollar augments the value of foreign assets owned by U.S. investors. If a Japanese stock is valued at 500 yen per share, the stock is worth $4.17 when the exchange rate of the dollar is equal to 120 yen. But if the dollar rises in value to 130 yen, that stock will be worth $3.85. On the other hand, returns on foreign stocks increase when the dollar's value falls versus other currencies. If the dollar's value were to fall to 110 yen, a share of Japanese stock valued at 500 yen would be worth $4.55.

Table 6.4 shows how changes in the dollar's value affected returns from international markets during 2000. Changes in the relative value of the U.S. dollar augmented returns in Europe and the Pacific region, but increased losses for U.S. investors in Europe and the emerging markets. For the MSCI Europe Index, a stronger U.S. dollar increased a 1.89 percent loss in local currencies to a 8.14 percent loss in dollar terms. For the MSCI Emerging-Markets Free Index, the rising dollar changed a 25.4 percent loss in local currencies into a loss of 30.61 percent in dollars.

Currency risk can be high in the short term (one-week moves of as much as 25 percent have occurred in recent years), but the impact may be reduced for longer holding periods because the changes in the relative value of the U.S. dollar tend to even out over time.

Liquidity Risks

Investing in foreign countries, particularly small foreign countries, introduces the risk of illiquidity. Liquidity, as we've discussed with regard

TABLE 6.4
IMPACT OF CURRENCY EXCHANGE RATES: TOTAL RETURN
(ONE YEAR ENDED DECEMBER 29, 2000)

Index	Local Currency Return (%)*	Currency Impact (%)	U.S. Dollar Return (%)*
EAFE	−7.11	−6.85	−13.96
Europe	−1.89	−6.25	−8.14
Pacific Free	−17.56	−8.09	−25.64
France	2.43	−6.49	−4.06
Germany	−9.53	−5.73	−15.27
Japan	−19.74	−8.32	−28.07
EMF (Emerging Markets Free)	−25.40	−5.21	−30.61
Brazil	1.47	−7.55	−6.07
Mexico	−19.55	−0.99 ·	−20.54

Sources: Wilshire Associates Inc.; Morgan Stanley Capital International, Inc.
*Total Gross Return

to U.S. stocks, is the ease with which an investment can be sold without impairment of value. Liquidity risks increase in small amounts with thinly traded shares. Significant purchases may cause a run-up in prices; a few large sales may cause a market to deteriorate rapidly. This illiquidity is often seen in some international mutual funds.

Higher Correlations

As stated above, one of the primary benefits of international investing is the low correlation between international and domestic securities. However, some research has shown (although not without debate) that these correlations are increasing. Also worrisome is the fact that there is stronger evidence that the correlation between international and domestic securities is not constant. In fact, correlations may increase during down markets and decrease during up markets. This is troubling because, in down markets, investors need the international and domestic securities to perform differently! From the research, it appears that this trend may be more common in established markets than in emerging markets.

Higher Costs

Investing in foreign markets involves higher transaction (commissions, market impact costs) and portfolio management costs (greater cost of research, and so on). This can negatively impact investors' returns.

This is especially true when foreign investment taxes are thrown into the mix. Reporting taxes earned on investments in far off lands isn't as hard as you might think (your fund firm, broker, or financial planner will send you dividend statements informing you of your tax liability and what to do about it) but some little known tax rules can bite you in the ankles. For instance, in some countries, there may be unexpected taxes, such as withholding taxes on dividends. And remember, transaction costs such as fees, broker's commissions, and taxes often are higher than in U.S. markets. Mutual funds that invest abroad often have higher fees and expenses than funds that invest in U.S. stocks, in part because of the extra expense of trading in foreign markets.

Investor Psychology

If you become a long-term investor, capable of holding on to foreign investments until their likely rebound takes place instead of locking in your losses by selling, you'll benefit from the discipline. One of the greatest factors inhibiting the growth of international investing is the notion that international markets are volatile and great losses and gains are not only probable, but likely. Volatility does exist, but it can be diminished by investing in a diversified international mutual fund. However, even in this environment, investors are very watchful of their investments. When investors see a loss in an international investment, they will most likely sell it more quickly than they would sell a domestic investment (with a similar risk level). They will often point toward a loss, remember it in detail, and then sell other international holdings to avoid future losses. Rarely will they view it on a total portfolio basis, especially if the domestic market is strong. It's important to remember that international investments may exhibit volatility, but one needs to look at their performance from a *total portfolio perspective* and not examine each investment in isolation. With certain individuals, this approach is nearly impossible.

The Euro

Most countries have their own unique currencies. The euro is a common currency now used by 12 countries participating in Europe's Economic and Monetary Union (EMU). The advent of the euro in January 1999 was part of a broader plan that aims to more closely integrate European countries and create a single European market. Although the common currency eliminates the uncertainty of exchange-rate fluctuations among the 12 countries that adopted it, the exchange rate of the euro and the dollar will continue to fluctuate. For U.S. investors, when the dollar strengthens in value versus the euro, it will reduce returns on European investments; a weaker dollar will augment returns on European investments.

POLITICAL RISK

Political events pose a considerable risk to the stability of returns from foreign markets. Some countries with emerging markets are especially vulnerable to dramatic events such as coups, assassinations, or civil unrest, any of which could upset their markets.

Equally important is the risk of changes in economic policy that could hurt U.S. investors. These could include imposition of currency

ADDING UP

American investors have poured more than $313 billion into gross purchases of global and international stock funds over the past two years. At the end of 1999, assets of international stock funds exceeded $580 billion, according to the Investment Company Institute, the mutual fund industry trade group.

controls, changes in taxation, or (in a worst-case scenario) outright seizure of foreigners' assets. Or, a government could decide to nationalize its domestic industries or to adopt restrictive trade policies. Any such developments could disrupt markets, possibly with little or no warning.

Costs

In addition to greater risk, international funds typically incur higher operating expenses, transaction costs, taxes, and sales charges (loads)—all of which reduce investors' returns.

The average 1999 expense ratio (annual expenses as a percentage of net assets) was 2.19 percent for emerging-markets' stock funds and 1.72 percent for international stock funds. For U.S. stock funds, the average expense ratio is about 1.46 percent. A mutual fund's expense ratio typically covers a wide variety of costs, including administrative and management fees.

What's more, international stock funds typically have higher transaction costs than funds that invest only in U.S. stocks. Traditional brokerage costs—as well as exchange fees, custodial fees, taxes, and other charges—considerably increase the cost of buying and selling foreign securities. Transaction costs for international stock funds are estimated to be as high as 2 percent of assets per year, or more than double the estimated cost for U.S. funds. Moreover, it's important to understand that these costs are not included in expense ratio disclosures, which

WATCH OUT FOR GLOBAL MARKET SCAMS

Make no mistake about it, unscrupulous scam artists see that U.S. investors are paying increasing attention to overseas investment opportunities. Hence, they're taking an active interest in global markets. Here are some simple steps that investors can take to protect their interests:

- Don't be stampeded into the rush to international investing. If you listen to other investors and read the business news columns, you may easily get the impression that everyone is investing overseas. Don't give in and send your dollars overseas just to "join the crowd." Make sure your investment is appropriate for your financial objectives and, in particular, for your ability to assume risk.
- Learn something about foreign markets. How are investments regulated in the nation where you are thinking about sending your money? To what extent are investors in this market protected from investment fraud and abuse? To what government agency would you go for assistance in resolving your problem?
- Remember: Even if investing overseas is one of the "hottest" activities going, it doesn't mean that the quality of the investment opportunities in other nations is any higher than those in the United States. In fact, because of enforcement complications, the actual level of risk in overseas investments—even in mainstream market products—may be considerably higher than in the well-regulated U.S. markets. (Once your money is gone, it may be impossible to recover it, due to the practical difficulties involved in pursuing court action against foreign entities and individuals.) Keep your head on your shoulders when it comes to the hoopla about international investing.
- Consider U.S. investment alternatives that provide foreign exposure. Many American corporations listed on U.S. exchanges have large operations in foreign countries and get a significant portion of their revenue from sales overseas. Investing in the stocks and bonds of these companies, or in mutual funds made up of several

of these companies, is one way to participate in the growth of foreign markets while keeping your dollars invested in U.S.-regulated
corporations. The business reference section of your public library
is a good place to research these companies.

- Check with your state securities agency and Better Business Bureau (BBB): Have they received complaints? If an investment is
being sold to you, its promoter should be registered with your state
securities agency. (For the number of your state's agency, call
NASAA at (888) 8-4-NASAA) or check the Web site (www.Nasaa).
Ignore claims that overseas investment promoters are somehow
exempt from state and federal securities law registration requirements; they aren't. Also, take the time to ask your BBB about the
company in question. It may have a record of customers' experi-
ences with (or government actions against) the company.

Source: Datastream.

makes it difficult for investors to know how much these costs reduce a
fund's gross returns.

If you believe that international funds have a place in your investment program, you then must decide how much of your portfolio to
allocate to foreign securities. Carefully consider your investment objective, time horizon, risk tolerance, and financial resources. As a rule,
most investors should limit international stock investments to 10 percent or no more than 20 percent of their overall equity holdings.

Remember that you have a variety of options when you choose to
invest in equity markets overseas. When you are making your selection, keep your investment objective and your time horizon firmly in
mind. Several types of mutual funds invest overseas. International
funds invest broadly across countries and industries outside of the
United States. Global funds do the same, but include U.S. securities in
their portfolios.

More aggressive funds focus on a single geographic region, such as
Latin America or Western Europe. Others may focus on certain types of

ARE EMERGING MARKETS FOR YOU?

Some foreign bourses are riskier than others—and, in some instances, a lot riskier. Among emerging markets, gains of 100 percent in a single year are not uncommon—nor are losses of 100 percent.

Emerging markets are countries considered to be developing from an agricultural to an industrialized economy or from a government-controlled to a free-market economy. Generally, growth rates in developing economies are higher than those in mature, developed economies. Therefore, stocks from emerging markets offer the possibility of higher returns during some periods. In fact, some of the highest single-year returns during the past two decades have come from emerging markets. The MSCI Emerging-Markets Free Index (an index of about 25 countries, including Brazil, South Africa, Mexico, and Argentina) climbed 65.0 percent in 1989, 74.8 percent in 1993, and 66.4 percent in 1999.

But the potential for higher reward comes at a price: higher risk. Emerging markets carry all the risks of international investing—market risk, liquidity risk, and currency risk—and then some. Generally, among developing countries, markets are more unstable, currencies are more volatile, liquidity is scarcer, and political upheaval is more prevalent. Emerging markets rose sharply in 1989, 1991, and 1993, but they have also suffered steep declines: down 10.6 percent in 1990, 11.6 percent in 1997, and 25.3 percent in 1998.

The addition of emerging markets to an investment portfolio can increase diversification and may help provide superior returns. But because of the additional risk involved, even the most aggressive investors—those who can withstand wide fluctuations in the value of their investments—should probably allocate no more than 15 percent of their international holdings to developing countries. More conservative investors should invest less—or maybe nothing—in emerging markets.

securities such as emerging markets, small capitalizations, or developed markets.

Foreign Currency Fluctuations

Investments in overseas equities can benefit greatly from positive exchange-rate movements. The converse, of course, is also true. However, with prudent management of foreign currency exposures, and with selective hedging of exchange rate risk, international long/short equity investors can achieve significantly higher risk-adjusted returns by investing in overseas markets. An example was the experience of U.S. investors in the Japanese stock market between 1985 and 1996. During that period, U.S. investors benefited significantly from a currency-related boost to their portfolio returns. They enjoyed far stronger performance than local investors in the Japanese equity market. Over this 11-year period, the cumulative return achieved by local investors in the Tokyo Stock Exchange (TSE) was approximately 50 percent. Because of the currency effect, however, dollar-based investors enjoyed cumulative currency-adjusted returns of almost 300 percent from the exact same market.

The Size of the World Stock Markets

In 1974, the share of world stock market capitalization represented by the United States was over 65 percent. At that time, apart from occasional investments in large overseas multinational companies such as BP (British Petroleum) or Royal Dutch Shell, investment professionals and individual investors rarely allocated specific tranches of their portfolios to dedicated international investing.

This changed in the late 1970s and early 1980s. Spectacular investment returns in foreign markets during this period attracted the attention of U.S. investors and reduced the percentage of the U.S. market capitalization in the MSCI World Index. By the early 1980s, the U.S. share of world capitalization had fallen to 40 percent; by the early 1990s, it was down to 32 percent. Today, it stands at 45 percent of total world market capitalization; due largely to the appreciation of the S&P 500 stocks in recent years.

PICKING THE RIGHT FUND

How suited to international investing are you? Some investors are more comfortable than others casting their lines into international waters, according to a recent report from Invesco Funds on international investing. At the top of the list of those who are comfortable are younger investors who are investing for the long term; investors in their peak earning years, who seek to maximize their capital; and mature investors who need to ensure that their capital is not eroded by inflation or by the performance of any one economy.

At the bottom of the list are investors who are risk-averse, can't afford to ride out the inevitable fluctuations of international markets, and perhaps seek capital preservation.

Some advice for those who do dip their toes into foreign markets: Stick to no-load mutual funds rather than individual stocks, and pick well-diversified funds. Familiarize yourself with one or two international funds that are tied to an index, and then consider a couple that are managed by experienced professionals who have superior long-term records. Here are some tips to help you begin to narrow down your fund selections:

- Compare past performance. Start by reviewing five years' performance, and pay particular attention to the fund's performance during and after the 1998 bear market, during which the average diversified international fund dropped 25 percent.

- Find out where the fund invests. It's crucial to find out whether they invest in risky emerging markets, such as Mexico, and in established developed markets, such as Japan and the United Kingdom. To find out how much a fund has allocated to different regions and countries, contact the fund or check Morningstar Mutual Funds (www.morningstar.com).

- Understand each fund's basic investment style. For example, is its strategy growth- or value-oriented? How is the fund managed? Is it directed by one person, a team, or a lead manager and a group of analysts? What are its top holdings? Look up each fund's top holdings to see what industry sectors it invests in.

- Kick some tires. What is the fund's expense ratio, and how does it compare with those of its peers? The average diversified international fund has an expense ratio of 1.73 percent, compared with 1.46 percent for its U.S. counterpart.

- Use the right benchmark. Comparing an international fund with U.S. indexes is like comparing apples with oranges. Use an international benchmark, such as the widely used MSCI EAFE Index, which is published daily in newspapers such as *The Wall Street Journal*. You can also find it at the Morgan Stanley Web site. The Index is based on market capitalization and includes the markets of 21 developed countries.

As with domestic funds, it's a good idea to compare fees, charges, and other expenses. In foreign markets, expenses are more critical than in domestic investing simply because they are higher. It costs more to learn about foreign stocks and bonds and to trade them. Plus, most managers claim a premium fee for their expertise in foreign markets. But few managers beat the market indexes over time, so this fee is usually not worth the extra expense. Monitor the expenses annually. Beware of funds that raise expenses after a single good year or at the end of a year of heavy advertising. Weed out funds that have heavy sales loads and expenses before you hone in on the ones that are worth studying in detail. You can almost always find no-load funds and funds with reasonable expenses that perform as well or better than funds with loads and above-average expenses.

Volatilitys tend to be greater overseas than in most domestic sectors. A common pitfall awaits international investors and domestic investors: chasing the hot hand (or hot country or hot region). But, because of the greater volatility, the consequences are worse. Ask yourself: If you were buying anything but stocks, would you eagerly buy merchandise that has been marked up 50 percent or more? Markets like Taiwan, Turkey, and Colombia may triple in a short period, *but* they often get cut in half soon afterward. Buy them when they are out of favor, and not when you are in an anxious rush to join a bandwagon that is already rolling downhill.

Because of this volatility, many fund managers, like Mark Mobius of the Templeton funds, recommend dollar cost averaging. This technique

of buying a constant dollar amount of an investment at regular intervals—for example, $10,000 every quarter—ensures that over time, you
pay a relatively low cost for your shares. The downside of dollar cost
averaging is the capital gain computation you or your accountant ends
up doing when you sell the shares.

The good news is brokerages seem to be finally adopting reports
that track your cost basis and include it in your tax report at the end of
the year.

Also, beware of the hot hand. Studies have shown, time and
again, that a fund manager who is currently at the top of the performance charts will rarely be there for long. Performance attribution
studies show the reason for this phenomenon. The manager has
made a lucky sector bet (or, internationally, a lucky country bet). Sector selection is responsible for 80 percent of the performance of an
equity portfolio but apparently is very unreliable, despite what you—
and those who have full-time staffs and expensive research reports—
may think.

SELECTING YOUR FUNDS

After you've chosen the type of fund that best fits your program, turn
your attention to selecting a specific fund or funds. When you are making a selection, weigh several factors, particularly the following:

- *Investment approach.* Decide whether you want to pursue an
  active or an index approach—or a program that combines the
  two. Actively managed funds buy and sell stocks in an effort to
  outperform the overall stock market or a specific segment of it.
  Index funds mirror a market benchmark as a low-cost way of
  achieving a return that matches that of an index.

- *Investment objective.* Consider the differences between growth
  and value stocks. Growth funds emphasize fast-growing companies whose stocks are expected to appreciate over time, thus
  providing capital gains. Value funds typically invest in stocks of

companies that may be out of favor with investors. The funds expect that the companies' prospects will improve.

- *Investment strategy.* Choose between funds that select stocks by country weighting or by fundamental analysis. Country-weighted funds emphasize stocks in countries where overall market conditions appear most attractive. Funds that take a fundamental approach to stock selection choose companies thought to have the best prospects.

Other important factors to consider are: past performance, risk characteristics (including such factors as a fund's volatility, or its concentration of assets in certain companies, countries, or sectors), and the cost of buying and owning fund shares. How an international fund—or an international market—has performed in the past is not a reliable indicator of future performance, but a fund's record of returns may give you an idea of how volatile the fund may be in the future. If a fund's return has fluctuated widely from year to year, it could very well continue to be volatile, and therefore risky. The goal, of course, is not to eliminate these funds from consideration but to understand, before investing, the risk they represent.

SOME TIPS ON INVESTING OUTSIDE MUTUAL FUNDS*

Because of their professional management and ability to diversify among companies, industries, countries, and even regions, mutual funds provide an excellent way to invest internationally, but if you're determined to use them as a way to get your feet wet for picking individual foreign stocks or bonds, here are some handy reference tricks:

- Set a "hurdle rate" that your individual stock or bond choices must substantially exceed in order to merit their purchase and the time you must spend monitoring them.

* *Source:* DataStream.

- Use your funds to scan for good stock or bond ideas or to confirm your own ideas. If an excellent fund holds a stock you believe is a good value, or has added it to its list recently, you may have found a good holding. If three of your funds hold or have bought your stock idea, that is strong confirmation that you may be onto something. (The converse may be true, too.)

- If any of a fund's largest holdings have not gone up since they were purchased by the fund (or since the last block was bought), they may be excellent bargains. Remember that a manager theoretically allocates his or her time according to the percentage a holding represents in the portfolio. For example, if one stock is 5 percent of a portfolio, you can be sure the manager knows that company intimately and watches it every day.

- If you're investing in foreign stocks, watch out for a double layer of commissions when you buy a foreign stock through a U.S. broker. The broker may simply be including a commission for his or her firm on top of a commission for the foreign affiliate who actually executed the transaction. Make sure you ask explicitly about *all* the fees you will be charged, before you commit yourself to a broker and to a trade.

HOW SHOULD YOU INVEST?

The well-known advantages of mutual funds—professional management, diversification, convenience, and low cost—stand out even more clearly when you are looking at the world's securities markets.

There is no single global stock exchange. Even in the current technological age, time-zone differences must be considered. You can't trade stocks in Jakarta at 3:00 P.M. New York time.

Then, too, your local stockbroker may not have access to timely information about corporate management and financial reports for companies overseas when you need to make individual securities selections. (Of course, some brokers do have offices around the globe while others specialize in global trading.) The commissioned cost of acquiring an adequately diversified portfolio of foreign stocks can be prohibitive. Making investment decisions on foreign securities and then trading them can present major obstacles for individual investors. Mutual funds may be your best solution. They can offer management by professionals who specialize in countries and industries around the world. You may also gain a crucial edge when those managers live and work in the overseas regions where they invest.

Another option is to invest in American Depository Receipts or ADRs (see page 166 for more information). For more adventurous investors, this may be a more attractive option.

WHEN SHOULD YOU INVEST?

International equity mutual funds are designed for the more aggressive portion of your portfolio. They are well suited for investors seeking greater diversification allied to strong capital growth and income potential. The extent of their foreign exposure will probably be different, but each investor may find that global or international mutual funds are an appropriate option. However, this is not the place for families to stash their emergency cash reserves, or for a retiree to seek stable income. The special risks involved in international investing include: different securities regulations and accounting standards, lower liquidity of foreign securities markets, generally higher commissions, longer settlement periods, potential restrictions on the flow of international capital, and political instability. Currency fluctuations are another concern. Generally, when the U.S. dollar declines against foreign currencies, returns on foreign securities for a U.S. investor tend to escalate.

DIVERSIFYING YOUR INTERNATIONAL STOCK PORTFOLIO

When you have determined a percentage allocation for your international stock portfolio, you are ready to make your selections. You can implement your strategy using one broadly diversified international fund that focuses mainly on established markets, or you can add other types of more specialized funds to further diversify your holdings.

Consider as your core holding a well-diversified foreign stock or a global fund that invests in larger companies listed in established markets. That fund may serve as the anchor of your portfolio and represent the majority of your international investments. International stock funds invest exclusively in foreign companies.

A broadly diversified fund that invests in established markets may be your core holding, but, for greater diversification, you can complement your investment with a fund that focuses on emerging markets. Funds that invest in Latin America, Eastern Europe, or the emerging markets of the Far East offer the potential for gains as these countries seek to expand their economies and raise their living standards. This strategy may also enhance your return without significantly increasing the overall risk of your international portfolio because emerging markets generally have low correlations with established foreign markets and therefore provide greater diversification. As individual funds,

SHOULD YOU INVEST INTERNATIONALLY?

Despite their growing popularity, international stock funds are not for everyone. Before you invest in an international fund, you must decide whether such a fund is right for you. Consider international funds only if you:

- Already maintain a balanced portfolio that includes domestic stock, bond, and money market holdings.
- Want the added diversification brought by exposure to international markets and economies.
- Can tolerate the higher risks—such as currency risk—that accompany an investment in foreign stocks.

however, they may be very volatile. The progress in these countries may be erratic, and the setbacks can be severe.

You can also supplement your core holding and your emerging-market stock fund with an international small-cap fund. Like their U.S. counterparts, fast-growing smaller companies offer greater return potential than large-cap stocks. Also, because of their size, many of these small companies are overlooked and undervalued by investors. Small companies provide diversification, but investors must be willing to take on the additional volatility inherent in small-cap investing.

When you have a mix of large-cap, emerging-market, and small-cap funds, depending on your interests, you may wish to invest part of your assets in funds that focus on a region (such as Europe) or a single country (such as Japan). This strategy may enhance your overall return; however, your individual funds may be more volatile because they are less diversified. This strategy could be used if you have a positive view of a particular region and would like to increase your exposure to that area.

Domestically, you can reduce the volatility of your portfolio by about 45 percent through diversification. Internationally, for the same return, you can reduce the volatility by another 15 percent or more.

If you decide that international funds have a place in your investment program, you then must decide how much of your portfolio to allocate to foreign securities. To do that, carefully consider your investment objective, time horizon, risk tolerance, and financial resources. As a rule, most investors should limit their international stock investments to between 10 percent and 20 percent of their overall equity holdings.

If you are choosing your first international investment, look for a broadly diversified international fund. If such a fund is already part of your investment program and you seek additional opportunity for growth, an investment in a more aggressive fund—such as an emerging-markets fund—may be appropriate.

As this chapter has outlined, international investing should be a measured exercise. It's a mistake to overweight emerging market, international, or global stocks, bonds, and mutual funds in your portfolio.

But it's also detrimental to ignore them entirely, since wide global indexes have outperformed the U.S.'s stock market repeatedly. As you begin adding an international component to your portfolio or set about increasing your holdings, you can rely on the risk diversification and fund selection guidelines in this chapter to help you identify promising funds while you minimize costs and risks.

CHAPTER 7   BE YOUR OWN RESEARCH ANALYST

"Dr. Livingston, I presume?"

—*Sir Henry Morton Stanley*

Success isn't accidental, it's intentional.

When the late President Lyndon Johnson was a freshman Senator, he would leave his office as often as ten times a day to go to the bathroom. He would never use his own bathroom. He made these walks on purpose—to accidentally bump into other Senators. Why? To make contacts and pick up information.

To succeed in picking the right stocks and the right mutual funds, you, too, have to go out of your way to cover all the bases and get the best information you can.

Luckily, there have been numerous successful investors (analysts among them) who have laid the groundwork for meaningful research analysis. And with the growing number of tools at your disposal, the job of finding winning stocks and mutual funds that can go the distance is getting easier.

One of the most formidable tools for analysis is the Internet, which has given curious and dedicated investors the ability to move beyond former boundaries so they can locate the best investment information in real time, online, and worldwide. Real time access to information along with the long-running bull market has given scores of investors the confidence and incentive to do their own research and make their own decisions without the aid of a broker.

The result has been a profound new wave of self-directed investors. Some are day traders. Others are do-it-yourselfers who prefer to roll up their sleeves and build longer term, needs-based portfolios.

One trendy term, coined by financial writer Todd Trometer, defines all these types of market enthusiasts as "new age investors." A new age investor is a person who:

- Actively and aggressively monitors his or her portfolio and market conditions.

- Focuses on investing in growth stocks and continually upgrading his or her portfolio based on the market conditions, as new and more profitable stocks are identified.

- Is always looking for news and information that indicates the pulse of the market.

- Aggressively researches stocks and performs technical analyses, to minimize his or her investment risk.

- Uses a combination of investment strategies to increase portfolio appreciation.

In the April 2000 issue of *Rogue Investor* (www.rogueinvestor .com), Trometer expanded on what it takes to be a new age investor. "As an investor you need to adopt a strategy to be successful," he wrote. "At the root of this strategy should be gaining information, information, information. Without information, you, the investor, are ill prepared and not likely to be successful." Figure 7.1 explains the advantages individual investors can have over professionals.

WHAT TO MAKE OF ANALYSTS' REPORTS

Gaining information is one thing. Gaining meaningful information is quite another.

Consider the venerable stock analysts. Most are experienced and forward-thinking stock evaluators who are not always right.

Advantages You Have over Analysts:

- You only have to answer to yourself, so you can make decisions based on reason rather than on worrying about how they will be perceived (by your peers, your clients, or the companies you like or dislike). You don't have to jump on the bandwagon, window-dress, or dump your underperformers.
- You have a long-term perspective. You're not consumed by the day-to-day fluctuations. You are not ruled by emotions like greed and fear. You can't be coerced into selling when conditions are unfavorable, just to appease others.
- Your investment decisions are driven by thorough research and analysis, not by rumors, canned presentations, and conference calls. You invest within your circle of competence; you're not making phone calls all day to find out what a company's products do, you're out using the products.

Advantages You Have over Mutual Fund Managers:

- You only have to answer to yourself, not shareholders. You don't have to window-dress by dumping your underperformers and scooping up yesterday's winners just before the quarterly reports. You don't have to worry about appearance, only results. You don't have to worry about shareholders pulling out assets all at once the way a mutual fund does.
- You don't have to concern yourself with advertising, marketing, accounting, legal, and other matters facing a mutual fund company.
- Your job isn't at stake, so you don't have to be afraid of taking calculated risks. You don't feel the need to hold small positions in a hundred mediocre companies rather than large positions in eight great ones.
- You don't have so much money that you have difficulty finding enough good stocks to go around (if you do, give us a call). You can invest whatever part of your portfolio you feel appropriate in any company. Due to SEC limits, most mutual funds have trouble buying large positions, especially in small companies.

Figure 7.1   Why You Can Do It Yourself

Source: InvestorsGuide.com.

According to financial writers Amitabh Dugar and Siva Nathan, in an article titled "Research Reports: Buyer Beware" (*Journal of the American Association of Individual Investors*),[1] investors should take analysts' reports with a moderate grain of salt.

The authors point to "many" studies that have found analysts' earnings forecasts and investment recommendations to be overly optimistic.

---

[1] Summarized in *Peoria Journal Star*, February 20, 2000.

"We argue that incentives within an analyst's firm are a major source for this optimistic bias; these incentives arise from the conflicts of interest within firms that issue research reports and at the same time have other business relationships with the companies that are the subject of their reports," say these authors.

Briefly, here's how analysts work. They are employed by brokerage houses to research the business practices, industry trends, and annual reports of a small niche in the business world. One analyst might specialize in the toy industry, another in steel, and another in construction machinery.

Stockbrokers use the analysts' expertise to advise clients on the good stocks to sell, the good stocks to buy, and the good stocks to hold on to. Good advice allows customers to buy stocks in advance of increasing values; bad advice could have customers selling stocks at irretrievable losses.

Good analysts sometimes write bad reports, so an individual investor may be confused. Whose analysis is trustworthy and whose isn't? Dugar and Nathan offer the following tips for getting the most out of analysts' reports:

- Read the fine print at the end of the report. If the author is a representative of the company he or she is writing about, the report is not objective. If it's based on research paid for by the company, avoid that investment.

- Check the writer's credentials. Anyone who adds CFA (Chartered Financial Analyst) after his or her name has gone through three years of testing and has mastered some pretty tough hurdles.

- Know the players. Much of the skepticism directed toward some analysts originates from the inherent conflict of interest in their relationship with the companies and industries they analyze. Analysts live and die by detailed information; often, it is provided directly by CEOs and other top company officials. But when an analyst reports negatively on a company's future performance and investors act on that information, the value of the company's stock may fall drastically. When that happens, a CEO could easily feel betrayed by the report and freeze the analyst out of future information.

DO YOUR HOMEWORK

Without question, one of the biggest mistakes that investors make, over and over, is diving into stocks, funds, or any other kind of investment without doing enough research. Does this mutual fund have a load? What do analysts think about that company right now? What are the tax consequences of those bonds? Sometimes, no amount of research can protect against a bad investment, but, in the long run, doing homework really can pay dividends.

- Research the analyst. There are ways to analyze the analysts. Sites such as Bulldog Research (www.bulldogresearch.com) actually review an analyst's record for prediction accuracy while newspapers like *The Wall Street Journal* publish annual analyst ratings.

- Beware an analyst wearing rose-colored glasses; it may be only in the analyst's best interest to be overly optimistic in a company report. Positive reports reap positive sales in stock, and that's good for the investment banking side of the analyst's brokerage house. Most analysts, however, are objective and are not going to sacrifice their objectivity for short-term gain.

- Take the long view. Measure an analyst against his or her record—not over days, weeks, or months, the authors say, but over a period of several years. If an analyst keeps hitting singles and doubles, and a home run or two are thrown into the mix, start reading more of that analyst's stuff.

WHAT INVESTORS WANT FROM THEIR RESEARCH

Analysts or not, investors seem to have their own ideas about what to look for.

In December 1999, a study of investors' self-directed research habits, authored by the National Association of Investors Corporation (NAIC) and PR Newswire, revealed a savvier, choosier market player.

Respondents ranked news and financial Web sites over brokers' traditional media sources and tips from family and friends as sources of investment information. "Although the survey was conducted online, skewing the results toward Web access, it clearly indicates that individual investors are the audience for corporate Web sites," says Michelle Savage, director of investor relations services at PR Newswire. "Separately, the survey also provides investor relations professionals with informed direction on what these investors need to see on corporate Web sites to make their financial decisions."

Of the 622 individuals surveyed, more than 95 percent stated that they want to see breaking news on corporate Web sites. Further, 74 percent visit the corporate Web site before investing in a company, and 53.6 percent visit often before making a final decision to invest.

What information is key? Prospective investors seek industry comparisons and financial data such as valuation ratios, annual reports, balance sheets, and income statements before they make investment decisions. After they become shareholders, their top information needs are: Timely news releases, income statement and balance sheet data, and profiles of company ownership. Over 90 percent of the respondents said that annual reports should be available online. Only slightly more than half said that, as shareholders, they would be willing to accept financial documents electronically. By contrast, e-mail is highly regarded as a means of receiving information among individual investors. More than 85 percent of the survey respondents would like to receive financial data that way; 78 percent would like to have news releases sent to their e-mail addresses.

WHAT THE EXPERTS SAY TO LOOK FOR

Can amateur investors handle all this information? How does the wheat get separated from the chaff?

According to *Rogue Investor*'s Trometer, taking a bottom-up approach to stock market analytics is best. "First and foremost is obtaining knowledge on the industries that are experiencing or are expected to experience super/hyper growth," he says. "Simply put, you want to look for companies where revenues are growing or will be growing in the near future by at least 30 to 40 percent per year. And you want to invest in companies that aggressively increase market share through new products, technology advancements, acquisitions, and mergers."

Here are more tips from Trometer on what to look for when researching—and buying—stocks:

- Always look for stocks that consistently meet and beat market expectations.
- Take profits when stocks are at a premium, to take advantage of market corrections.
- If a stock moves significantly lower after you make a purchase, don't worry. In fact, add to your position as long as the fundamentals of the stock remain positive.
- Keep a diversified portfolio of 8 to 12 stocks from various industries, to reduce market risk. Increase your position in growth stocks that perform well over time and meet or beat market expectations.
- Use market volatility and dips as buying opportunities.
- Adopt a strategy that considers stock valuation to be important but understands that historical multiples do not apply to many new economy stocks.
- Always keep a level head and watch market conditions. Be sure you are not overpositioned in any given sector when the market signals otherwise.

"Looking at a company" means thoroughly researching its balance sheet, income statement, and subsequent ratio analyses. This is because you are deciding not only whether to buy, but when. It's most advantageous to buy stock at the lowest price possible before its ascent. For that reason, it's important to look at the price chart for each potential stock investment. Trends can be identified by looking at a company's price chart over time. This information can then be used to determine an entry point, or, good time to buy, for any given stock investment. According to Trometer, one example would be to use the 50-day or 200-day moving average as a starting point to help make an entry point determination. It's also important to identify the lower and upper trending ranges for stocks, to help determine entry and selling points. Other technical analyses will also help to make entry point determinations and to decide whether and when to purchase a stock. For example, good investors follow the money. To identify a ceiling or possible selling point, they watch how fast money is flowing into a stock. Money flow and on-balance volume are indicators that help to make this determination. For a more detailed look at technical analysis and its various terminologies and definitions, check out Chapter 9.

COVERING THE WEB ANGLES

As we mentioned in Chapter 1, the Internet has had a huge influence on individual investors particularly those who prefer to do their own stock market research.

Some investors insist on accumulating and dissecting investment research the old fashioned way—i.e., thumbing through old copies of *The Financial Times,* studying annual reports, or paying their broker to do these chores—but a growing number, especially among younger investors, are using the Web. In fact, the younger the investor, the more likely he or she is logging onto the Web for financial research. A 1999 survey, conducted on behalf of Fidelity Investments, showed that a new generation of younger investors is using the Internet as one of its main sources of information when making an investment decision. Over one-third (35 percent) of investors under the age of 35 said they used the Internet to help make their last investment decision, compared to 17 percent of investors between 35 and 55, and only 10 percent of those over 55. The telephone-based survey was carried out among

Fidelity clients and other people who had expressed an interest in the company's products.

What's driving the move toward finding stock market research on the Web? Lower costs and easier access to good information. According to *San Francisco Chronicle* financial columnist Arthur M. Louis, investors are turning to Web sites to wean themselves from expensive financial advisers.

"Many well-to-do people these days are turning away from professional investment advisers and financial planners, opting instead to manage their own money with help from the Internet," writes Louis. "The Internet abounds with Web sites offering information and advice to help you optimize your finances. Many of these sites are free, while others charge just a few dollars per month."

Louis adds that a professional money manager typically will charge an annual fee of 1 percent to 1.5 percent of a client's assets per year. That's $2,500 to $3,750 on a $250,000 portfolio, which is about the minimum size that most professionals consider worthy of their attention.

Do-it-yourselfers can find not only investment advice, but also scads of retirement planning calculators and advice on the Internet. They also can collect tips on how to plan for college, draft wills, minimize taxes, and determine their insurance needs.

ONLINE TOOLS

There's no shortage of good market research out there and it is the investor's job to determine which sources are best for him. Some serious investors like to tune in to CNBC. Others like to peruse *The Wall Street Journal, Investor's Business Daily,* or *Business Week.* Still others comb the Net for clues and tips on which stock to buy and which stock to unload.

One source of information is a good investment brokerage firm. For example, TDWaterhouse and E*Trade both provide free real-time quotes, research (e.g., Zachs and S&P Reports), and advanced charts to monitor and compare the performance of one stock against another or against an industry. In addition, several free Internet sites contain valuable information. These include www.clearstation.com, www.cnbc.com, www.flextrader.com, www.fool.com, www.forbes.com, www.moneycentral.msn .com, www.morningstar.com, www.personalweath.com, www.quicken .com, www.thestreet.com, www.siliconinvestor.com, and www.zdii.com, to name but a few. Flextrader.com, Moneycentral.msn.com, and quicken.com provide some of the most in-depth free information available. (Descriptions of some leading Web sites appear later in this chapter.)

It's also getting easier to find out what institutional traders are doing, which can alert investors to what stocks are likely to be bought or sold in large blocks. Institutional purchases are often viewed as a tip that a stock's price is likely to rise. Block selling, in contrast, is viewed as a precursor to a sell-off that may mean the stock's price is decreasing. To help on this front, other "direct" market information providers include Thomson Investors Network, which is extending some of its professional products to private investors via its Web site.

One such brand is AutEx, an electronic network of institutional traders that tracks pretrade activity. Before institutions place orders, they indicate on AutEx the size and price of trades they are interested in placing. These huge blocks of shares, when traded, can move a stock's market value in seconds. Institutions view the interests of others and can shop around for the shares they are also interested in trading.

With AutEx, individual traders can view the institutional pretrade activity and get a bird's-eye view of the activity on the New York Stock Exchange floor. AutEx also delivers pre- and postmarket newsletters with commentary on and analysis of the market's activity.

Hearing what's happening from the proverbial horse's mouth can also be helpful to finding out what company executives are telling investors and analysts—or what they are not telling them. If you're a fan of conference calls, try logging on to Bestcalls.com, a service that delivers conference-call information to individual investors. The company has embarked on a long-term campaign to increase awareness and has gained enough clout to force every company to open these calls to all shareholders, not just the largest shareholders and Wall Street analysts.

GET IT FOR FREE: THE WEB'S BEST RESEARCH

Much has been said about how the Internet has leveled the playing field between institutional and individual investors. Institutional investors retain the edge in good market information, but the Web is helping to narrow the gap somewhat. Here's a list of some of the best Web sites where individual investors can get good market information—in many cases, for free.

Much like the CNBC network, the CNBC site—www.cnbc.com—offers real-time investment news for serious investors.

Other recommended sites are:

www.aaii.com—Offers articles from the *Journal of the American Association of Individual Investors* on topics such as building logical stock screens, devising a contrarian strategy, and learning how tax-law changes affect IRA options.

www.allexperts.com—Offers professional analysts who are willing to answer general questions about the stock market for free.

www.bigcharts.com—Provides an array of price charts illustrating a stock's performance versus the appropriate benchmark. A good source for finding stocks on the move, based on price and volume momentum.

www.bloomberg.com—Features online news and market updates as well as features from *Bloomberg Personal* magazine. Click the analysis button for interactive tools such as mortgage and educational cost calculators.

www.briefing.com—Offers sector ratings and analyses, an economic calendar, features on intriguing-story stocks, and intraday charts.

www.cyberinvest.com—Provides links to a variety of sites, advice from market gurus, updates on stocks in the news, and guides to related financial subjects such as online banking.

(continued)

www.datachimp.com—Includes educational resources on various investing topics: financial statements, risk, Roth IRAs, and more.

www.e-analytics.com—A site with information on stocks, bonds, options, futures, commodities, technical analysis, and Dow history, as well as financial planning, insurance, and retirement planning. Also offers market quotes on many stocks, indexes, world currencies, bonds, futures, and commodities.

www.edgar-online.com—Source of SEC filings and related business intelligence.

www.financialengines.com—Top-of-the-line retirement calculator, devised by Nobel prize economist William Sharpe of Stanford University.

www.financialweb.com—A family of sites with links to Stock Detective, offering advice on protecting oneself from scams; Small Cap Investor, spotlighting overlooked growth stocks; and Wall Street Guru, with picks and pans from investor newsletters.

www.firstcall.com—Features an earnings scoreboard that highlights the top recent positive and negative surprises, revisions by analysts, and upcoming announcements, and special charts on the Dow Jones industrial stocks.

www.401kafe.com—Predicts annual growth in a 401(k), based on investment strategies. Basic articles on retirement issues.

www.hoovers.com—Source of company information and late-breaking news.

www.interquote.com—Offers real-time quotes of stocks, options, indexes, futures, and funds.

www.investools.com—Offers nine preset stock screens keyed to factors such as insider ownership, low price-to-book ratio, and high dividend yield.

www.investoreducation.org—A clearinghouse for investor education materials.

www.investorguide.com—Has a personal finance section with advice on topics such as insurance and saving for college, and an investing section with Securities and Exchange Commission filings, links to home pages of public companies, a stock splits calendar, and updates on share buybacks.

www.investorwords.com—Offers a huge glossary of investment and finance terms.

www.marketguide.com—Includes price charts, a what's-hot/what's-not list, and Company of the Day.

www.moneynet.com—A Reuters site loaded with market and company news.

www.morningstar.com—Offers articles on topics such as selecting your first mutual fund, interviews with portfolio managers, and short lists on things like bargain coffee stocks.

www.motleyfool.com—Showcases the Fool's team's wise-cracking commentary, A-to-Z company message boards, updates on Dow theories, and features such as the Daily Double and Daily Trouble, which single out stocks that have recently doubled or been halved in price.

www.noloadstocks.com—Includes commentary from *No-Load Stocks* (newsletter) Editor Charles B. Carlson, model portfolios, and news on stock splits and dividend hikes. More Carlson commentary and information on direct-purchase stocks and dividend reinvestment plans can be found at www.dripinvestor.com.

www.rapidresearch.com—Offers access to 8,000 research reports and lives up to its name with quick stock-screening tools. Click the advanced interface if you're stoked enough to fill 29 criteria.

www.stockpoint.com—Offers a wide range of most commonly used investment data. Perfect for the personal investor. Provides daily charts, indexes, news, analysis, and a natural language search of stock data.

www.stocksmart.com—Includes daily news on dividends and detailed sector summaries. Use the Fund Wizard screen to produce a customized list of mutual fund choices based on criteria such as asset size and sector preference; click the "advanced" button to add

(continued)

factors such as manager tenure, expense and turnover ratios, and performance year-to-date or for periods stretching back as many as 15 years.

www.thestreet.com—Includes Jim Cramer's brash commentary; value plays on low-priced stocks; and information on what mutual fund managers are buying and selling.

www.vanguard.com—Offers the Investor Education University, a huge collection of educational resources focused on mutual funds investors.

www.w100.com—Offers stock quotes on the biggest U.S. and global public companies, with links to their home pages.

www.younginvestor.com—Helps teach kids and parents about money and investing.

www.yourfunds.com—Includes net asset value charts and a flash-mail feature that offers customized alerts on news and price changes affecting portfolios.

Net Roadshow offers a similar service with a twist—Webcasts of roadshow presentations for its investment-bank clients.

BUYERS BEWARE

Still, in today's multimedia age, when information is dumped onto the personal computers of millions of individual investors, you've got to be careful about what you're reading, hearing, and watching. Fortunately, the Securities and Exchange Commission has developed a list of "do's" and "don'ts" for investors who conduct their own research.

TOP NINE INVESTMENT SCAMS

The SEC has also come up with a list of common investment scams that have ensnared unsuspecting investors:

1. *Internet.* Investors should be careful about taking advice from strangers. Never invest based on a "tip" found on the Internet unless the advice matches your own research.

2. *Investment seminars.* Be wary of expensive seminars conducted by self-appointed gurus who imply that you can get rich quick. It's usually the gurus who get rich, from charging admission and selling their books and audio tapes.

3. *Affinity groups.* Members of closely knit religious, business, political, or ethnic groups are targeted by con artists of the same background. The crooks take advantage of a natural trust of "people who are like us." They use advertising to identify potential victims, often adding offers of employment or financial advice.

4. *Abusive sales practices.* Investors should hang up on aggressive cold-callers.

5. *Telemarketing.* New "boiler rooms" feature high-pressure telephone sales operations that are always open and sell fraudulent investments. Promoters try to capitalize on the headlines, from the Year 2000 computer bug to the Asian currency crisis to breakthroughs in computers or biotechnology. To avoid telemarketers, screen phone calls with an answering machine or hang up on cold-callers.

6. *Promissory notes.* In this growing area of fraud, the notes are supposedly insured and backed by real assets. In fact, they are backed only by an often worthless promise to repay. Some notes are issued on behalf of companies that don't exist. Even if a company is legitimate, investors should realize that the reason these notes are offered to small investors is that banks and venture capitalists have declined to invest.

7. *Entertainment.* Con artists focus on investors who hope to "hit it big" with a stake in the next Hollywood blockbuster, cable television shows, video games, and other entertainment products.

8. *Ponzi/pyramid schemes.* Always in style, these swindles promise high rates of return. The only people who make a killing are the promoters who concoct them. Inevitably, later investors lose their money when the house of cards collapses.

9. *Franchise offerings.* Promoters target people who are attracted by the prospect of owning their own business. Some states have taken actions relating to inadequate disclosure and fraud involving franchises, which often are marketed at business opportunity and franchise trade shows.

STUDYING ANNUAL REPORTS

Annual reports can be extremely important documents for finding out not only where a company thinks it's going, but where it has been. They can help give you a sense of where a company's executives believe

TEN DO'S AND DON'TS FOR INVESTORS

1. Be cautious when strangers offering get-rich-quick schemes contact you via "cold" phone calls, e-mails, or unannounced visits to your home. The phone calls could be "boiler room" scams, in which the operators rent offices at impressive addresses, hire unlicensed salespeople to work banks of phones, and call individuals whose names are on lists the promoters buy. The promises of fast profits usually don't come true.
2. Question any fantastic promises of extraordinary returns on your investments.
3. Shy away from high-pressure sales techniques that require hurried money commitments. Some fraudulent schemes have used messengers to pick up investors' checks almost as soon as they ended a phone call.

4. Avoid investments offered by a seller who has little or no written information about the company or its past performance. Even printed materials can be fakes. Read all materials carefully, ask questions, and check with experts.

5. Be wary of investments that are sold on the basis of rumors, tips, or supposedly "inside" information.

6. Ask the seller to give you written information about the investment, including the prospectus (also called an offering circular) and the most recent financial statement. Such information is required for many types of investments, including stock and franchise offerings, limited partnerships, and mutual funds. Read this information before you sign a purchase order to pay for an investment.

7. Consult with your registered stockbroker, banker, lawyer, or accountant. Check with the Better Business Bureau, your state's Securities Commission, or a knowledgeable friend.

8. Contact government agencies to find out whether a company or an individual is licensed to do business or has any history of violating the law. Failure to register, or a history of trouble with authorities, should raise a red-flag warning to prospective investors.

9. Deal with established businesses—those with reputations that are known in the community.

10. When in doubt, wait. Even legitimate investments carry a risk of losing money.

its greatest competitive threats lie and provide details about any lawsuits against the company or failures it had in executing its market or financial strategies. Gone are the days of the bulky, complicated tomes that were hard to read and even harder to glean pertinent information from. Under a new rule by the Securities and Exchange Commission, publicly traded companies must produce more "user-friendly" annual reports and new-issue prospectuses.

Thanks to those measures—and the competitive nature of the stock market, which has forced companies to spruce up their annual report production efforts—the vast majority of investors rate annual reports as the most important source on which to base an investment decision. Some 91 percent of investors said that a company's annual report was the most credible source of information, above the financial media and analysts' reports, according to a survey by Research-Strategy-Management Inc. (RSM) for the Public Relations Society of America.

Yet, ironically, only 8 percent of Americans polled said they request such information first. Most tend to check a likely company's Web site, which was among the least credible sources in RSM's National Credibility Index.

Unfortunately, one of the most common problems companies have is clarifying revenue reports. The Securities and Exchange Commission is particularly strict in this area, and many companies have been forced to go back and change their reporting.

The credibility of annual reports is also enhanced by objective reporting. The minute people get a sense of subjectivity in a corporate document, they tend to shy away from it.

BE A SKEPTIC

Overall, the wealth of information available is a boon to those who are thorough and cautious, and a portfolio-choking albatross to those who believe everything they read. Which category are you in?

TAKING ADVANTAGE OF INVESTMENT CLUBS

Throughout most of this book, we've extolled the virtues and benefits of being your own investor. We've shown you how to conduct your own research, pick your own stocks, get online, and trade on your own.

But not everyone wants to trade as a loner. Some investors may not want to pay the stiff fees that a full-service brokerage firm demands, but they need some help in picking the right investments for their portfolios.

One way to maintain your financial independence from the big-commission brokerage firms, and still get help in picking great stocks, is through an *investment club.*

Investment clubs are groups of members who form a "partnership" to invest together. Each member puts in a minimum required amount, and then all money is put into the group account for investing. The club will make investments based on members' recommendations. The members will then incur a pro rata share of each stock's gains or losses. In previous times, investment clubs didn't do a lot of research; they relied only on safe and conservative stocks. That approach seems to have changed. Investment clubs now do more research, invest in riskier stocks, and realize higher profits than before. Due to their higher visibility, investment clubs are popping up all over. Even Digital-Dollars has a newly started investment group! The number of investment groups is increasing at a tremendous rate, and it's a lot of fun to join one.

Investment clubs are usually groups of 10 to 15 people who come together for fun, education, and profit. They started around 1900. Many clubs have flourished as long as 20 to 30 years. Some have accumulated over $1 million in assets. Members (of both genders) range from teens to senior citizens.

Investment club members pool their funds to buy stocks. Monthly "dues" per member range from $10 to $100. Dues are used to purchase shares of stock. Low-cost dues indicate that shares are being accumulated slowly.

Over time, this approach generally pays well. More than 60 percent of investment clubs show lifetime annual returns equal to or greater than the Standard & Poor's 500 Stock Index. Most clubs lose money during their first two years, but the average club has a portfolio valued at about $89,000.

The National Association of Investors Corporation (NAIC); (www .better-investing.org) based in Royal Oak, Michigan, was formed in 1951. It recommends four conservative principles for investment clubs:

1. Once a month, invest a set sum in common stocks, regardless of general market conditions. This helps you obtain lower average costs.

2. Reinvest dividends and capital gains immediately. Your money will grow faster if earnings are reinvested. This puts compound interest to work.

3. Buy growth stocks (companies whose sales are increasing at a faster rate than their industry in general). The companies should have good prospects for continued growth. They should be stronger companies five years from now.

4. Invest in different fields. Diversification helps spread both risks and opportunity.

Investment clubs are not a get-rich-quick scheme. They are programs for learning and for accumulating and building toward long-term gain. Successful clubs demand this long-term commitment; many hold stocks several years or until they have doubled in value. A falling stock may be considered a buying opportunity.

How do investment clubs work? An investment club is a lot like a mutual fund. You pool your money with several other people so that you can buy a diversified portfolio of stocks. Together, you and the other club members make decisions on which stocks to buy and sell. Each club member does independent research to come up with good stock picks, and then shares the results with the rest of the club. Club members vote on the different stock picks to determine which stocks the club should invest in.

As an investment club member, you end up owning your share of the investment club's assets. If you are one of ten investment club members who contributed equal amounts of money, your share is 10 percent of the value of the club's portfolio.

Advantages

Don't view investment clubs as the purview of elderly women or novice investors—though they can serve both well. Their track record as a whole shows they equal or outpace many of their competitors, as well as market benchmarks. Investment clubs tend to outperform professionally managed mutual funds because the mutual funds charge a fee for managing your money (about 1.4 percent of your assets, on average). There is no such charge with investment clubs.

Secondly, investment clubs are a great way to learn about the stock market AND have fun at the same time. You can form them with your best friends or with people whom you don't see often because of your busy schedules. The weekly meetings are a great way to catch up with friends and help each other learn about investing.

How much does it cost to join? That depends on the entry amount that you and the other club members are most comfortable with. We recommend that each person should invest around $2,500 to start, and then about $50 to $100 per month thereafter. If you and your friends can't afford a $2,500 starting investment, settle on an amount that you can afford, and contribute that. Your goal should be to reach about $70,000 in assets within one to two years. With $70,000, your club could own 15 to 20 stocks and would be appropriately diversified. To keep things on an even keel, all club members should invest the same amount of money at the start and at the meetings.

Meeting Schedules

One meeting each week is ideal, but if that doesn't work for the members, once every two weeks is okay. You really should make a commitment to meet at least once every two weeks. Otherwise, enthusiasm wanes and club members become less serious about investing.

Time Commitment

A five-year commitment is ideal. Five years is enough time to give your investments a chance and see how well the club is functioning. Often, excellent investments will perform poorly in the short term (over the course of a year or a couple of years), but over a time period of five or more years, most solid investments generate a decent return. This doesn't mean that all members will be forced to stay in the club for five years; members can always leave after 30 days' notice. It just means that you will be starting your club with a five-year time horizon in mind.

Investment Club Strategy Tips from the NAIC

The NAIC offers investment clubs these tips on how best to invest their money:

1. Invest in companies you know well. This includes companies from whom you buy products and services, companies you've worked for or competed against, and companies you've read a great deal about. You may not realize it, but you are probably an expert on a certain company or industry. If you shop a lot, you should invest in companies in the retail industry that you think have hot products and good long-term prospects. If you are a Web site programmer with a high level of knowledge about the Internet, you should invest in technology companies that you respect. Your area of expertise or knowledge can give you an advantage over investors, even professionals, who don't have your exposure to certain industries, products, or services. So use it to your advantage.

2. Make sure your portfolio is adequately diversified, so that if one stock goes down, the loss can be offset by other investments that do well. To be adequately diversified, your club should own at least 13 stocks, and the stocks should be in different industries. Don't worry if you don't own 13 stocks right away; most clubs, at the start, do not have enough money to buy 13 different stocks. But after 18 or 24 months, you should reach this milestone. And once you do, you should aim to maintain this level of diversification.

3. Hold on to your stocks for the long term. Most investors buy and sell stocks far too often, and they lose a lot of money as a result. Every time you buy or sell a stock, you have to pay a brokerage commission. Even worse, when it comes time to do your taxes, you have to calculate profits on stocks you've sold, and pay taxes on these profits. Selling stocks can be very expensive. Your stock sales can cost thousands, even millions, of dollars over the course of your lifetime.

STRAIGHT TO THE SOURCE

In December 1994, the Securities and Exchange Commission (SEC) approved what are known as dividend reinvestment plans (DRPs) and direct stock purchase plans. These plans allow investors to buy and sell shares directly through companies and save on brokerage commissions. The plans typically feature statement-based accounting and certificate safe keeping for record-keeping purposes, similar to the systems used by brokerage firms. They put companies on a more equal footing with brokerage firms by offering popular services formerly available only through street-name ownership. These modified DRP plans aren't suited to every individual investor, but they appeal to those who plan to buy and hold their shares, like families saving for retirement or for a college fund for their children.

If you simply sell your stocks less often, you will save a lot of money in brokerage expenses and taxes. Target to establish a 25 percent turnover limitation when you start the club. This means that the club will not be allowed to sell more than 25 percent of its stocks in a single year unless all members agree.

Of course, the most important issue to consider when it comes to investment clubs is, where does the club fit in with your overall investment plan? Is the club the core of your investment strategy or is it to be reserved for your more "disposable" money? This depends upon the nature of the club and its investment philosophy. If the club is more aggressive, it is probably best not to put your core money into it.

PRACTICE MAKES PERFECT

If you're still a little tentative about diving into the stock market with your hard-earned money, consider creating mock portfolios or investing

BUY DIRECT? HERE ARE THE PROS AND CONS

A well-informed investor is a productive investor. But is a well-informed investor smart enough to buy stocks directly from publicly traded companies? Some industry gurus think so.

Currently, about 1,000 domestic and international stocks are available directly to investors, sold straight from the issuing company without a sales charge, and providing monthly statements like those you might expect from a no-load mutual fund.

Direct-purchase stocks function virtually the same as a mutual fund. You contact the company (or its transfer agent), fill out an application, and mail in a check. As with funds, you invest whole dollar amounts—say, $100—which are fully invested down to a fraction of a share, rather than buying a set number of shares from a broker. In many plans, accounts can be opened for a few hundred dollars. You can even get phone withdrawals, automatic investments, and dividend reinvestments, just as you can with most funds.

The advantages to direct-purchase stocks include the cost of ownership, superior ability to avoid tax liabilities, and the sense of accountability that comes with making decisions rather than having a professional manager make them for you.

Disadvantages include the fact that you're on your own. With mutual funds, you have a seasoned stock picker handling your stock selection. With self-directed programs, you have *you*. Plus, self-directed stocks seem to generate a lot of paperwork.

Direct-purchase stocks typically charge fees for initial purchases ($10 to $15), additional purchases (capped at $3), reinvesting dividends (topping out at $3), and selling out. Many of these fees are waived if you set up automatic monthly investments.

For a complete list of available direct-purchase stock plans, check out www.netstockdirect.com, or call *The DRIP Investor/No-Load Stock Insider* newsletters at (800) 233-5922.

fake money in real ones to see how you fare. A number of Web sites give investors this option. Creating and monitoring a portfolio of real stocks, before you put your money on the line, can give you a sense of how individual stocks perform, whether you have the stomach for volatility and if your research was diligent and on the money. It will also give you a sense of whether or not you have the discipline to stay in the market during times of tumult or whether you might prefer investing in mutual funds, where the active management is performed by a money manager.

Web sites that give investors a chance to build mock portfolios or invest in practice portfolios include www.FOLIOfn.com and www.morningstar.com. The exercise is a good one to help you refine your stock picking and investing skills, including your research analysis, your ability to build a portfolio, and your temperament for staying invested in good times and bad—all skills outlined in depth in this chapter. All of these tools will serve you well as you move forward to create investment wealth.

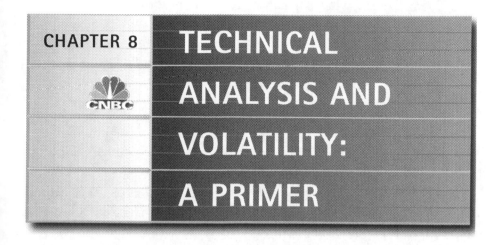

CHAPTER 8

TECHNICAL ANALYSIS AND VOLATILITY: A PRIMER

"He who lives by the crystal ball soon learns to eat ground glass."

—Edgar Fiedler

When it comes to analysis, there's good news and bad news. First, the good news: There are numerous methods and programs for picking stocks and this chapter helps you sample some of the more prominent systems. Now, the bad news: There is no *one* indicator that can tell you when to buy or sell a stock. A variety of factors influence whether a stock's price rises. That's why this chapter helps you understand and pick and choose from a variety of different systems and programs for charting, tracking, and analyzing different aspects of a stock's characteristics, from volatility to price. Zeroing in on these factors, and the direction in which they're moving, can help you refine your stock selection and begin to narrow your choices. Of course, it bears repeating that no one indicator, data point, or trend line can be all-knowing in forecasting winning stocks. It's one thing to miss the next Dell Computer or Microsoft, but imagine losing out on the internal combustion engine or air travel because you didn't do your homework!

That's exactly what has happened to some of our most reputable and prominent business and government leaders over the years. Opportunities to cash in on new inventions were cast away with a sneer without even looking into their potential. Try the following missed opportunities for size:

- In 1943, Thomas J. Watson Sr., chairman of the board at IBM, said that there was no future for the personal computer.

- In 1962, a record industry exec said of the Beatles: "We don't think they'll do anything—guitar groups are on the way out."

- This, from renowned physicist Lee DeForest: "I have not the smallest molecule of faith in aerial navigation other than ballooning."

- Prior to Waterloo, Napoleon to Robert Fulton: "What, sir, would you make a ship sail against the wind and currents by lighting a bonfire under her deck? I pray you excuse me. I have no time to listen to such nonsense!"

Perhaps Napoleon could have learned much from his nemesis, the Duke of Wellington. Leaving little to chance, the British military mastermind fought the battle of Waterloo dozens of times—before he engaged Napoleon in battle. It seems that the Duke, for days before the encounter, fought the battle on a huge map laid out on his desk, using pins and needles to represent the two armies.

Leaving nothing to chance is a good way to pick winners on Wall Street, too. Much of the previous chapter was spent preparing yourself to invest by doing your own analysis and your own research. In this chapter, we go a bit deeper into identifying some investment trends and cycles that may not be recognizable to investors who don't do their homework. Understanding analysis strategies—for example, technical and fundamental analysis, and how volatility impacts the financial markets—will give you a huge leg up on investors who don't take the time to understand how these issues can mean the difference between a portfolio written in black ink or one written in red.

It's not always easy, but it's worth it.

TECHNICAL ANALYSIS

Anyone who has pored over a spreadsheet 20 minutes before the opening bell or downloaded a quantitative analysis program to uncover the next dot-com supernova knows that technical analysis offers enough mind-numbing complexity to satisfy even the most seasoned market analyst.

Okay, so your average online stock trader isn't really interested in stochastic technical analysis or moving-average convergence/divergence. But in a country where 50 percent of all Americans have access to the Internet, getting technical analysis that can improve the quality and timing of your investments is easier to come by—and a bit easier to understand.

First, a little background on technical and fundamental analysis.

Technical analysis is the study of stock price behavior. Historically, traders have used it to uncover trends in stocks (specifically) and the stock market (in general). By identifying and knowing when to take advantage of trends, individual investors have the opportunity to enter and hold profitable positions in stocks on the move. It's worth noting that technical analysis and fundamental data are not the same thing. Fundamental data provide helpful background information on a company, such as the strength of its management team or its earnings, but they cannot fully explain the movement and behavior of the stock itself.

It's important to remember that fundamental analysis relates to the basics of a company: how much profit it's making, and what sort of earnings return it gets on its assets—in other words, the reality of the business. An investor paying close attention to the fundamentals would consider the potential for the business to grow, how much money is being returned to shareholders, and the extent to which profits are being ploughed back to reinforce the company.

Fundamental analysis means buying only stocks that show consistent earnings improvement, have improving sales, and have either strong profit margins or a high return on equity. Earnings per share (calculated by dividing a company's total after-tax profits by the number of common shares outstanding) can be used as an indicator of growth and profitability.

Technical analysis differs from fundamental analysis primarily by helping traders understand the direction in which a stock price is likely to move, based on its track record, which fuels decisions on when to buy, sell, or hold the stock for maximum performance.

A technical analyst focuses simply on movements in the share price over time, or the prices people are prepared to pay for stocks. For example, a technical trader would begin buying XYZ shares when they were down around $14. As they went above $18, the trader would probably seek to lock in the profit and then begin hunting around for another company to buy and sell.

FUNDAMENTAL VERSUS TECHNICAL ANALYSIS

Fundamental analysis seeks to determine a future stock price by understanding and measuring the objective "value" of an equity. In contrast, the study of stock charts, known as technical analysis, is based on a belief that the past action of the market itself will determine the future course of prices.

The company itself may not have changed significantly over that period. Indeed, if the market is valuing it more highly, the outlook for the future may suggest that the company actually offers better value at the higher price. That sort of comfort would sustain fundamental investors. They're not overly concerned with buying at the very bottom and selling at the absolute top.

Fundamental analysts want to acquire some value in return for their money. They want a company that will continue to provide profits (dividends), coupled with long-term share-price growth.

But technical analysis tells a slightly different story that is every bit as compelling as a Steven King or John Grisham yarn. Specifically, it tells the story of a company's movement of its stock price (or "price action"). No matter what the fundamentals say, only price action tells you what actual buyers and sellers think about the company, and what they think is all that matters in determining whether a stock rises or falls. That study of price action, and its visual representation in patterns and trends on a graph, is the cornerstone of technical analysis.

Stock market technicians say that trends and patterns in a stock's price action often repeat themselves in predictable ways—not because trends and patterns continue by magic; but because the underlying psychology of investor behavior toward a stock tends to produce repeated patterns. As Edwards and Magee note, in *Technical Analysis of Stock Trends,* a technical analyst will look at the graphic depiction of a stock's "actual history of trading (price changes, volume of transactions, etc.)" and deduce from that "pictured history" its "probable future trend." Look at 100 historical stock graphs and you'll notice

HOW TO PICK WINNING STOCKS

When it comes to choosing high-return stocks, fundamental and technical analysis can come into play. According to *Investor's Business Daily* Chairman William O'Neil, the main thing that separates really successful investors from those who get only so-so results is *good analysis.*

"The objective is not to be right in the market," says O'Neil. "It's to make big money when you're right, and to get out early when you appear to be wrong. To make big money, you've got to buy the very best companies that are number-one in their fields—the real leaders."

To find those stocks, your analysis should point toward several crucial data points, adds O'Neil. "We've found that strong sales and earnings were among the most important characteristics of winning stocks. This becomes obvious when you see what really great companies looked like in terms of their sales, earnings, and profit margins before they launched price increases of 200 percent to 1,000 percent. So you're looking for strong increases in quarterly sales and earnings compared to the same quarter the year before. You also want an acceleration in the rate of increase in the latest quarter over the previous quarter."

that stocks do indeed tend to trend, and investing at opportune points near the beginning of a trend can be a profitable move. As Wall Street traders like to quip, "The trend is your friend."

UNDERSTANDING VOLATILITY

Believe it or not, one factor worth charting or observing on a rolling basis is volatility. The underlying reason for changes in stock prices is *volatility*—a measure of a stock's tendency to fluctuate over a range of prices during a set period of time.

Volatility has several uses and potential interpretations. First, the degree of volatility of a particular security can be used to determine whether a stock should be considered for selection. Low degrees of volatility can suggest that a stock will tend to stick to its underlying trend. High degrees of volatility can suggest that a stock will move greatly about its trend. This knowledge can be valuable for trading and investment strategies. Is a price change likely to be a trend change? Is price movement related to industry or market movement? Is a stock more appropriate for longer-term or shorter-term analysis? And so on.

Watching a stock's volatility in graphic form can also give you an indication that its price may be ready to move up or down. When a stock tends to have a certain range of volatility over an extended period of time and then breaks out of the range and moves upward, it may predict a change in trend. If it breaks out of the range downward, it can mean that the frequency and severity of short-term price swings will decrease as the overall trend establishes itself among investors.

Recognizing cycles in volatility can be useful in determining appropriate times to anticipate a price breakout. Many stocks can have cycles with a high degree of regularity. Volatility's tendency to be autocorrelative (meaning that reversals often continue in the new direction) can help create circumstances that yield a powerful leading indicator.

Measuring volatility can open the door to successful price prediction. But first take the time to understand exactly what it means. TASC volatility has been said to be "a measure of a stock's tendency to move up and down in price, based on its daily price history over the latest 12 months." "Over time," writes analyst Alan Farley of Traderswheel.com, "markets take on unique characteristics that can be measured through price swings. One well-known example is price rate of change or the average number of points that a stock moves over a specified period of time."

Farley's position is that volatility builds on this quantitative analysis of price by removing direction from the equation. "It stretches pure increments of price change so that their relative travel can be measured," he adds. "The greater the distance over time, the more volatile the market. But pure volatility has little value for traders if they can't base price prediction upon it. Fortunately, volatility has a characteristic that contributes to profitable trading. It tends to move in cyclical patterns."

Markets expand and contract endlessly, so volatility moves cyclically between active and inactive states. Relatively new (outside the options world, at least) techniques for analysis of this phenomenon have developed over the past 15 to 20 years. Many tools now focus on the relationship between price swings over time and their current movement. Others predict the future through the pattern of wide- and narrow-range price bars.

As ranges contract, so does volatility. Like a coiled snake, markets approach neutral triggers from which sharp price movements erupt. Properly tuned indicators can identify these trend-range interfaces and offer a powerful supplement to classic pattern analysis. Using charting software with range analysis functions can extract this information directly from chart patterns. (See Figure 8.1.)

Regardless of whether a trader undertakes the study of fundamental or technical analysis, his or her primary mission is understanding how volatility impacts the financial markets.

At the top of the list of most technical analysts' goals is the "popular models" theory of stock price volatility. First credited to financier Robert Shiller, the popular models theory proposes that investor reactions, due to psychological or sociological beliefs, exert a greater influence on the market than commonsense economic arguments. Shiller says that because excess volatility exists in the stock market, volatility

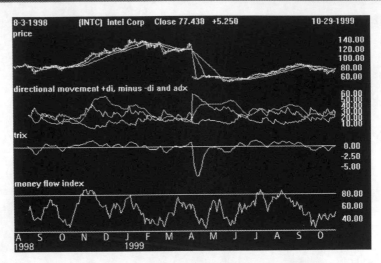

GLOSSARY OF TECHNICAL INDICATORS SHOWN

Moving Average

A Moving Average is an average of the closing prices over a selected number of days. A simple Moving Average is calculated by adding the prices for a number of periods and dividing by the number of periods. *When the stock prices rise above their downward trend line and then also rise above their moving average, you have additional confirmation that a bottom has occurred in the stock.* On an actual graph, the 30-day average line is shown in red, the 15-day average line is shown in green, and the 5-day average line is shown in white.

Directional Movement

The Directional Movement Index is a unique filtered momentum indicator developed by Welles Wilder in 1978. It is based on the assumption that markets exhibit strong trends only about 30% of the time and provides entry into trades only when markets exhibit significant trending character-istics. This indicator uses exponential moving averages and ratios using the high, low, and close price data on a scale that ranges from 0 to 100. *The basics indicate that you should enter long when +DI crosses over the −DI line and sell or sell short when −DI crosses over the +DI line.* On the actual graph, the +DI line is shown in red and the −DI line is shown in green.

TRIX

The TRIX indicator was developed by Jack Hutson in the early 1980s. This indicator shows the per-cent rate of change of a triple exponentially smoothed moving average of a security's closing price. This indicator filters out insignificant cycles and produces a smoothed line that closely follows price. *One interpretation of this indicator suggests that trades should be placed when it changes direction.*

Money Flow

The Money Flow Index (MFI) is a volume weighted indicator that gives an interpretation based on activity and not solely on price movements. The up and down stock price averages are multiplied by the respective volumes to produce an index that tracks money flow activity in a stock. *The basics suggest that when the index is below 20 a long position should be considered. A short position should be considered when the index is above 80.*

Figure 8.1   Stock Trend Analysis with Technical Indicators

Source: www.globalstocktrends.com/products/sample/charts/naup/intc.html.

TRADING ANALYSIS DO'S AND DON'TS

Many short-term players view trading as a form of gambling. Without planning or discipline, they throw money at the market. The occasional big score reinforces this easy-money attitude but sets them up for ultimate failure more like a gambler than an investor. Without defensive rules, insiders easily feed off these losers and send them off to other hobbies.

Technical analysis teaches traders to execute positions based on numbers, time, and volume. This discipline forces traders to distance themselves from reckless gambling behavior. Through detached execution and solid risk management, short-term trading can finally "work."

Markets echo similar patterns over and over again. The science of trend allows investors to build systematic rules to play these repeating formations and avoid the chase. Forget the news, remember the chart. You're not smart enough to know how news will affect price. The chart already knows the news is coming.

Source: Alan Farley, editor/publisher, Hard Right Edge, www.Hardrightedge.com.

cannot be totally explained. He claims that substantial price changes result from a collective change of mind by the investing public, which can only be explained by investors' thoughts and beliefs on future events—that is, investors' psychology.

Another rationale for stock market volatility is the efficient markets theory. "One of the basic notions of modern finance is that the stock market—in fact, all securities markets—are efficient in the sense that, at any given point in time, the price of the stock reflects all that's knowable about the company," says Robert A. Haugen, in his recent book *Beast on Wall Street: How Stock Volatility Devours Our Wealth.* "Over the last 10 years, a lot of evidence has come forth that has shaken the belief of many academics in this concept of efficient markets."

Haugen attempts to show that, by far, the prime mover of stock prices is not new information about, say, corporate profits or economic prospects; instead, it is recent changes in stock prices themselves—

what he calls "price-driven volatility." Explaining what he calls a "spectrum of efficiency," Haugen says that at one end are perfectly efficient markets, and at the other end are markets that are in total chaos. His view is that we're closer to the chaotic side.

"Over the century, there is evidence that returns on stocks have been too high relative to securities that are risk-free," says Haugen. "There is also evidence that stock prices have been too volatile relative to the cash flows—earnings and dividends—being generated by corporations. And it's also the case that we can only explain a very small fraction of the movements in stock prices, month to month, on the basis of real economic variables."

Haugen's position is light years away from the traditional belief among "market technicians that stock performance can be predicted from past price movements, without regard to a company's earnings, sales, or management style. Rare is the fundamental analyst who gleans nothing from looking at a chart of a stock's price over the past 12 months.

TERMS TO KNOW

Technical and fundamental analysis and volatility are the cornerstones of a solid stock prognosticator, but myriad other research terms come into play as well. Here's a breakdown of the more important ones. Oh, and check out CNBC and see how these terms are put into play by the pros. Or use CNBC.com for further analysis or use some of its technical screens to narrow the field of interesting stocks. The site's tools, like "Stock Search Criteria," will help you apply both fundamental and technical screens that can show you how the market is reacting to some of the companies you begin following.

Moving Average (MA)

No, it's not the number of times you switch households in your lifetime. According to Hardrightedge.com's Farley, the "moving average" is the oldest and the most widely used technical indicator, demonstrating the average value of a security's price over time. A moving average is plotted in graph form as a line connecting the average daily prices over some historical or lookback period. It makes it easier to discount "noise," such as short-term spikes or drops in a stock's price, especially during more volatile markets. This moving average value is calculated based on each day's stock prices and is designed to highlight trends. "The purpose of the moving average is to show the trend in a smooth fashion," he says. "The user specifies the time span." For stocks, Farley says the most common time periods for moving averages are 10 days, 30 days, 50 days, 100 days, and 200 days. Most technicians, however, use variations of these numbers to suit their individual needs. There really isn't just one "right" time frame. Moving averages have different time spans, and each tells a different story. The shorter the time span, the more sensitive the moving average will be to price changes. The longer the time span, the less sensitive or the more smoothed the moving average will be. The other component a person needs to specify is what value to use for the price of the stock. The most common value to use is the closing price for that particular day.

To do it yourself, bring a calculator to the table, because moving averages can be calculated in a number of ways. First the easier stuff. A simple moving average is calculated by adding the prices over a given number of periods, then dividing the sum by the number of periods. For example, a nine-day simple moving average would add together the closing prices for the past nine days, and then divide that number by nine. An exponential moving average gives more weight to recent prices and is calculated by applying a percentage of today's closing price to yesterday's moving average. The longer the period of the exponential moving average, the less total weight is applied to the most recent price. The advantage to an exponential average is its ability to pick up on price changes more quickly. Moving averages are very flexible and can be incorporated into most trading and investment philosophies or screens.

FINDING THE TREND

Many Web sites have developed tools that allow you to use moving averages to track and chart average stock prices over any period of time you designate. These tools are helpful to look for stocks that have the potential to move up in price or breakout (the term used to describe when a stock crosses its moving average). To show you how using different time periods will give you different results, here's a moving average chart of XYZ Company. It shows the actual price movements, the 50-day simple moving average, and the 200-day simple moving average over a 22-month period through January 2001.

If you absorb any of this, let it be this line: The shorter the time period, the more reactionary a moving average becomes. (See Figure 8.2.) A 50-day moving average is much more sensitive to price swings than a 200-day moving average. However, a shorter period also means that there may be a greater number of false moves within an existing trend. You'll hear about terms like "market noise" or a "whipsaw" when you reach this level of security analysis. Experts say these events are considered a false move. Also remember that moving averages can be used to evaluate

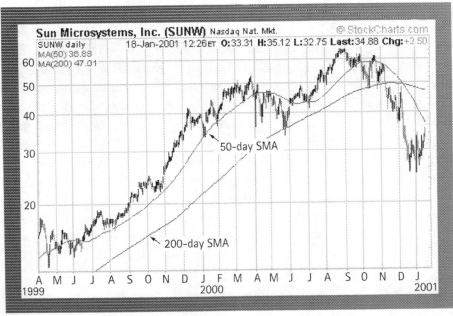

Figure 8.2   Moving Averages—Part 1

Source: Stockcharts.com.

trends in both the short term and the long term. A typical short-term moving average ranges from 5 to 25 days. An intermediate-term range is from 25 to 100 days, and a long-term range is 100 to 250 days.

Momentum

Like Derek Jeter picking up speed rounding first base, momentum means movement on Wall Street, too. There, the term momentum means a relatively straightforward indicator that measures the rate of change in price as opposed to price itself. It is calculated by subtracting the price of x periods ago from the price now. This indicator can also be referred to as rate of change (ROC).

The conventional interpretation is to use momentum as a trend-following indicator. That means that when the indicator peaks and begins to descend, it can be considered a sell signal. The opposite conditions can be interpreted when the indicator bottoms out and begins to rise. If momentum reaches very high or low values relative to its range historically, a continuation of the current trend is likely, and a change might not be considered until the actual price begins to dip down or rise, respectively. (See Figure 8.3 for a typical stock chart.)

Money Flow

Sure, we all want money flow. But it means a lot more than just hitting a hot streak at the track or having Regis call your name on "Who Wants to Be a Millionaire." Money flow is one of the more sophisticated and powerful technical indicators that links price to volume. It is calculated based on each tick during the trading day. Money flow increases by the shares traded on the level of an uptick, and decreases by the shares traded on the level of a downtick. Therefore, if there is an uptick on 5,000 shares traded, money flow will increase by 5,000. If there is then a downtick on 600 shares traded, money flow will decrease by 600. If these two trades comprise the entire trading day, money flow will have increased by 4,400.

Signals are generated when there are divergences between the money flow and price:

1. When price is increasing while money is flowing out of the security, it is a warning of an impending collapse in the price of the stock.

2. When the price is trending downward while money is flowing into the security, it is a sign that some savvy buyers are accumulating the stocks.

Bollinger Bands

Investors use trading bands—lines drawn above and below the moving average to isolate a range of prices for a given security—to represent the concept that a stock generally trades within a predictable range on either

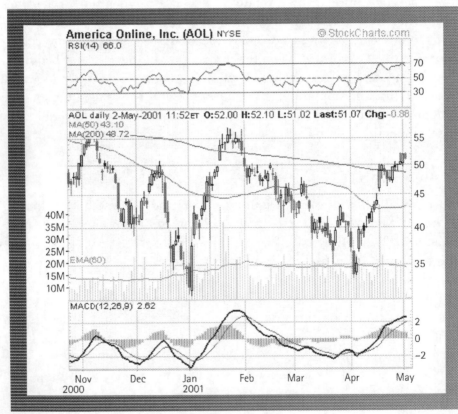

Figure 8.3   Stock Chart Illustrating Momentum

Source: Stockcharts.com.

side of the moving average. When a stock is near the upper or the lower limits of the trading bands, an investor should pay closest attention, according to conventional wisdom. Bollinger bands are considered some of the most useful bands in technical analysis, for they vary in distance from the moving average of a security's price, based on the security's volatility. During periods of increased fluctuation, the bands widen to take this into account; when the fluctuation decreases, the bands are tapered for a narrower focus to the price range. The upper band is the standard deviation multiplied by a given factor above the simple moving average, and the lower band is the standard deviation multiplied by the same given factor below the simple moving average.

On-Balance Volume (OBV)

OBV relates price to volume and tries to capture the buying and selling pressure in the market. It assumes that when a security closes up for the day, the shares transacted represent buying power. Conversely, the amount of volume on a down day represents selling power. Therefore, if the price ends up for the day on 10,000 shares traded, OBV's value will increase by 10,000. Should the price decrease on 25,000 shares, OBV's value will decrease by 25,000.

Proponents of on-balance volume maintain that trend changes in OBV occur before trend changes in price. Therefore, if OBV is going down over time and price is increasing, a price collapse is possible. If OBV is trending up and price is trending down, the security could be heading for an upswing in price.

Patterns and Indicators

The oldest form of interpreting charts, *pattern analysis,* gained popularity through both the writings of Charles Dow and *Technical Analysis of Stock Trends,* a classic book written on the subject just after World War II. The newer form of interpretation is *indicator analysis,* a math-oriented program in which the basic elements of price and volume are run through a series of calculations in order to predict where price will go next.

Pattern analysis gains its power from the tendency of charts to repeat the same bar formations over and over again. These patterns have been categorized over the years as having a bullish or bearish bias. Some well-known patterns include: "head and shoulders," "triangles," "rectangles," "double tops," "double bottoms," and "flags." Chart landscape features such as "gaps" and "trend lines" are said to have great significance for the future course of price action.

Both patterns and indicators measure market psychology. The core investors and traders who make up the market each day tend to act with a herd mentality as price rises and falls. This "crowd" tends to develop known characteristics that repeat themselves over and over again. Chart interpretation using these two important analysis tools uncovers growing stress within the crowd that should eventually translate into price change.

Relative Strength Ranking (RSR)

The idea here is that most successful stocks must rank well when they are compared to the overall market, using several criteria. RSR measures the performance of a stock based on the past year's worth. Relative strength ranking is measured on a scale of 0 to 100, where each number can be considered a performance percentile out of all available individual stocks in the market.

Relative strength ranking can be used as part of an overall selection criterion for purchasing new stocks, and as verification for a stock that has limited potential for a major price advance. Many of the biggest price advances in recent history have been for stocks with an RSR topping 80. Remember:

1. Choose leading stocks with high RSR.
2. Avoid laggard stocks with low RSR.

Relative Strength Index (RSI)

This oscillator, introduced by J. Welles Wilder, Jr., could be more appropriately called the *internal strength index,* for it compares the price of a security relative to itself. The RSI is based on the difference between the average closing price on up days and the average closing price on down days over a given period, and is plotted on a vertical scale of 0 to 100. An oscillator refers to a momentum or rate-of-change indicator that is usually valued from −1 to +1 or 0 percent to 100 percent. Wilder advocated a 14-day RSI, but shorter and longer periods have gained popularity when the market exhibits certain characteristics. Generally, RSI is measured in a period between 5 and 25 days.

Stock Charts

A stock chart is a simple two-axis (x–y) plotted graph of price and time. Each individual equity, market, and index listed on a public exchange has a chart that illustrates this movement of price over time. Individual data plots for charts can be made, using the closing price for each day. The plots, connected together in a single line, create the graph. A combination of the opening, closing, high, and/or low prices for that market session can be used for the data plots. This second type of data is called a *price bar.* Individual price bars are overlaid onto the graph, creating a dense visual display of stock movement.

Stock charts can be created in many different time frames. Mutual fund holders use monthly charts in which each individual data plot consists of a single month of activity. Day traders use one-minute and five-minute stock charts to make quick buy-and-sell decisions. The most common type of stock chart is the daily plot, which shows a single complete market session for each unit.

Stock charts can be drawn in two different ways. An arithmetic chart has equal vertical distances between each pair of price units. A logarithmic chart is a percentage growth chart. It has equal vertical distances between the same percentages of price growth. For example, a price movement from 10 to 20 is a 100 percent move. A move from 20 to 40 is also a 100 percent move, so the vertical distance from 10 to 20 and the vertical distance from 20 to 40 will be identical on a logarithmic chart.

Stock chart analysis can be applied equally to individual stocks and major indexes. Analysts use their technical research on index charts to decide whether the current market is a bull market or a bear market.

On individual charts, investors and traders can learn the same thing about their favorite companies.

Trends

Professional stock traders use stock charts to identify current trends. A trend reflects the average rate of change in a stock's price over time. Trends exist in all time frames and all markets. Day traders can establish the trend of their stocks to within minutes. Long-term investors watch trends that persist for many years.

Trends can be classified as up, down, or range bound.

In an uptrend, a stock rallies, often with intermediate periods of consolidation or movement against the trend. In doing so, it draws a series of higher highs and higher lows on the stock chart. In an uptrend, there will be a positive rate of price change over time.

In a downtrend, a stock declines, often with intermediate periods of consolidation or movement against the trend. In doing so, it draws a series of lower highs and lower lows on the stock chart. In a downtrend, there will be a negative rate of price change over time.

A rangebound price swings back and forth for long periods between easily seen upper and lower limits. There is no apparent direction to the price movement on the stock chart, and there will be little or no rate of price change.

Trends tend to persist over time. A stock in an uptrend will continue to rise until some change in value or conditions occurs. Declining stocks will continue to fall until some change in value or conditions occurs. Chart readers try to locate tops and bottoms—the points where a rally or a decline ends. Taking a position near a top or a bottom can be very profitable.

Trends can be measured using trend lines. Very often, a straight line can be drawn under three or more pullbacks from rallies or over pullbacks from declines. When price bars then return to that trend line, they tend to find support or resistance and bounce off the line in the opposite direction.

John Murphy, bestselling author and stock analyst, said, "The trend is your friend." For traders and investors, this wisdom teaches that you will have more success taking stock positions in the direction of the prevailing trend than against it.

TOOLS AT YOUR DISPOSAL

If you're already picking your own stocks, this chapter should have served as a refresher for you, perhaps giving you insight into new ways you can winnow down the market of available stocks and monitor those you think are worth following. If you are just getting started, this chapter is a primer to explain the tools available to you for screening entire stock markets or the stocks of individual industries to find those that have the traits that interest you most. These technical tools, whether you use moving averages, money flow, relative strength rankings, or a combination of all three, can also tell how stocks on your watchlist are faring over a period of time and in different types of market climates. Coupled with fundamental research into how a company is performing, technical analysis can help you determine which trends are worth watching and aid you in your overall decision-making process of which stocks to buy, which to hold, and which to sell.

SOURCES

John J. Murphy, *Technical Analysis of the Futures Markets,* Prentice Hall Press, 1987.

Martin J. Pring, *Technical Analysis Explained,* McGraw-Hill; 1991.

Stan Weinstein, *Stan Weinstein's Secrets for Profiting in Bull and Bear Markets,* Irwin Professional Publications; 1988.

CHAPTER 9

ASSET ALLOCATION STRATEGIES

> "If you don't know where you're going, you might wind up somewhere else."
>
> —*Yogi Berra*

Without a plan, it's tough to move from point A to point B, much less make your way toward investment success. That's why it is so important to develop a good asset allocation plan that can be your guide. Many things—varying interest rates, turbulent stock market performance—can hamper a portfolio's performance.

But that impact is diminished, if not negated, by a good asset allocation plan.

What's the alternative to having such a plan? In an old yarn (attributed to the late President Lyndon Johnson), a young man is applying for a job as a flagman for a railroad. The railroad manager says the young man can have the job if he answers just one question correctly. When he agreed, the fellow was told to imagine that he was a flagman at a crossing. The Continental Express was bearing down on him from the east at 95 miles per hour, and the Century Limited was bearing down from the west at 100 miles per hour.

What, the manager asked, would the young fellow do in that situation? Without hesitation, the applicant said he'd call his brother-in-law.

Vexed, the station manager asked why. "Because he ain't never seen a train wreck before," the young man replied.

That's what happens when you don't have a plan.

ASSET ALLOCATION

If you think that picking top performing stocks or mutual funds is the best way to build a sound long-term portfolio, you're likely to be wrong.

Many academic studies have shown that the actual equities chosen account for 5 percent of a portfolio's success. The other 95 percent can be attributed to the allocation of a portfolio among stocks, bonds, and money market instruments, whether through direct investment or mutual funds. Ibbotson Associates, which has done the most widely cited study on the subject, places the number at 90 percent.

Asset allocation is a blueprint investors use to make their investment decisions. It's a method of structuring an investment portfolio with a mix of investments from various types of financial assets and geographical markets to suit an individual investor's goals. Rare is the fund manager or financial planner who doesn't think that asset allocation is a good method for maximizing long-term returns while maintaining a comfortable level of risk.

ASSET ALLOCATION

Dividing an investment into different categories, such as stocks, bonds, and mutual funds.

Here's how it works. Asset allocation operates on the principle that not all investments behave the same way at the same time. Some, such as equities or equity mutual funds, have greater short-term price fluctuations; others, such as short-term Treasury bonds or money market mutual funds, are generally more stable. More volatile investments, however, offer the potential for greater long-term gains. Financial markets also vary in performance cycles. If U.S. stock markets are on the rise, those in other areas of the world may be in decline. When interest rates are dropping, shorter-term bonds generally outperform longer-term bonds. Moreover, when stock markets are strong, bond markets may be weak.

Generally, proper allocation of your investment dollars means assembling a portfolio from the three major asset categories: cash, fixed-income, and equities. Cash includes money in the bank, short-term investments such as Treasury bills, and money market mutual funds. Fixed-income investments include bonds, guaranteed investment

AMATEUR HOUR?

According to *Wall Street Journal* columnist Holman W. Jenkins, a woefully common misapprehension is that adults in positions of authority know what they are doing. In politics, we correct this with elections; in business, we keep a daily watch on the stock market.

That's why, when it comes to market risk, you should try not to put too much faith in what the so-called professionals have to say.

A recent study by Wilshire Associates, a Santa Monica, California-based financial consulting firm, estimates that regular investors could have earned an average of 280.6 percent over the past 10 years by following the asset allocation advice of brokerage specialists.

But left to our own devices, we could have done even better. According to the study, investors could have earned 286 percent simply by buying and holding a portfolio of 55 percent stocks, 35 percent bonds, and 10 percent money market investments. (By themselves, money markets may not be a good investment, but a 10 percent stake protects some of your money from a market crash.)

One other thing. The 280 percent earned by following the market experts' advice comes with strings attached—fees, commissions, and other expenses that would have dragged that percentage down even more.

certificates, and other interest-generating securities. Equities, or stock market investments, can be further subdivided into different styles, such as "value" and "growth."

Through asset allocation, you can use these variations in the performance of securities and financial markets to your advantage. Asset allocation ensures that your portfolio is diversified; you reduce the degree of short-term fluctuations while maintaining the potential for long-term returns. You can also reduce the risks associated with putting all your eggs in one basket. (See Figure 9.1.)

To do that, it's important to put your own needs and comfort level first. The following four considerations should help you determine that so you can build the right asset allocation:

1. *Your investment goal.* The most common goals are: retirement, education, and a down payment on a first home.

2. *Your investment horizon.* Once you have determined your goal(s), a time horizon is easy to calculate. If you expect to work for another 20 to 30 years, you can build a more aggressive portfolio because you can ride out the highs and lows of a volatile stock market. If your primary goal is to save for a home, you don't want to risk facing a dip in the stock market just as you are ready to withdraw the funds for the down payment. In that case, you would be better off with money market instruments. Saving for educational expenses usually fits in somewhere between the other two goals, depending on how far in the future you will need the money.

3. *Your risk tolerance.* Take this Q&A quiz to determine how you should allocate your portfolio assets:

   • Do market fluctuations keep you awake at night?
   • Are you unfamiliar with investing?
   • Do you consider yourself more a saver than an investor?
   • Are you fearful of losing 25 percent of your assets in a few days or weeks?

   If you answered "Yes" to these questions, you are likely to be a "conservative" investor.

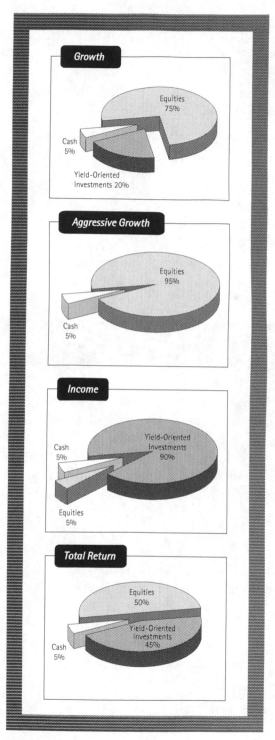

Figure 9.1 Choosing the Right Asset Allocation Strategy

Source: www.gruntal.com/asset.html.

- Are you comfortable with the ups and downs of the securities markets?
- Are you knowledgeable about investing and the securities markets?
- Are you investing for a long-term goal?
- Can you withstand considerable short-term losses?

If you answered "Yes" to these questions, you are likely to be an "aggressive" investor. If you fall somewhere in between "conservative" and "aggressive," you could call yourself a "moderate" investor.

4. *Your financial resources.* The amount you have available to invest will be a factor in the risk you might want to take.

KNOW WHAT YOU WANT—AND WHAT YOU CAN HANDLE

Wall Street pros have varying opinions on how to best use asset allocation to maximum advantage. One interesting outlook on the allocation picture comes from Martin L. Leibowitz, TIAA-CREF vice chairman and chief investment officer.[1]

Leibowitz recommends pondering the following seven points to get yourself in the right frame of mind for creating your asset allocation program.

1. *The future may really be different.* We've all heard that past performance is no assurance of future results. It's perfectly natural to think (or, these days, to hope) that the stock market will act tomorrow like it did yesterday. But in our heart of hearts we know it's impossible to be certain of *any* future market performance—in the next few years, or next month, or tomorrow. That's why the advice to avoid extrapolating from the past applies to risk levels as well as returns. Stock market

[1] Martin L. Leibowitz, "Please Check Your Asset Allocation Seat Belt" (October 13, 2000; www.tiaa-cref.org/siteline/archive/assets.html).

volatility has been relatively high in recent years. As for returns, we don't know whether daily, monthly, and yearly changes in the market will continue to occur within a fairly large range or whether volatility will decrease.

2. *You never know when a dip is just a dip.* Because of recent history, some people may believe that market retreats are likely to be temporary dips followed by rallies. It would then be logical to believe that any decline would always be an opportunity to buy more stocks. The stock market cliché tells us to buy low and sell high, but it doesn't say anything about how to know when a drop is as low as it will get. In the midst of a significant market decline, no one will be sure how much lower the market might go. In other words, only in retrospect can a downward market move be safely described as a "dip."

3. *Equities don't always beat other assets.* Over long periods of time, equities have historically provided better returns than cash, bonds, or real estate. But remember, that's *on average* and *over time.* For any future period, there are no guarantees. Over significant spans of years, bonds have sometimes outperformed stocks. If your allocations are heavily weighted toward stocks and your time horizon isn't as long as it used to be, you may want to think about some of the advantages of more conservative assets.

4. *Your asset allocation mix will almost surely have drifted.* If you have been investing in stocks or stock mutual funds for a while, it won't be unusual for your asset allocation to become too heavily weighted in stocks, as they did in many investors' plans during the bull market of the 1990s. Check whether your investment goals and asset allocations line up. A significant discrepancy raises questions that deserve answers.

5. *Everyone finds it hard to overcome inertia.* Most people don't want to fiddle with a winning strategy. Nor do they like to confront a losing strategy. As you might guess, this means that asset allocation plans are often left untouched for a longer time than makes sense. Circumstances change—in your portfolio, in the markets, and in your life situation. Besides your retirement assets, how have your other holdings changed in recent years? How have your spending patterns evolved? What new financial obligations have you adopted, such as commitments

USING ASSET ALLOCATION TO MANAGE RISK

Of the three major investment classes—stocks, bonds, and money market securities—stocks usually pose the greatest risk, bonds the second greatest risk, and money markets the least risk. The returns from the three investment classes are reversed. Stocks offer the best chance of investment gain; bonds, the second best chance; and money markets, the least chance for gains.

In the stock market's worst year, according to the *Los Angeles Times*, the value of big-company stocks fell 43.3 percent. In the market's best year, big-company stocks rose 53.9 percent. There's no shortage of volatility—or good returns—in stocks. The returns of small-company stocks, which are more volatile than big-company stocks, have varied by as much as 78 percent in a given decade, whereas the returns on Treasury bills have varied by less than 1 percent. T-bills are a sure bet, but the returns on that bet are pretty slim pickings.

In fact, $1 invested in big-company stocks in 1926 would have earned you $1,114 by the end of 1995, even though big-company stocks lost money in 20 of those 70 years. Conversely, if you had invested $1 in Treasury bills in the same period (with only one down year that yielded minuscule losses), you would have earned only $12.87. But some people would be happy with that. "You never know what the stock market is going to do."

Creating a risk profile for yourself is critical to your financial fortunes. Some investors can go about their business, knowing that their portfolios are invested in higher-risk funds like international and aggressive growth funds. Others can't, so they bulk up on conservative bonds funds. Whether you consider your investment philosophy to be aggressive, moderate, or conservative, you need to form an opinion of yourself as a risk investor and determine how you're going to feel about possibly losing 5 percent or 10 percent of your investment at certain times. Will you be all right with that? Or will it send you into a fit of sheer panic and have you pacing your bedroom floor at 4:00 A.M.?

Either way, a good asset allocation strategy can help.

to children, parents, other relatives, or charitable organizations? What retirement plan contributions have you made recently that you need to fold into your financial planning? You can—and should—adjust your allocation as your circumstances change.

Liebowitz also encourages investors to be realistic about their risk tolerance during rough times and to avoid the "herd mentality" that permeates much of Wall Street trading. No matter what happens, stick to your plan and try not to let others—meaning family members, Wall Street pundits, and/or coworkers—influence your investment decisions. "The best way to approach your asset allocation," sums up Liebowitz, "is to first make sure you don't have any illusions about your money; imagine it all to be fresh cash in your pocket. Second, figure out how your asset allocation mix may have changed. Third, examine whether your retirement and other needs have changed. And lastly, consider whether you need to modify your asset allocation mix in light of any changing circumstances or plans."

6. *Think of your entire portfolio as new money.* This revision may involve adopting a new mind-set. As a first step, take the attitude that all of your retirement savings are equal, including your and your employer's original contributions, previous earnings on those contributions, and recent gains. Consider all of them to be cash in your pocket—cash that should be invested thoughtfully in light of your goal—your retirement. It may help if you "forget" about where the money came from. View it as an inheritance that you just received from your favorite uncle. You've been following a path that has led to your portfolio's current value. Your family is protected, and other investment goals are secure. Now, starting fresh, how would you invest this new-found legacy? Your answer to this question would be clearer reflection of your real appetite for risk during the rest of your lifetime and, in some cases, beyond.

7. *Don't let "the crowd" dictate your choices.* Almost everywhere, you can read or hear stories about how everyone is putting their money into this or that stock. New money flowing into stock mutual funds, for example, set a new record in eight out of the past ten years. Many Americans developed a love affair with stock mutual funds during the

ASSET ALLOCATION SNAPSHOT

Modern Portfolio Theory is the cornerstone of asset allocation. It tells us that the risk of a portfolio is lowered when two (or more) asset classes are combined.

As an example, Portfolio A is composed of:

100 percent Small Capital Growth stocks.

Portfolio B is composed of:

20 percent Large Capital Value stocks;
30 percent Large Capital Growth stocks;
30 percent "First World" International Stocks;
20 percent Small Cap Growth stocks.

Asset allocation theory would suggest that, over a market cycle (three to five years), portfolio return and risk (as measured by volatility) would be lower in Portfolio B.

Asset allocation is certainly not confined to equities. In its purest sense, the concept refers to allocating among all asset classes:

Fixed income (bonds, money markets, cash, and so on).
Equities (small, large, growth, value, international, and so on).
Hard assets (real estate, gold, raw land, and so on).
Other (venture capital, hedge funds, derivatives, and so on).

Source: ElectronicAdvisor.com

1990s. But you shouldn't feel compelled to follow others, especially when your decisions affect your own personal investments.

Above all, Leibowitz says, choose an asset allocation program that comforts you and allows you to sleep better at night. In the end, it's your money—not your neighbor's, not your coworkers', and not your mail carrier's. Do what feels right for you and your family.

ASSET ALLOCATION STRATEGIES

You have probably already guessed that asset allocation needn't be complicated. The asset mix is essentially the percentage of a portfolio that is represented by each class of investment—stocks, bonds, or cash and cash equivalents. For example, a portfolio may be comprised of 40 percent stocks, 50 percent bonds, and 10 percent cash. Research has proven that asset mix is the single most important determinant of a portfolio's rate of return, so the correct asset mix is crucial.

If the Ibbotson study (mentioned earlier in this chapter) is right, 90 percent of a portfolio's return stems from the asset mix decision. That leaves about 5 percent for market timing and 5 percent for security selection. Returns are compounded over time, so, over the life of a portfolio, even modest changes in asset mix can lead to significant changes in the return. See Figure 9.2.

FACTORS THAT IMPACT INVESTMENT RETURN

Asset mix = 92.5%

Securities selection and market timing = 6.4%

Other factors = 2.1%

Source: Barron's.

Evaluating Risk

As we saw in Chapter 4, an appropriate asset mix depends primarily on the investor's tolerance for risk.

RISK

Risk relates to the chances of your investment diminishing in value.

Year-Ending Date	Total Return—12 Months
12/31/81	1.86
12/31/82	41.39
12/31/83	20.48
12/31/84	−19.53
12/31/85	22.38
12/31/86	−8.43
12/31/87	−6.90
12/31/88	25.85
12/31/89	9.37
12/31/90	−10.80
12/31/91	55.90
12/31/92	13.02
12/31/93	15.41
12/31/94	0.54
12/31/95	26.60
12/31/96	14.04
12/31/97	14.57
12/31/98	3.52
12/31/99	37.26
12/31/00	9.22

Figure 9.2   Portfolio Time Series

Source: The Vanguard Group.
Annual performance: Vanguard Explorer Fund.

Although the cornerstone of asset management is the establishment of clear and concise objectives, it is essential to define risk before an asset allocation plan can be formed. Risk is mostly defined as "the probability that a plan will not meet its long-term objectives." The key risk factors to consider are inflation, interest rates, the economy, the markets, and specific risk. In theory, an older adult's portfolio should be structured to provide growth of income without assuming significant risk. The real challenge is to provide enough growth to stay ahead of inflation. For example, a conservative portfolio for a 70-year-old retired couple may be comprised of 30 percent stocks, 60 percent bonds, and 10 percent cash. A portfolio weighted heavily in stocks may be exposing the couple to higher levels of risk than are appropriate. On the other hand, a portfolio invested primarily in bonds may be secure but will not outpace the effects of inflation over time.

How Many Funds to Choose

One rule is: The more money you have on hand to invest, the wider your fund choices can be.

Typically, you can build a suitable investment portfolio with as few as four funds, although some investors have as many as 20 or more.

Don't worry when a certain fund class, like emerging-market funds or international funds, doesn't sit well with you. The absence of one fund group isn't going to damage your portfolio. The added comfort you gain by *not* investing in such a fund is probably worth any moderate gains you might miss out on. With mutual funds, you're already diversified. That's what a mutual fund with investments in 60 or 70 companies can do for you.

One rule says that you should use your age as a barometer when you are creating an asset allocation plan. It works like this. A 30-year-old train conductor named Kevin subtracts his age from 100 percent, giving him 70. That 70 percent represents how much money Kevin can invest in stocks; the remainder should be invested in bonds or other conservative investments.

When he turns 40, Kevin bumps his bond holdings up to 40 percent, leaving 60 percent invested in stocks. He repeats the adjustment each decade, until he retires. This interesting formula makes a lot of sense. But, as we explain later, it might not be aggressive enough to capitalize on the higher historical stock market returns we've seen over the past 50 years or so. (See Figure 9.3.)

Whatever asset allocation program you use, try to include a mix of big-company ("big-cap") stock funds, small-company ("small-cap") stock funds, and international funds. Then toss into the mix some short- and long-term U.S. Treasury funds and corporate bonds funds. Throw in a money market fund for added protection. This asset allocation should provide you with the high performers (stocks) and conservative funds (bonds) you need to rest comfortably.

The Right Combination

There are two choices when investing in the stock market: size and style. Size refers to the size of the firm. In general, the 500 stocks comprising the S&P 500 are considered "large" stocks, which account for almost 75 percent of the market value of all U.S. stocks.

Style refers to the investment style or philosophy to which a company is most likely to appeal. Growth investors seek growth stocks—firms with fast-growing earnings. They tend to have low dividend yields, high price-earnings ratios, and high price-to-book-value ratios. Value investors seek value stocks—firms whose shares are selling below their "real" value. They tend to have high dividend yields, low price-earnings ratios, and low price-to-book ratios.

| Age | Conservative | | | Moderate | | | Aggressive | | |
	Stocks	Bonds	Cash	Stocks	Bonds	Cash	Stocks	Bonds	Cash
20–49	65%	35%	0%	75%	25%	0%	90%	10%	0%
50–59	45	45	10	65	35	0	85	15	0
65+	15	65	20	30	50	20	50	40	10

Figure 9.3   Asset Allocation Chart

WHERE DO YOU FIT IN, RISK–WISE?

The following groups of investments can help you decide what mix of investments fit your attitudes, risk profile, and needs as an investor.

Ultra-Aggressive Portfolio

%	Investments
35	Small-cap funds
20	International stock funds
20	Sector funds
15	Large-cap funds
10	Emerging-market funds

Aggressive Growth Portfolio

%	Investments
30	International stock funds
35	Large-cap funds
35	Small-cap funds

Growth Portfolio

%	Investments
40	Large-cap funds
25	International stock funds
30	Small-cap funds
5	International bond funds

Growth and Income Portfolio

%	Investments
40	Large-cap growth and income funds
20	Large-cap growth funds
15	International stock funds
15	Small-cap funds
10	Intermediate-term bond funds

(continued)

Conservative Income Portfolio

%	Investments
25	Large-cap growth and income funds
25	Long-term bond funds
20	Intermediate-term bond funds
15	International bond funds
10	International stock funds
5	Small-cap funds

Conservative Portfolio

%	Investments
40	Money market and short-term bond funds
25	Intermediate-term bond funds
10	International bond funds
10	Large-cap funds
10	International stock funds
5	Small-cap funds

As you've learned, your choices when you buy specific stocks, bonds, or mutual funds are not nearly as crucial as maintaining the right mix of asset classes. Remember, asset allocation is a systematic approach to diversifying a portfolio of investments. You start with an overall allocation among stocks, bonds, and money market securities. Then, within each category, you select assets that react differently to the same economic condition. This strategy effectively reduces risk and increases returns over the long term. Returns may be less during bull markets, but asset allocation tempers the impact of unpredictable market swings, thereby increasing your probability for long-term financial success.

A portfolio diversified both within and among asset classes offers the only effective way to manage the risks inherent in investing. For example:

- Including both domestic and foreign stocks in your portfolio may moderate the effects of a slow domestic market if foreign stocks are performing well.

- Allocating some of your assets to domestic bonds usually lessens the risk of stock investments and helps stabilize your income if that is one of your objectives.

- Small-capitalization companies are likely to lead the market at the beginning of a market expansion.

- Large-capitalization companies generally perform better when the economy is slowing.

The expectation of asset allocation is that all investments in the portfolio will not produce high returns, but losses in one class will be offset by gains in others. Investments that move together are considered highly correlated. The purpose of asset allocation is to mix assets that have lower correlation, to reduce investment risk (i.e., diversification).

Investments will not be protected against market risk (an increase or decrease in the overall market for a particular class of assets) if diversification is only within one class. Tactical asset allocation adds an element of "market timing" by attempting to forecast returns of several asset classes and periodically adjusting the mix to increase returns or minimize market risk.

Diversification

The stock market may have been one of the longest running headlines during the 1990s, but investors in 2000 and 2001 learned a quick lesson in asset allocation: Whoever put too many eggs in one basket wound up with a lot of broken eggs when the market stumbled. That's why it is important to diversify within the stock portion of a portfolio. In particular, an investor should always have an exposure to large-value and large-growth stocks.

Diversification within a stock portfolio consists of investing some portion in each of these areas: large- and small-capitalization stocks (with proportions roughly equal to their weighting in the total stock market, a 75–25 percent large-cap/small-cap mix) and growth and value stocks.

Here are some tips to help you determine which types of stocks fit your age and risk profile:

- International stocks should be included in everyone's portfolio, with the possible exception of the elderly. Recommendations for international exposure start at about 15 percent to 20 percent for younger investors and gradually decrease as investors get older. One source recommends no exposure for investors age 75 or older.

- Young investors should put more emphasis on international stocks, small stocks, and growth stocks; older investors should put more emphasis on large-cap stocks, especially value stocks. Broad diversification is always encouraged, but younger investors can take more risk and can therefore place greater emphasis on the riskier portions of the stock market. Older investors can still invest in these areas, but their emphasis should be on more stable, large-capitalization companies.

- As investors age, they should shift the bond portion of their portfolio. Primarily long-term bonds should diminish and primarily intermediate-term or short-term bonds should increase. Bond prices become more stable as maturity is shortened. Thus, the advice to shorten bond maturity as one ages is consistent with the advice to move toward assets that have more stable prices.

- As one ages, the cash portion of the portfolio increases. Increasing cash assets aligns with shortening the bond maturity for increased price stability.

- High-grade corporate bonds and Treasury bonds of similar maturity are close substitutes because the returns on these bonds are very close. (High-grade corporate bonds tend to have slightly higher yields.) In contrast, high-yield bonds have a much higher default risk and, consequently, are lower-graded.

They are not close substitutes for high-grade corporate or Treasury bonds.

Maintenance and Rebalancing

Your financial picture will change over time. Your income will vary. You may have several children and even more grandchildren. You may start and sell a business, get a golden handshake for a company and trade up to a new position, or decide to retire earlier or later than you ever imagined. Wherever life takes you, after you develop and implement your asset allocation strategy, don't forget to make periodic adjustments to reflect your own changing lifestyle and needs.

After an allocation strategy is developed and implemented, periodic adjustments will be required to maintain it. Investments will need to be rebalanced to correct the asset mix and allow the investor to continue his or her long-term strategy. Rebalancing of asset classes can be done annually or when the investment value moves a certain percentage in one direction or the other. The basic idea is simple: A stable asset mix gives an investor a risk exposure that is stable *and* appropriate for on-going financial needs (typically dictated by his or her stage in life). A "fixed-weight" strategy—a long-run contrarian strategy—is an example. When stocks rise from being fairly valued to becoming overvalued, the investor sells the overvalued stocks and buys bonds (or takes the proceeds in cash); or when new money is needed to replenish the portfolio, the investor purchases bonds or cash rather than stocks. When stocks fall from being fairly valued to undervalued, the investor sells bonds or uses new money and buys the undervalued stocks. In short, a fixed-weight strategy allows the investor to profit from market misvaluations while maintaining a stable risk exposure.

The method of rebalancing will depend on many factors. One important factor is whether investments are in taxable or tax-deferred (retirement) accounts. Adjusting tax-deferred investment accounts can be done at little or no cost. Rebalancing of taxable investments should be considered carefully because transactions usually trigger taxable income. A change in the allocation of taxable investments could be accomplished by directing the inflow of any additional funds to the appropriate asset class, to achieve the desired investment mix overtime. "An asset allocation strategy that has a long-term focus will help take the emotion out of investment decisions, especially during times of market volatility," notes Greg Sandor, a member of the financial counseling services group at Deloitte & Touche LLP.

ASSET ALLOCATION STRATEGIES

How long you plan to stay invested in the markets and when you'll need to cash in investments to meet your goals or needs are crucial components to developing a meaningful asset allocation plan. Here are three scenarios to choose from:

Long-Term Strategy. Tends to emphasize growth to build assets by investing in stocks. This strategy may also include a commitment to income investments such as bonds, in order to moderate risk. A portfolio that employs a long-term strategy might have 70 percent equities, 25 percent bonds, and 5 percent short-term instruments or cash.

Mid-Range Strategy. Provides a balanced approach with investments in both equities and bonds. The goal is to provide some growth potential along with current income. A portfolio that employs a mid-range strategy might have 50 percent equities, 40 percent bonds, and 10 percent short-term instruments or cash.

Short-Term Strategy. Designed to emphasize current income, capital preservation, and liquidity, while maintaining a smaller portion of the portfolio in stocks that have growth potential. A portfolio that employs a short-term strategy might have 50 percent bonds, 20 percent equities, and 30 percent short-term instruments or cash.

These examples are for illustrative purposes only. Ask your investment professional to help you determine a mix of investments that is suitable for you.

FACTORS TO CONSIDER

The goal of asset allocation is to maximize potential return based on your acceptable level of risk. As we stated above, there is no correct or perfect allocation for your specific situation. It is up to you (and a financial planner or adviser if you choose to use one) to build a plan you believe can go the distance and allow you to live comfortably, both in terms of risk and return. Before determining a target asset allocation, investors should understand the principles of risk and return and the potential impact of an allocation strategy on their financial situation. Here are some rules of thumb that can help you maximize your plan and avoid common mistakes.

1. *Avoid market timing.* Market timing calls for sharp swings in the stock/bond/cash mix, based on expected near-term market prospects. For example, a market timing service may recommend shifting the stock allocation from 80 percent one month to 10 percent in the second month and 60 percent in the third. By definition, market timing advocates an unstable risk exposure. All sources are unanimous in their discouragement of market timing.

2. *Moderate your portfolio's risk by mixing stocks and debt.* Stocks are claims against real assets. Bonds and cash are debt; they usually promise fixed returns. Stock and debt are fundamentally different; consequently, their returns tend not to follow similar patterns. Combining stocks and debt moderates a portfolio's risk. On a broader scale, individuals who hold stocks and debt in their investment portfolio *and* own their own home have a broad portfolio that is diversified among stocks, debt, and real estate—three asset types with widely varied returns.

3. *Young investors: lean toward stocks.* Young investors who are years from retirement can invest more of their portfolio in stocks than the elderly. Although year-to-year stock returns are volatile, the young can be reasonably confident that the good years will more than offset the bad years over their investment horizon. As they age and their investment horizon shortens, they are less confident that there will be

enough good years to offset the bad ones, and they decrease the recommended allocation to stocks.

4. *Whatever your age, stocks matter.* Historically, the returns on a portfolio of long-term Treasury bonds have been more volatile (that is, riskier) than a portfolio with 90 percent bonds and 10 percent common stocks. Stocks held alone are riskier than bonds held alone, but, given the magic of diversification, investors can add some stock to an all-bond portfolio and actually reduce the portfolio's risk. Diversification means not putting all your eggs in one basket even if the basket looks safe. Since 1926, the volatility of an 80 percent bond/20 percent stock portfolio has been equal to that of a 100 percent bond portfolio. This helps explain why no one recommends a stock weight of less than 20 percent.

STICK WITH THE PROGRAM

After you've chosen your asset allocation strategy, stick with it. The investment experts at Vanguard Funds say that investors who give up on an asset allocation strategy take on "far more risk" than they may realize.

MORE ASSET ALLOCATION STRATEGIES

Dollar cost averaging consists of investing a constant dollar amount in common stocks at fixed intervals, over a long period of time. "Fixed intervals" can be weekly, monthly, annually, or whatever schedule matches your abilities. The secret is to keep the interval consistent.

For example, you could invest $600 a month in common stocks, or you could invest $1,800 every quarter. The goal of dollar cost averaging is to invest smaller amounts of money on a regular basis, thus forming your long-term strategy.

There are specific advantages to this system:

1. It guards against purchasing too many shares when prices are too high.
2. It allows you to take advantage of buying opportunities when prices are low.
3. Its consistent purchase system usually makes the average cost of the shares purchased less than the actual market price.

But, there are disadvantages to the system as well. One is the possibility of having to liquidate the portfolio when stock prices are low, causing a loss. You can offset this problem by creating a plan to liquidate your shares well in advance of the actual liquidation time. Once in place, you can begin to pick and choose the best time to liquidate each holding.

A second disadvantage is created when the investor's income stream is not as steady as had been assumed. This can force the investor to limit purchases at inopportune times.

In an article on asset allocation on the fund company's Web site, Vanguard's fund managers pointed to the whopping returns (135 percent) in the technology stock fund sector in 1999 and said they were too tempting for some investors. Many funds with triple-digit returns that year were relatively new and are small in asset size, so their chances of repeating these returns are low. As a fund's assets grow, it becomes increasingly difficult for the manager to pick stocks that consistently outperform the market.

"It makes sense, now more than ever, to allocate," said Richard W. Stevens, Principal, High-Net-Worth Services. "No one could have predicted that we'd go through a decade of incredibly high equity returns. No one can outguess the markets, so the best thing to do is diversify your assets."

It's All About You

As TIAA-CREF Vice Chairman and Chief Investment Officer Martin L. Liebowitz indicates, the key to a solid asset allocation strategy is knowing your own limits and not getting caught up with what the guy down the hallway from your office thinks about the market. You know your financial goals, you know your risk tolerance levels, and you know your time frame for meeting your investment objectives. You can lean on a financial adviser or stockbroker for support, but the real impetus to a successful long-term asset allocation strategy is staring right back at you from the mirror every morning. Swinging for the stands can seem like the thing to do during periods of market euphoria, but if you build an asset allocation plan and follow it, you'll be better off than just about any investor who tries to buy only winners. As history has taught us, successful investing isn't about home runs or picking winners. It's about designing a suitable asset allocation plan so that one type of assets will offset the losses of another type. The never-ending noise of the markets can be pretty distracting and the lure of easy money, well, alluring, but consider your asset allocation plan the foundation of your investing house. Build it right from the start and it will withstand harsh rain, sun, and snow. Sure, from time to time you'll have to make adjustments, just as you will with your asset allocation plan, but if you maintain them they will serve you well over the years, far better than jumping from investment to investment ever can. In addition to underscoring that fact and giving you guidelines for building a plan that fits your needs, this chapter also discussed how asset allocation can help you avoid unnecessary volatility.

You also learned to modify your plan over the years as your assets grew and your needs changed. At the core of your plan, you learned to put your own needs first, by using your own goals and risk tolerance as your core building blocks.

CHAPTER 10

WEB SAVVY: USING THE INTERNET TO TRADE AND TRACK YOUR PORTFOLIO

"Get your feet off my desk, get out of here, you stink,
and we're not going to buy your product."
—*Hewlett-Packard executive, responding
to Apple Computer founders Steve Jobs'
and Steve Wozniak's pitch to invest
in the duo's "personal computer" in 1976*

Who knew? Today, you can sit at your computer, put in a limit order at your online broker for shares of IBM or Microsoft, attach a FOK (fill or kill limit) and still have most of your lunch hour left. We take the ease and immediacy of online research and investing completely for granted these days because we can. And if you don't know what a limit order or FOK is, don't worry. You soon will. This chapter is designed to give you the information you need to harness key tools like the Internet and on-line trading, in addition to providing you with an insider's view so you can control your transactions and your exposure.

Back in 1976, who could possibly have imagined the coming tsunami—the personal computer. Several years prior to Apple's launch, even IBM's legendary founder and president, Thomas Watson Sr., had said that there was no market for personal computers. As recently as the mid-1980s, Digital Equipment founder and computing legend Kenneth Olsen had added that there was "no use" for the personal computer. Today, there is no Digital. It was swallowed up by Compaq—a personal computer maker.

Thanks to computer technology (primarily, the personal computer and the Internet), schoolchildren 200 years from now will know the names Jobs and Wozniak—and Bill Gates, too—just as well as children in the mid-1900s knew the names Henry Ford and Orville and Wilbur Wright.

A NEW WORLD ORDER

Make no mistake, technology is making history these days, too.

According to Forrester Research, at the end of 1999, there were 34 million U.S. households with Internet access. This number is expected to grow to approximately 107 million U.S. households by 2003. As the number of U.S. households on the Internet increases, so does the number of U.S. households accessing financial products and services online. At last count, at least 18 percent of investors used the Internet to buy or sell stock. According to the research firm Cerulli Associates, the collective financial services industry held more than 26 million online accounts at the end of 1999. By 2003, the company estimates, the industry will hold 80 million accounts online.

There's no doubt that the Internet has democratized Wall Street by providing retail investors access to investments and information previously open only to professional investors. It has allowed online firms to open up IPOs to retail investors, and issuers to communicate more readily with their shareholders. And, it has enabled financial service companies to harness the Web to give their clients unprecedented access to accounts, research, portfolio strategies, and other financial planning data.

But although the breadth and scope of what investors can do on the Internet today is nothing short of phenomenal, the Web has also raised significant regulatory and compliance issues that financial advisers need to address. The Internet is changing things for investors and for financial advisers, but there may be roadblocks ahead in the form of Web compliance challenges.

Why the big attraction to the Web?

Many investors are lured to the Web by lower transaction fees and service fees. The most prominent example has been investors' rapid migration to online brokerage firms to trade stocks and no-transaction-fee mutual funds. Investors using online brokerage platforms can easily cut their trading costs in half, compared to the old brick-and-mortar brokerage industry alternatives.

The rise of the Net has spiraled nicely with the shifting attitudes displayed by individual investors. The benefits that investors previously associated with an intermediary's ability to deliver information and execute trades have been diminished—at least in the eyes of investors.

ONLINE INVESTING FACTS AND FIGURES

Average income of an online investor: $78,300.

Online stock traders use the Internet an average of 11.6 hours a week; nontraders log on for only 8.4 hours every week.

About a quarter of Internet visitors say they use the Net to get financial information. About half say they log on for news and entertainment.

More people trade securities than purchase books, CDs, or any other products online.

By 2004, more than 17.4 million American households will invest electronically.

Percentage of Americans trading online: 5 percent.

Number of online brokerage accounts in the United States: 13 million.

Source: eMarketer, Money.com, and Securities and Exchange Commission.

To a great extent, the financial intermediary sector has rallied to the cause by launching programs that enable them to serve as catalysts for cyberinvestors, helping them to refocus on the quality and consistency of the advice and guidance they're receiving online.

REASONS INVESTORS LOVE THE WEB

As a recent report in *Business Week* indicates, Wall Street has come a long way from the days when eighteenth-century merchant bankers sent stock tips to favored customers via carrier pigeons.

Thanks to the Internet, superior financial advisory services are now available to a larger base of customers—not just the $1 million-and-up crowd. With the technological advances and increasing competition that the Internet has created in the financial services industry, the average American now has access to financial planning tools and resources that were once available only to the rich, if at all.

Correspondingly, if you are among the increasing number of Americans with a net worth of $1 million or more, you may soon have access to the personalized, comprehensive, and far-reaching advice and services once reserved for families with $100 million.

But even more important than its broadening of the base of financial service options for consumers, the Internet has been instrumental in educating investors on the complexities of stocks, bonds, and mutual funds, and how to properly incorporate them into an investment portfolio. Rare is the financial company Web site that doesn't offer investment tutorials, interactive classrooms, and plain old descriptions of investment terms and how they impact investors.

Investment company sites have had great success hammering home basic investment tenets like investing for the long term, investing on a regular basis, and creating solid investment goals. Twenty years ago, when most Americans depended on their company pension and Social Security income for their retirement savings, investors weren't paying much attention to mutual funds and the financial markets. Today, thanks in part to their own self-empowerment and the evolution of

FIVE REASONS WHY YOU SHOULD LOVE THE NET

1. *Convenience.* The Internet gives you the ability to access your financial information from anywhere and at any time. By employing the Internet, consumers are no longer restricted to making financial transactions at a physical location or during a firm's hours. The Internet is especially convenient for customers who travel frequently or work off-site—for example, oil industry workers or construction managers.

2. *Efficiency.* The Internet gives you a platform for managing all of your finances. With a click of a mouse, consumers have access to past account statements and transaction histories without stockpiling paper. Furthermore, the Internet now affords consumers the ability to review information from multiple financial providers on one site.

3. *Access to information.* The Internet provides you with previously unavailable information on financial products and services. Investors interested in trading online can receive breaking industry news, analysts' reports, and real-time quotes and account updates—all from one Web site. They can also use the Internet to get the best deals on financial products and services by easily comparing offerings from a number of different financial providers.

4. *Control.* You don't have to rely on your brokers' being in the office at 9:30 A.M., when the markets open, and you don't have to worry about a broker's being out to lunch when you want to make a purchase. The purchase ultimately is the client's decision, and a broker won't be urging the client to buy stocks to meet his or her quota. Investors can log on, punch a few buttons, and buy or sell their investments in an instant. They don't have to call their broker, wait for a call back, or listen to a spiel about the mutual fund the broker's company is trying to sell. Plus, if they're too busy during the day, they can place their trades at any time when they are free to log in.

(continued)

> 5. *Low cost.* Because of heated competition among online brokers, you'll enjoy commission rates that have gone through the floor Purchasing 50 shares of a $20 stock from a traditional broker may cost you $80. You could do it online for $10 to $15. By taking the online route, you could buy another three shares. And those buys can really add up.

technology and the Internet, investors are more highly educated than ever and are subsequently playing a greater role in their long-term financial choices.

LOGGING ON

No computer? No problem. For the uninitiated, getting on line has never been easier.

Prices for PCs have sunk so low that there's no longer any real excuse not to have one. For only $600, you can get a personal computer that performs any digital investing functions, runs applications like Word and Excel at decent speeds, and plays glitzy games. To hedge against rapid obsolescence, your best bet is to buy a midlevel PC— priced today at about $999. The higher-priced machines often come with key application software like Microsoft Word and Excel already installed. Look for a package that also offers a CD-ROM encyclopedia and personal finance software such as Intuit's Quicken or Microsoft Money. If you're a Macintosh loyalist, you'll have to spend around $1,500 for similar power and speed.

To invest in cyberspace, you'll need the following basics in a PC.

Monitor

For as low as $250, you can grab a user-friendly, easy-to-see computer monitor. A 15-inch screen may come bundled with your computer, but aim for 17 inches, even though it will cost you a bit more cash. Get a screen with a "dot pitch" rating of 0.28 or smaller. It will guarantee a crisp picture of your finances.

Modem

Look for the fastest possible access when you buy your computer. The best choices are the new cable modems or high-speed DSL—Digital Subscriber Line—phone lines that are being rolled out. If neither is available, you may want an ISDN line, which can cost you roughly double the price of a standard phone line. If all else fails, go for the newest 56k bps (bits per second) modems, which by now are standard in most new personal computer purchases.

Keyboard/Mouse

The keyboard for a new system is usually barely adequate. If you plan to do a lot of typing, upgrade to a better one. Try different keyboards in a store or at friends' computers, or find one made by IBM or Keytronics ($50 to $100). If your desk space is limited, you may want a trackball (an upside-down mouse) or a touchpad.

RAM (Random Access Memory)

With Windows '98, 32 megabytes (MB) of RAM would be the minimum; 48 MB or 64 MB would be better. Windows 2000 is likely a better fit for that kind of speed and capacity when shopping for a new computer, but if you already own an old 486 or 586 Intel series PC, you can get by with 32 megabytes. The more applications you run at once (for example, Word, Excel, and an investing program), the more memory you'll need—and memory is cheap now.

Processor

The chip that serves as the brains of your computer is the biggest factor in how fast your system runs. These days, a midlevel computer should have a speed of 600 megahertz (MHz), although you might get by on the old 233 MHz boxes.

Hard Drive

Bigger is definitely better because this is where your computer stores applications and documents. Storage space is measured in gigabytes, or thousands of megabytes. Get at least a 20-gig hard drive on a new system. If your entire family plans to use the computer, move up to a 30-gig or higher.

CD-ROM/DVD

The CD-ROM is standard on desktop PCs, and most software comes only in this format. Resist pressure to "upgrade" to DVD, which holds a lot more data than a standard CD-ROM and also runs movies. There's very little DVD software, and it's doubtful that you'll watch movies on your PC.

ONLINE TRADING—BASICS

To open an online trading account, you will typically need a minimum balance—often $1,000 or so—with an online broker. You choose the broker. We can't recommend one over another, but we can provide you with these tips from Kassandra Bentley, president of CyberInvest.com.[1]

1. *Size matters.* If you regularly make trades of 100 or 500 shares, check the commission schedule for trades of those sizes. A highly touted rock-bottom rate may apply only to trades of 1,000 or 5,000 shares. Or, you may have to maintain a minimum level of assets in your account or make *x* number of trades each month.

2. *Look for hidden costs.* Nasty surprises may be lurking on the fee schedule: Fees for delivery of stock certificates, fees for late payments or bounced checks, transfer fees, wire fees, IRA fees, annual maintenance fees, termination fees—to name a few. A pesky little transaction or "postage and handling" fee is still tacked onto all trades

[1] *Source:* Cyberinvest.com.

by a few brokers. Be sure to check out the fee schedule. SmartMoney .com gives a separate rating for fees in its broker survey.

3. *Find out the exact meaning of zero.* Some brokers do not require a minimum investment to open an account. But, unless you establish a credit line, funds must be in a new account before you make a trade. All stock trades must be settled by the third day after the trade.

4. *If you want kiwis, be sure to plant a kiwi tree.* Broker surveys and broker guides are geared toward stock trades. But maybe you want to trade options or bonds or mutual funds. Maybe you like penny stocks or Canadian stocks or ADRs (American Depositary Receipts). If so, be sure the broker you choose trades these securities. And check out the commissions. Even if the broker trades them, they may not be traded over the Internet and may incur a higher-than-desirable commission.

5. *Real time is the best time.* Real-time quotes are becoming more prevalent on the Net. But understand what your broker means when you're being offered free real-time quotes. Is it for each trade you make? Or for accounts of a certain size? Are there bonus quotes with each trade, to be drawn upon as needed? Can you update your portfolio with real-time quotes? Do they have streaming real-time quotes?

After you have opened an account, you will be provided with a user ID, an account number, and a password. You can then execute transactions through this account via the broker's Web site. When your orders are executed, you usually receive an e-mail notification, followed by a notification via the U.S. Postal Service. Online brokers typically charge a certain amount of commissions per trade for some (or any) number of shares. Real-time quotes are available at all times, usually at no extra cost. Charts, news, and research information are also available on the broker's Web site, and you would have access to these as a customer (see Figure 10.1).

Your Trading Screen

For most online brokers, your order screen usually consists of a form with a few boxes to fill in, such as: buy or sell, number (#) of shares,

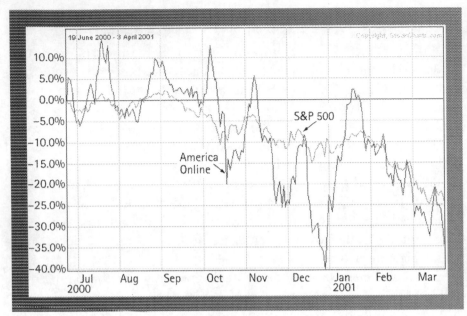

Figure 10.1   Online Stock Chart—Advanced

Source: StockCharts.com.

stock symbol, type of order (market, limit, and so on), and length of time for the order to be open (good until canceled, good for the day only). After submitting your order, a second screen appears: the confirmation screen, which allows you an opportunity to cancel your order if you entered any part of it improperly (perhaps you set up a sell when you meant to set up a buy) or if you have changed your mind. At this point, you enter your password to confirm your order, and you then become responsible for the outcome of the trade. If you made an order entry mistake, this second or confirmation screen allows you to review your transaction a second time and change it (if necessary) before you submit it. Confirmation screens are a very important safeguard against any mistakes you make while entering your order. Imagine the horror of buying 1,000 shares of a stock when you only wanted 100 shares.

A Note on "Express Servers"

Some online brokers offer their customers an "express server"—a direct order (buy and sell) entering system. But amateur investors should be wary of express servers. When an order is entered with an express server, you don't get the confirmation screen to review your order a second time for accuracy. You get just one opportunity to get it right. Express servers are usually used by hyperactive traders (people who buy and sell multiple times within a day or an hour) because of the speed of order execution offered by the system.

An express server is an advantage if you are buying and selling volatile stocks. These stocks move in price very quickly, and a very fast execution could mean the difference in an extra $25 or $100 made or lost on just 100 shares. (See Figure 10.2.)

Placing an Order

When you place an order, it's generally sent either to an exchange, such as the New York Stock Exchange, or handled through the Nasdaq dealer market. Your order will be executed by being paired with its complement. If you wish to buy a stock, your order will be paired with the order of someone who wants to sell, and vice versa. For over-the-counter (OTC) stocks in which your brokerage firm makes a market, it will usually act as market maker; that is, the brokerage firm, acting as principal, generally will sell stock to you or buy stock from you.

The Execution Process

When you place an order to buy or sell stock, you might not think about where or how your broker will execute the trade. But where and how your order is executed can impact the overall costs of the transaction, including the price you pay for the stock. Here's what the Securities and Exchange Commission (SEC) says you should know about trade execution.[2]

---

[2] www.sec.gov/consumer/tradexec.htm Last update: March 20, 2000.

TSE: CN

Call-Net Enterprises Inc.		Toronto Stock Exchange		Last traded: September 26, 2000 03:55 EST	
Last	Volume	Net Change	Open	High	Low
$2.36	35,040	−0.140	$	$2.50	$2.36
Bid Price	Bid Size	Ask Price	Ask Size	# Trades	% Change
$2.36	4	$2.41	30	80	−5.60%
TICK Trend	52 Week High		52 Week Low	Last Date/Time	
-+-===	$10.40		$2.36	September 26, 2001 03:55 EST	

TSE: CN.B

Call-Net Enterprises Inc.		Toronto Stock Exchange		Last traded: September 26, 2000 03:55 EST	
Last	Volume	Net Change	Open	High	Low
$1.48	365,617	0	$1.55	$1.55	$1.46
Bid Price	Bid Size	Ask Price	Ask Size	# Trades	% Change
$1.46	3	$1.48	6	215	0.000%
TICK Trend	52 Week High		52 Week Low	Last Date/Time	
=+=-+=	$9.35		$1.46	September 26, 2001 03:58 EST	

Figure 10.2   Sample Web Stock Chart

According to the SEC, many investors who trade through online brokerage accounts assume they have a direct connection to the securities markets. But they don't. "When you push that *enter* key, your order is sent over the Internet to your broker, who decides which market to send it to for execution," says the SEC. "A similar process occurs when you call your broker to place a trade."

The SEC advises investors that security prices can change quickly, especially in fast-moving markets. "Because price quotes are only for a specific number of shares, investors may not always receive the price they saw on their screen or the price their broker quoted over the phone," the SEC reports. "By the time your order reaches the market, the price of the stock could be slightly—or very—different."

SEC regulations do not require a trade to be executed within a set period of time, but investment firms aren't supposed to exaggerate or fail to tell investors about the possibility of significant delays.

More on Trade Executions[3]

The SEC also tells us that just as you have a choice of brokers, your broker generally has a choice of markets where your trade can be executed.

- For a stock that is listed on an exchange, such as the New York Stock Exchange (NYSE), your broker may direct the order to that exchange, to another exchange (such as a regional exchange), or to a firm called a "third market maker"—a firm that stands ready to buy or sell a stock listed on an exchange at publicly quoted prices. As a way to attract orders, some regional exchanges or third market makers will pay brokers for routing orders to a particular exchange or market maker. A penny or more per share may be paid for your order. This is called "payment for order flow."

- For a stock that trades in an over-the-counter (OTC) market such as the Nasdaq, your broker may send the order to a "Nasdaq market maker" who handles the stock. Many Nasdaq market makers also pay brokers for order flow.

[3] *Source:* SEC (www.sec.gov/consumer/tradexec.htm).

- Your broker may route your order—especially if it is a "limit order"—to an electronic communications network (ECN) that automatically matches buy and sell orders at specified prices. A "limit order" is an order to buy or sell a stock at a specific price.

- Your broker may decide to send your order to another division of his or her firm and request to have it filled from the firm's own inventory. This is called "internalization." Your broker's firm may make money on the "spread"—the difference between the purchase price and the sale price.

Broker Obligations

The SEC says that in any decision on how to execute orders, your broker has a duty to seek the best execution that is reasonably available for customers' orders. "Your broker must evaluate the orders received from all customers in the aggregate, and periodically assess which competing markets, market makers, or electronic trading networks offer the most favorable terms of execution," says the SEC.

The opportunity for "price improvement" (an opportunity, but not a guarantee, for an order to be executed at a better price than is currently quoted publicly) is an important consideration when a broker is executing customers' orders. Other factors include the speed and the likelihood of execution.

Here's an example from the SEC of how price improvement can work: Let's say you enter a market order to sell 500 shares of a stock. The current quote is $20 per share. Your broker may be able to send your order to a market or a market maker where a price better than $20 is possible. If your order is executed at $20 1/16, you would receive $10,031.25 for the sale of your stock—$31.25 more than if your broker had only been able to get the current quote for you.

Trader's Options

SEC regulations state that if for any reason you want to direct your trade to a particular exchange, market maker, or ECN, you may be able to call your broker and request that this be done. Some brokers charge for this service. Others now offer active traders the ability to direct orders in Nasdaq stocks to the market maker or ECN of their choice.

The SEC advises that you ask your broker about the firm's policies on payment for order flow, internalization, or other routing practices, or look for that information in your new account agreement. To find out the nature and source of any payment for order flow that may have been received for a particular order, write to your broker.

Reading a Stock Quote

When you get ready to place an order for a stock, look at the stock's quote. Before placing an order to buy a stock, check the ask price (the price at which the security is offered for sale in the market). Before placing an order to sell a stock, check the bid price (the price a buyer is willing to pay). Doing so will provide you with an indication of the price that you will pay or receive for the security. The volume of a stock, often provided along with the price quote, will tell you the number of shares traded from the current day's market opening until the reported trade time (see Figure 10.3).

Most stock quotes given in news reports and through online information sources are often delayed for 15 to 20 minutes. This is fine when a stock's price is moving slowly, or when you simply want to get a general sense of the price. When you wish to make a transaction, however, you should obtain a real-time quote, comprised of the current bid and ask quotes and the last sale price.

Real-Time Quotes, Fast Markets, and Order Queues

It is important to realize that a real-time quote is not a guarantee that your order will be executed at that price. In a quickly changing market ("fast market"), the bid and ask prices may change rapidly. Securities of companies that have recently made initial public offerings (IPOs) may be particularly prone to price volatility. If a large volume of shares is being traded in that stock, there may be a delay in the execution of your order. From the time you obtain a real-time quote and place your order,

Trade times, 15 minutes delayed, are local to the exchange.

[CN] as of Sep 26 03:57:27 on the TSE *52 WEEKS*

LAST
$2.36

AVERAGE
WEEKLY VOLUME
72,034

52-WEEK HIGH
$10.40

52-WEEK LOW
$2.36

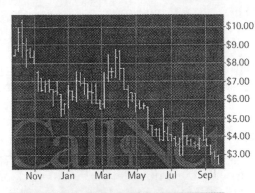

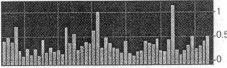

[CN.B] as of Sep 26 03:57:27 on the TSE *52 WEEKS*

LAST
$1.48

AVERAGE
WEEKLY VOLUME
276,957

52-WEEK HIGH
$9.35

52-WEEK LOW
$1.46

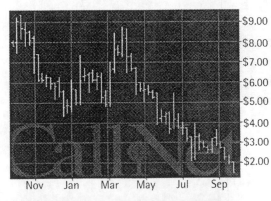

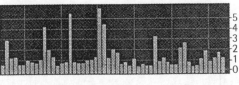

Figure 10.3 Trading Volume

to the time the order is actually executed, the price may change substantially. For example, if you get a real-time quote that says a stock is selling at $100, and the price moves up to $110 by the time your order is filled, you will pay $110. You should be especially cautious if you place orders during fast markets.

Market and Limit Orders

An order to buy or sell a stock at the current price is known as a market order. When you place a market order (except in the last few minutes of the trading day), you are guaranteed that it will be executed. But you are not guaranteed a specific execution price. You're allowing "the market" to set the price you pay, even if that market winds up being your broker-dealer's inventory department. To handle pricing uncertainties, you may want to place what is known as a limit order.

A limit order lets you specify the price at which you are willing to have the order executed. If you are placing an order to buy a stock, you can set a price limit, which says you are willing to buy only at or below a specified price. For example, if a stock is trading at $100 but you are expecting the price to rise quickly, you may choose to place a limit order at or near $100. Your order may then be executed if the price remains at $100 or drops lower. If the price moves up, however, your order will not be executed. The advantage of a limit order is that you will be protected from having to pay more than $100 for the stock. The downside is that if the market moves higher, your order will not be executed, and you will not own the stock you had tried to purchase.

Limit orders guarantee a particular price, but they do not guarantee that your order will be executed. Market orders, on the other hand, guarantee that your order will be executed but do not guarantee a particular price. Depending on your preferences, limit orders may or may not be appropriate tools. Additionally, always consider whether buying highly volatile stocks is suitable for your investment strategy.

Most stocks move at a slow pace (their price changes very slowly during the course of the market day), which allows the use of a market order, but you might be surprised—or disappointed—if you use a market order to buy or sell a stock in a fast-moving market (the price of the stock changes very rapidly over a short period of time). If you use a market order during a fast-moving market, the price of a stock may change tremendously before your order can get executed, because market orders are taken and filled (executed) in the order received. If hundreds, or thousands, of orders are coming in almost simultaneously, your trade may not be executed until many minutes after you enter it. You may find that your execution price is significantly different from the price quoted to you at the time you placed your order.

Here is an example of how market and limit orders to buy and sell work. The order here is for 100 shares of XYZ stock.[4]

Market Order: 100 Shares of XYZ Stock

Order Type	Current Price	Execution Price
Buy	30⅛	30⅛
Sell	30⅛	30⅛

Limit Order: 100 Shares of XYZ Stock

Order Type	Current Price	Limit Buy Price	Execution Price
Buy	30⅛	29	Did not execute
Buy	30⅛	30½	30⅛

Order Type	Current Price	Limit Sell Price	Execution Price
Sell	30⅛	29	30⅛
Sell	30⅛	30½	Did not execute

With limit orders, you must specify the length of time that your order will remain open (executable). Usually, you will be able to select either "Good For The Day" (your order remains open for the length of the current trading day, unless executed) or "Good 'Til Canceled" (your order remains open for the current trading day and each successive trading day until you cancel it or the order gets executed). Using limit orders is another way you can protect yourself while attempting to make

---

[4] *Source:* MsFiscallyFit.com.

your fortune trading online. While some broker-dealers provide limit orders for free, make sure you read the fine print. Others may charge between $15 and $25 for the privilege of controlling your order.

Time Limits on Orders

You may also place orders with time limits. A day order that is not executed will expire at the end of the trading day. (If you place the order after market hours, it will expire at the end of the next trading day.) If you place a limit order to buy a stock at $100, for example, and the price does not trade at $100 or less that day, your order may expire and not be executed. If you wish to try again the next day, you will have to place another order.

A good-'til-canceled (GTC) order, on the other hand, is good for 30 days and will remain in force until it is executed or until you choose to cancel it. If you place the same limit order as described above, and the price does not trade at $100 or less that day, the order will remain open until the price does hit $100 or less. (Note that if the order is not renewed within 30 calendar days, it will be systematically canceled at the end of the trading day indicated on the order. All orders with Saturday or Sunday expiration dates expire at the end of the previous trading day.)

Most online brokerages will allow you to place other types of time limits on your orders:

- Fill or kill (FOK): Execute the entire order immediately or cancel it.

- Immediate or cancel (IOC): Execute as much of the order as possible immediately, and cancel the remainder.

- All or none: Execute the entire order or cancel it.

Confirmations and Cancellations

Be aware that submitting a trade through the Internet is not the same as having that trade executed. When you submit a trade, you will receive a confirmation number, which indicates that the order has been received and transmitted to the market.

Margin Trading

What is the difference between a cash and a margin account? With a cash account, you must have full funds in your account prior to placing an order. A margin account allows you to increase your purchasing power by borrowing against your stocks. You may also borrow against mutual fund shares held in your account for 30 days or more. In the on-line brokerage industry, the average minimum initial deposit is $1,000 for a cash account and $2,000 for a margin account.

A WORD ON DAY TRADING

If you're thinking about giving up your day job to take advantage of on-line trading full time, think again.

Self-directed trading, also known as day trading, is a high-risk strategy that can result in substantial losses. From an SEC briefing on day trading: "Self-directed trading requires substantial capital, and there is no guarantee that you will achieve profits. It is important, therefore, that you carefully consider the risks and determine whether such trading is suitable for you in light of your circumstances and financial resources."

Self-directed trading is also highly speculative. The SEC advises individuals to invest in day trading only funds that they can afford to lose. "Day-trading accounts should not be funded with retirement savings, student loans or mortgage proceeds," says the SEC report. "You should be prepared to lose all of the funds that you use for day trading. In addition, day trading on margin may result in losses beyond your initial investment."

Time and money are huge challenges with day trading. Electronic day trading also involves a high volume of trading activity—the number of transactions in an account may exceed 100 per day. Each trade generates a commission, and the total daily commission on such high volume of trading can be considerable.

What do day traders do? Mostly, they sit in front of computer screens and look for a stock that is moving either up or down in value. They want to ride the momentum of the stock and sell before it changes course. They do not know for certain how the stock will move; they are hoping that it will move in one direction, either up or down in value. True day traders do not own any stocks overnight because of the extreme risk that prices will change radically from one day to the next and result in large losses.

Day trading is an extremely stressful and expensive full-time job. Day traders must watch the market continuously; they spend their workdays at their computer terminals. The need to watch dozens of ticker quotes and price fluctuations, and spot market trends, is extremely difficult and demands great concentration. Day traders also have high expenses. They must pay their firms large amounts for training, for computers, and in commissions. Any day trader should know, up front, how much income is needed to cover all expenses and at least break even.

Day traders depend heavily on borrowing money or buying stocks on margin. Borrowing money to trade in stocks is always a risky business. Day trading strategies demand using the leverage of borrowed money to make profits. This is why many day traders lose all their money and end up in debt as well. Day traders should understand how margin works, how much time they'll have to meet a margin call, and the potential for getting in over their heads.

Don't believe advertising claims that promise quick and sure profits from day trading. Before you start trading with a firm, make sure you know how many clients have lost money and how many have realized profits. If the firm does not know, or will not tell you, think twice about the risks you would be facing. Watch out for "hot tips" and "expert advice" from newsletters and Web sites catering to day traders.

Some Web sites have sought to profit from day traders by offering them hot tips and stock picks, for a fee. Again, don't believe any claims that trumpet easy profits from day trading. Check out their sources thoroughly, and ask whether they have been paid to make their recommendations. Remember that "educational" seminars, classes, and books about day trading may not be objective.

Find out whether a seminar speaker, an instructor teaching a class, or an author of a publication about day trading stands to profit if you start day trading. Check out day trading firms with your state securities regulator.

Like all broker-dealers, day trading firms must register with the SEC and the states in which they do business. Confirm a firm's registration by calling your state securities regulator. Ask whether the firm has a record of problems with regulators or with customers. You can find the telephone number for your state securities regulator in the Government section of your phone book or by calling the North American Securities Administrators Association at (202) 737–0900. NASAA also provides this information on its Web site: www.nasaa.org.

INVESTORS, FINANCIAL SERVICES COMPANIES, AND THE INTERNET: THE SEC IS CYBER-WATCHING

Day trading is one of the primary reasons that the Securities and Exchange Commission (SEC) began monitoring the Internet for fraud. With over 30 online investment fraud cases since 1995, and a current daily tally of 300 or so complaints by consumers against online investment firms, the SEC is beginning to take a hard-nosed stance against stockbrokers, stock promoters, and other investment professionals who commit fraud online. The number of advisers and money managers who actually commit such fraud is minimal, so the SEC is also taking steps, albeit at a glacial pace, to establish ground rules for all online investment sites. The rules will be enforced by the new Office of Internet Enforcement.

Besides the formation of the new enforcement unit in 1999, the SEC has 125 "cyber" enforcement attorneys dedicated to surfing the Internet, looking for fraudulent activity, and responding to investors' complaints, which have increased tenfold in the past four years. Of the 30 online investment fraud cases undertaken by the SEC since 1995, 22 have been successfully prosecuted.

The SEC is taking baby steps in its literal interpretation of what financial services companies can and cannot do online. Here are some of the major items on Uncle Sam's Web shopping list.

Privacy

Online financial advisory firms should try to give investors meaning-ful notice and information about their privacy practices and not just create a liability document. The "legal stuff" online seems to be buried and is often overlawyered. Some agreements are longer than a mortgage document. Would a plain-English agreement that investors can understand make for smoother investor relations down the line? Are firms concerned about investors' being able to control how infor-mation gathered about them is used? If you're interested in protecting your financial privacy, scan for disclosure that tells you what the firms' policy is regarding selling your name and financial particulars or sharing the information with affiliated companies, which might in-clude banks and insurance companies. If you're uncomfortable with those types of practices, make sure the firm has an "opt out" provi-sion that allows you to veto the marketing of your name and financial particulars.

Suitability

The suitability rule lies at the heart of a broker-dealer's responsibilities to investors. It very simply states that a broker-dealer must recommend to a customer only securities that are suitable for that particular cus-tomer. In making a suitability determination, a financial adviser must consider factors such as the investor's investment objectives and finan-cial situation.

Cyber-Chat Rooms

The Internet offers investors a plethora of online chat communities that cover just about every investment opportunity around the globe. At every hour of every day of the week, some new investment is being primed and pumped via a Web chat room. The SEC, however, wants Web site owners to know that it will hold them liable for what they say when they're engaging in online bull sessions.

ONLINE MESSAGE BOARDS: HELP OR HINDRANCE?

You come home after a hectic day at the office. You check your investments and find one of the stocks you have invested in has fallen 15 to 20 percent. After recovering from the shock, you immediately go to the stock message boards and read what the "self-labeled pundits" have to say. You search for the reason for the drop and wonder what to expect in the upcoming days. Some of the people posting on the board may have some valuable input for you to read, but many of those people are not to be relied on for accurate information.

The Internet has become an amazing medium for the transfer of information. Anyone today can access up-to-date information on almost any subject, and when the subject is stocks, real-time information is put up on the Internet instantaneously. Many of the stock message boards have resident "gurus" who post messages explaining the recent action of a stock and its future prospects. Buyer, Beware though! Anyone can post to a stock board under various aliases and never give anyone a shred of truthful information. Some people are even paid promoters, whose job it is to talk up stocks, oftentimes so insiders can sell the stock before its price plummets. You must sift through the "hype" to find people who post accurate information and thought-provoking analyses of stocks.

The way to separate "hype" from "help" is to visit the different message boards for a couple of weeks straight, and read the different messages posted by the "pundits." Make sure you also read the previous two or three weeks' messages. You will begin to see a pattern that shows who is accurately posting information about the stock and who is just spewing negative information or hyping the stock. Follow the different posters. Check their information independently, to validate their posts. This will give you some insight and some confidence in the recent action of a stock and its possible future.

On the stock message boards, there are professional traders, day traders, and knowledgeable people who like to talk about investments. When you are comfortable with a couple of these people, initiate contact through the message board and start to ask questions that you want answered about the stock: Why they bought into the stock, where they see the stock heading, and what investments they might be considering. These will do for starters.

A Broker's Fiduciary Obligations

As far as Uncle Sam is concerned, there is only one set of regulatory principles, whether an adviser is online, talking on the phone to a client, or sharing a cup of coffee at the office. Here is the National Association of Securities Dealers (NASD) statute on financial professionals and Internet chat rooms:

A [registered representative's] compliance responsibilities when communicating via the Internet are the same as they are in face-to-face discussions or in written communications with the public.

Consequently, Internet communications with the public cannot omit material information, be misleading or exaggerated, or contain predictions of investment results.

This listing of online resources may be helpful to readers who are interested in learning more about investing and other financial activities on the Web.[5]

ONLINE HELP

For more information about the topics in this chapter, visit the following Securities and Exchange Commission and NASD Regulation, Inc., Web sites:

- Electronic Investing: www.nasdr.com/2500_online.htm
- Tips for Online Investing: What You Need to Know About Trading in Fast-Moving Markets: www.sec.gov/consumer/onlitips.htm
- Guidance to Investors Regarding Stock Volatility and Online Trading: www.nasdr.com/2545.htm
- Possibilities and Pitfalls: The Internet as an Investment Tool: www.nasdr.com/2580.htm
- Purchasing on Margin, Risks Involved with Trading in a Margin Account: www.nasdr.com/2535.htm
- Understanding Margin Accounts: Why Brokers Do What They Do: www.nasdr.com/5700_understanding.htm

[5] *Source:* Datek Online.

GOVERNMENT AND REGULATORY AGENCIES

Federal Reserve Board—The central bank of the United States: www.federalreserve.gov

NASAA
The North American Securities Administrators Association, Inc.— The governing umbrella group for all state securities regulators: www.nasaa.org

NASD
The National Association of Securities Dealers, Inc.—The self-regulatory organization of the brokerage industry: www.nasd.com

SEC
The Securities and Exchange Commission—The federal regulator of the U.S. securities markets: www.sec.gov

Edgar-Online
The EDGAR—(Electronic Data Gathering, Analysis and Retrieval system) database contains searchable records of SEC filings: www.sec.gov/edgarhp.htm

Index of SEC Speeches—www.sec.gov/news/spchindx.htm

The Securities Industry Association—the membership and lobbying association of the securities industry: www.siainvestor.com

U.S. Treasury Department
The agency in charge of the collection, management, and expenditure of public revenue: www.ustreas.gov

The Washington State Department of Financial Institutions/Securities Division—the Investing Online Resource Center funded through the Investor Protection Trust: www.investingonline.org

EXCHANGES AND MARKETS

NYSE
The New York Stock Exchange: www.nyse.com

Nasdaq-AMEX
The merged markets share a Web site: www.nasdaq.com

Chicago Stock Exchange
Formerly known as the Midwest Exchange: www.chicagostockex
.com

Pacific Stock Exchange
Trades stocks and options: www.pacificex.com

Philadelphia Stock Exchange
Trades stocks, options, and other derivatives: www.philex.com

INVESTOR EDUCATION

Investopedia: www.investopedia.com

SEC Investor Education Site: www.sec.gov/oiea1.htm

The Motley Fool School: www.fool.com/school.htm

The Investment FAQ: www.invest-faq.com

INVESTMENT SITES

Bloomberg.com: www.bloomberg.com

Briefing.com
Briefing.com was started by a team from Standard and Poor's. The site provides investment opinions along with a standard package of free resources: www.briefing.com

CBS MarketWatch
The CBS MarketWatch site focuses primarily on financial news: www.cbs.marketwatch.com

ClearStation
Focuses on technical analysis. You can learn the basics of charting and delve into any indicator you want: www.clearstation.com

CNBC.com
The CNBC site offers real-time data and formats for investors: www.cnbc.com

Motley Fool, The
The Motley Fool provides investor education and several financial calculators: www.fool.com

Morningstar.com
A financial portal that emphasizes mutual fund information for individual investors: www.morningstar.com

MSN Money Central: A free, comprehensive, investment research site with market commentary five times a day, and some predefined stock selection screens: moneycentral.msn.com/home.asp

SmartMoney.com
Published by *The Wall Street Journal,* this Web site offers solid financial information: www.smartmoney.com

TheStreet.com
High profile Web site gives investors insightful and sometimes irreverent market observation: www.thestreet.com

BASIC TOOL KITS

Yahoo! Finance
Yahoo! Finance simply aggregates basic content, but also provides access to the Yahoo Web Directory and their many other content components: finance.yahoo.com

The Wall Street Journal
The online equivalent of *The Wall Street Journal* print edition, this Web site offers all of the news of the Journal as well as archives, charting, and research: www.wsj.com

BigCharts
Charting and basic investment information. Contains earnings estimates from Zack's and company profiles from Hoover's. Brokerage firm research reports through Multex are also for sale: www.bigcharts.com

Stockpoint
A basic toolkit of quotes, profiles, charts, and news. Stockpoint also provides a personalized daily market update, via e-mail: www.stockpoint.com

Market Guide
Aggregates information from Briefing.com, Stockpoint, and PR Newswire and Business Wire news:
www.marketguide.comMGI/home.asp

INVESTools
Along with a standard package of free quotes, charts, news, and profiles, you can also purchase data like S&P reports and investment newsletters: www.investools.com

News Alert
An aggregator of standard investment info such as quotes, charts and news: www.newsalert.com

MESSAGE BOARDS

Message boards can be interesting places to interact with other investors and get various points of view. However, you should use extreme caution in evaluating message board information.

- Silicon Investor: www.siliconinvestor.com/stocktalk/forum.gsp?forumid=31
- The Motley Fool: boards.fool.com
- Deja News: www.deja.com/channels/channel.xp?CID=11559
- Gomez Advisers: www.gomez.com/scorecards/index.asp?topcat—id=3

CONCLUSION

While the Internet has lead to explosive opportunities for investors, it has also brought added responsibility. How and when you place stock trade orders is totally up to you. For instance, whether or not you want

INTERNET TRENDS

How will the Internet shape the trends you need to watch? Some examples of the Internet's impact on financial services are self-evident: Interactive company Web sites, online trading sites, and electronic commerce (e-commerce) have been with us for a few years now and will continue to be with us for a long while. But in what other, less discernible ways will financial services be impacted by the Internet? And what drawbacks does the Internet bring to the financial services industry? Here's a glimpse into the future:

- Markets will be far more liquid and efficient. Trading volumes will explode as retail investors trade at the pennies-per-share rates of today's institutional investors. Markets will be open all the time. Auction markets for initial public offerings and other traditional investment banking products will spread. Customers will buy directly from issuers.
- Risk taking and risk management will increase. Financial engineers will tap into the Internet to develop and market sophisticated risk-management tools.
- Economic growth will pick up worldwide. A large body of research supports the observation that more efficient capital markets spur technological innovation and economic expansion.
- As individual investors become increasingly knowledgeable about finance, they will migrate toward the Internet for transactions—from mortgage loans to 401(k) investments. Computer programs will provide top-notch money-management guidance.
- Financial services companies will dismantle expensive sales, marketing, and product infrastructures to make room for a direct pipeline to customers. Some firms will concentrate on distributing financial products; others will focus on creating new ones. Partnerships will be commonplace.

INTERNET TREND

Online brokerage trading fees are fluid, but, late in 2000, an industry snapshot provided a glimpse of where the major players are, fee-wise:

AmeriTrade	$13.00 per trade
Charles Schwab	29.95 per trade
Datek Online	9.99 per trade (with 60 sec execution)
CSFBdirect	20.00 per trade + 2c per share
E*Trade	19.95 per trade
FirstTrade	9.95 per trade
InvesTrade	9.95 to 11.95 per trade
SuperTradeUSA	14.95 per trade
ScottTrade	7.00 per trade
Trading Direct	9.95 per trade
Waterhouse WebBroker	12.00 per trade

COMMISSIONS DO IMPACT PERFORMANCE

The more you pay in commissions, the more your stock/investment/mutual fund has to perform to cover your initial commission cost and begin making a profit. Here is an example.

Online broker. You buy 100 shares of XYZ stock at $20/share. Your commission is $10. If XYZ stock goes up in price only ⅛ point (⅛ point = 12½ cents) to 20⅛, you have a gain of $12.50 and you have a profit of $2.50. In this scenario, XYZ only needs to increase in value less than 1 percent and you would have a profit.

Full-service broker. You buy 100 shares of XYZ stock at $20/share. Your commission is $200. Now XYZ stock must go up in price 2 points (1 point = $1.00), to 22, in order for you just to recoup your commission cost. In this scenario, XYZ needs to increase in value more than 10 percent if you are to have a profit.

Source: MsFiscallyFit.com

STRAIGHT FROM THE HORSE'S MOUTH

STATEMENT BY CHAIRMAN ARTHUR LEVITT
SECURITIES AND EXCHANGE COMMISSION
CONCERNING ON-LINE TRADING

January 27, 1999

Investing in the stock market—however you do it and however easy it may be—will always entail risk. I would be very concerned if investors allow the ease with which they can make trades to shortcut or bypass the three golden rules for all investors: (1) Know what you are buying; (2) Know the ground rules under which you buy and sell a stock or bond; and (3) Know the level of risk you are undertaking. Online investors should remember that it is just as easy, if not more, to lose money through the click of a button as it is to make it.

In recent months, we have begun to identify a number of issues every on-line investor should be aware of. First, investors must understand the issues and limitations of on-line investing. You may occasionally experience delays on these new systems. Demand has grown so quickly that many firms are racing to keep pace with it. In the meantime, you may have trouble getting on-line or receiving timely confirmations of trade executions. You should not always expect "instantaneous" execution and reporting. There can and will be delays in electronic systems. You should investigate and understand options and alternatives to executing and confirming your orders if you encounter on-line problems.

Second, investors may sometimes be surprised at how quickly stock prices actually move. For example, many technology stocks have recently had dramatic and rapid price movements. When many investors attempt to purchase (or sell) the same stock at the same time, the price can move very quickly. Just because you see a price on your computer screen doesn't mean that you will always be able to get that price in a rapidly changing market. You should take precautions to ensure that you do not end up paying much more for a stock than you intended or can afford.

One way to do this is to use limit orders rather than market orders when submitting a trade in a "hot" stock. The result for investors that do not limit their risk can be quite surprising. Say an investor wanted to buy a stock in an IPO that was trading earlier at $9.00 and failed to specify the maximum they were willing to pay using a limit order. That investor could end up paying whatever price the stock has moved to at the time his order reaches the market—$60, $90, or even more. If, on the other hand, the investor submitted a limit order to buy the stock at $11.00 or less, the order would only be executed if the market price had not moved past that level. Investors should understand the risk associated with trading in a rapidly moving market and make sure that they take all possible actions to control their risk.

Third, I am concerned that investors buying securities on margin may not fully understand the risks involved. In volatile markets, investors who have put up an initial margin payment for a stock may find themselves being required to provide additional cash (maintenance margin) if the price of the stock subsequently falls. If the funds are not paid in a timely manner, the brokerage firm has the right to sell the securities and charge any loss to the investor. When you buy stock on margin, you are borrowing money. And as the stock price changes, you may be required to increase the cash investment. Simply put, you should make sure that you do not over-extend.

Fourth, while new technology available to retail investors may resemble that of professional traders, retail investors should exercise caution before imitating the style of trading and risks undertaken by market professionals. For most individuals, the stock market should be used for investment, not trading. Strategies such as day trading can be highly risky, and retail investors engaging in such activities should do so with funds they can afford to lose. I am very concerned when I hear of stories of student loan money, second mortgages, or retirement funds being used to engage in this type of activity. Investment should be for the long run, not for minutes or hours.

(continued)

Millions of new investors have taken advantage of the unprece- dented access and individual control the Internet provides. But, new opportunities present all of us with new responsibilities, challenges and risks. The SEC will do everything it can to protect and inform investors during this time of great innovation and change. But, investor protec- tion—at its most basic and effective level—starts with the investor. I say to all investors—whether you invest on-line, on the phone, or in- person—know what you are buying, what the ground rules are, and what level of risk you are assuming.

Source: www.sec.gov.

WHAT TO DO IF YOU HAVE A COMPLAINT

Act promptly if you feel you're getting the runaround from your online broker. By law, you only have a limited time to take legal action. Follow these steps to solve your problem:

1. Talk to your broker or online firm and ask for an explanation. Take notes of the answers you receive.
2. If you are dissatisfied with the response and believe that you have been treated unfairly, ask to talk with the broker's branch manager. In the case of an online firm, go directly to step number three.
3. If your are still dissatisfied, write to the compliance department at the firm's main office. Explain your problem clearly, and tell the firm how you want it resolved. Ask the compliance office to respond to you in writing within 30 days.
4. If you're still dissatisfied, send a letter of complaint to the National Association of Securities Dealers, your state securities administra- tor, or the Office of Investor Education and Assistance at the SEC, along with copies of the letters you've already sent to the firm.

Source: www.sec.gov.

to attach limits to your order, limit orders that specify what price you want to buy shares, or decide what sources you turn to for information is your call. This chapter was designed to give you maximum control over your trading and investing activity, while avoiding some of the pitfalls that have arisen as a result of the Internet. What is one challenge for investors? Instant information from less-than-savory sources who hang out in chat rooms just to pump up the prices of stocks so they can sell at the peak and leave you holding the bag. With a little care, you'll be able to navigate this new investing environment confidently. And if you have concerns, this chapter gives you a comprehensive list of both investing sites and regulatory sources that can help.

CHAPTER 11   RESOURCES, TIPS, AND PLACES TO GO

Throughout the book, we've done our best to support the text with graphs, charts, sidebars, and other complementary information to help you understand the material we've presented.

But, there's always room for more good information. In this chapter, we provide resource information that can help to make the wealth creation process a bit easier to manage. Whether you're looking for commonsense tips for reviewing your monthly cash flow or determining how long to keep vital documents like tax returns, the chapter was constructed to help you find answers easily. For added benefit, we've added Web sites on investment research, stock trading, bonds, mutual funds, and international investing. You'll also get the latest in news sites you can click on for stories and reports on the investments and economic trends you're watching. This chapter will help you flesh out your overall investment strategy and serve as an ongoing resource to you as you set out to create wealth.

I. PERSONAL FINANCE AND BUDGETING RESOURCES

HOW DO YOU CALCULATE YOUR NET WORTH?

Add the dollar amounts of your assets. Do the same for your debts. Subtract your debt amount from your asset amount. The difference is your net worth.

FINANCIAL PLANNING BASICS: YOU'VE CALCULATED YOUR NET WORTH—NOW WHAT?

After you've arrived at your net worth, work through the following questions and their related advice.

1. Has your net worth increased each year or since you compiled your last balance sheet? If it hasn't, determine the reason and perhaps make some changes in your spending, saving, or other financial habits.

2. Does your balance sheet reflect a preference for personal assets such as an expensive home, cars, furs, and jewelry? Make sure you're also accumulating investment assets. Keep in mind that personal items like cars and furs are depreciating assets that are far less likely to increase in value or produce income that will help you meet other financial goals.

3. Is your debt out of proportion? If your balance sheet shows excessive debt, especially for personal consumption, that's a signal to review your spending. Keeping debt under control is essential for good financial management.

4. Have you given enough thought to the money you'll need for retirement? If your balance sheet shows total neglect for accumulating funds for retirement, make some changes as soon as possible.

5. Are your assets diversified? Diversification is a good hedge against inflation and changes in the economy. Having all your eggs in one basket is seldom a good idea. Also, don't keep excess cash in no-interest or low-interest accounts unless you foresee an immediate need for the cash.

6. Where do you want to be three years, five years, and ten years from now, in terms of your net worth? You might determine this by doing projected balance sheets for three years, five years, and ten years in the future.[1]

CRAFTING A CREDIT CARD STRATEGY

Credit cards are a necessary evil; for many cardholders, they are more evil than necessary. Their interest rate ranges around 16 percent or more, the interest paid is not tax-deductible, and, quite often, the money owed is for something purchased so long ago that it will soon need to be replaced. Pay off the card debt!

But first, make sure the debt being charged is accurate. Analyze the bill. Make sure it matches your receipts. Sometimes, when you sign on the dotted line, you don't double-check the amount of the purchase. For example, amid the rush of holiday shopping, you might not have been charged the advertised sale price for an item; you might have been charged twice for a single purchase; or you might even have been charged for an item purchased by someone else in line. It happens. If you notice a discrepancy, call your credit card issuer and dispute the charge.

Meanwhile, don't fall for any credit card company's offer to lower your minimum payment or allow you, because you're such a good customer, to skip this month's payment. That may sound enticing, but the interest-rate clock is still ticking.

With all your holiday shopping, in addition to your regular expenses, suppose that your January credit card bill is $2,500, a typical

[1] *Source:* Hall, Kistler & Company LLP, CPA Firm. (220 Market Avenue S Suite 700, Canton, Ohio 44702–2100) Phone (330) 453–7633 FAX (330) 453–9366.

amount. If the annual interest rate is 18 percent, skipping January's payment could cost you about $38 in finance charges, which will show up in the next month's bill. No wonder the credit card company is so nice.

GREAT BUDGET IDEAS

Here are some more tips on building a better budget:

1. Don't make your budget too inflexible or, like a diet, it's unlikely you'll stick to it.

2. Use exact costs, not averages. You should know, at any point, exactly how much you need and how much you have.

3. Use a spreadsheet layout. Label the two main sections *Income* and *Expenditures.*

4. Categories should have broad titles so that your budget is not too complex. For example, include your doctor, dentist, other health professionals, and prescriptions under Medical.

5. People always underestimate what they spend. Remember extras such as lunches, public transport, and sports events or memberships.

6. A good strategy is to prepare your budget based on how often you get paid.

7. Review your budget every month for the first couple of months, to make sure you are on track.

8. When the economy enters a low-interest-rate period, as it did in the mid-to-late 1990s, take advantage of the low rates to refinance a home mortgage and make lower monthly payments. Among numerous Web sites that offer instant calculators to estimate your new payments are www.Quicken.com and www.realtor.com.

9. Review auto and home insurance rates, and comparison-shop for better values. Some companies offer discounts for senior citizens, for clients who buy multiple policies, and for installing

MONTHLY BUDGET CHECKLIST

Here's a ready-made list to help you keep track of your monthly expenditures:

Monthly Income

Net monthly salary/wages	$_____
Net monthly income from interest and dividends	$_____
Other monthly income (e.g., family allowances and benefits)	$_____
Total Monthly Income	$_____

Monthly Expenditures

Living expenses	$_____
Rent/Mortgage payments	$_____
Food and beverages	$_____
Utilities (e.g., electricity, water)	$_____
Clothing/Footwear	$_____
Daily expenses (e.g., lunch)	$_____
Household expenses	$_____
Insurance: House and contents, life, auto, health, other	$_____
Personal care (e.g., chemist, hairdresser, barber)	$_____
Medical (e.g., doctor, dentist, optician, therapist, prescriptions)	$_____
Transportation	$_____
Fuel for vehicle(s)	$_____
Repairs and maintenance	$_____
Registration/License fees, service club dues	$_____
Public transport, taxis, parking	$_____
Children's expenses	$_____

(continued)

Recreation (e.g., sports and activities)	$_____
Entertainment (e.g., dining out, movies, books, CDs, tapes)	$_____
Education (e.g., courses, associations)	$_____
Gifts (e.g., presents, donations)	$_____
Credit/Loan repayments	$_____
Credit cards/Charge account repayments	$_____
Rentals/Hires/Purchases	$_____
Personal loan repayments	$_____
Savings and investments	$_____
Unexpected events, replacements, and additions	$_____
Savings, special goals, holidays, etc.	$_____
Investments in shares, properties, etc.	$_____
Total Monthly Expenditures	$_____
Total Monthly Income	$_____
Less: Total Monthly Expenditures	$_____
Cashflow Position +/−	$_____

Source: Adapted from Money Manager Web site, www.moneymanager.com.au.

antitheft devices in autos. Consider raising your deductibles in exchange for lower payments.

10. Add up the fees on your bank statements and shop for a better deal or ask your existing bank about lower-cost accounts. Ask whether your employer will automatically deposit your paycheck to your bank account, to minimize the risk of bounced or lost checks and other mishaps. Consider starting an automatic savings plan that will route some money directly to a separate account before you're tempted to spend it.

11. Obtain an estimate of your future Social Security income by calling (800) 772–1213. Ask for a Personal Earnings and Benefits Statement Request form. The response time is quick, and it's a good opportunity to make sure your employment history is reflected accurately.

12. For an $8.00 fee, order a copy of your credit report from any of these reporting agencies: Equifax (800) 685-1111; Trans Union (800) 916-8800; or Experian (800) 422-4879.

13. Get rid of clutter and raise extra cash by holding a garage sale, or get a tax deduction by donating unwanted items to charities. Be sure to keep an itemized receipt of donated goods in case the IRS has questions.

14. Make a detailed household inventory to protect yourself in case of theft or disaster. Engrave your name and an identifying code on high-value items, and record any visible serial numbers. Most insurance companies offer guidelines or even workbooks. Call your agent or check out the Nationwide Mutual Insurance Company Web site at www.nationwide.com.

15. Taking out one manageable loan to pay off various scattered debts is often a smart way to lower your effective cost of borrowing. Credit card debt is the prime target for this strategy. Interest rates on credit cards are frequently two to three times higher than on consumer loans. Consider the possibility of borrowing on a personal line of credit to pay off credit cards. If your credit card spending has gotten that far out of hand, it's time to break out the scissors and begin cutting up some cards.

16. Draw a line between personal and professional debt. If you are self-employed, you may need to borrow for business purposes. Be sure your records are accurate enough to track personal and business borrowing separately. Better yet, use dedicated sources for your business borrowings. For example, use one credit card for your business spending and a different one for personal use. If your business borrowings become tainted with personal debts, you could jeopardize your interest-expense deduction.

17. Keep up with Uncle Sam. If you are self-employed or have substantial investment income, you are probably required to pay all or part of your taxes in quarterly installments. Interest and penalties on unpaid installments can currently reach 12 percent, compounded daily. Unlike a salaried taxpayer, who has tax withheld at the payment source, a self-employed person must pay each tax installment or slip deeply into debt owed to the government. Keep your tax money segregated, and fight the temptation to dip into it randomly.

18. Loan or lease? When you are trying to decide whether to buy or lease your next car, keep in mind that a lease is another form of financing. Find out the effective financing rate implicit in any lease proposal, and compare it to prevailing new-car loan rates.

19. Stay squeaky clean. Protecting your capacity to borrow is a worthwhile financial objective. Buying a house or a car, going into business for yourself, or jumping on a unique investment opportunity are actions that often require external financing. Also, normal cash reserves may be insufficient to deal with a financial emergency. Keep your credit rating clean. Do not take on debt you cannot handle. Do not miss payments. If you find yourself in a default situation, do not try to hide from your creditors. Take the initiative: Propose revised repayment schemes, and keep them fully informed at all times.

20. Inject some fun into your money-saving regimen. Open a bottle of wine, make a date with your loved one, flip a Dixie Chicks CD into your stereo. Saving money will put a smile on your face and make you feel good about yourself. It's time well spent.[2]

---

[2] *Sources:* CPA Australia and Gannett News Service "Getting organized? Some tips," August 26, 1998.

HOW LONG SHOULD YOU KEEP VITAL DOCUMENTS?

Just like a can of mushroom soup, there's an expiration date on your critical financial documents. Some you keep a year, some you keep a lot longer. Here's a snapshot of how long to hang on to the important stuff:

- Old credit card statements, pay stubs: one year.
- Bank statements, canceled checks: three years.
- Income tax returns: six years.
- Home improvement records: ownership plus seven years.
- Investment records (IRAs, pensions, insurance policies, and similar original documents), real estate records and transactions, stock records, personal records (birth certificates, military, marriage/divorce, adoption, custody agreements, naturalization papers): permanent.

II: TRADING AND RESEARCHING STOCKS

Here's a bevy of great trading and analysis Web sites for the avid investor:

GENERAL STOCK TRADING SITES

www.bigcharts.com   Interactive online charting service giving free and unlimited access to charts, reports, indicators, and quotes of 22,700 U.S. stocks, mutual funds, and major market indices.

www.briefing.com   Provides commentary and analysis on breaking news events faster than any site on the Internet. It covers upgrades, earnings reports, economic releases, technical trading points, market sectors, and technology stocks.

www.dailyrocket.com Pushes stock quotes, charts news, company profiles to your desktop portfolio.

www.cfsbdirect.com CFSBdirect is the online trading service of Credit Suisse First Boston.

www.galt.com A wide-ranging mutual fund Web site.

www.globalfindata.com Extensive, long-term historical indices on stock markets, interest rates, exchange rates, and inflation rates. The database provides historical data on more than 80 countries.

www.investools.com A site with useful information and tools.

www.investor.msn.com Microsoft Investor. A comprehensive investment site by Bill Gates' gang.

www.investorama.com Best feature? Links to more than 1,600 online finance-related Web sites.

www.investorsleague.com Site offers an effective way to learn about the stock market and to discover investment opportunities for your real dollar portfolio.

www.marketguide.com Dependable provider of fundamental financial information that offers fairly comprehensive company research.

www.metro.turnpike.net/holt Site offers lots of raw data, a few articles on growth companies, and good links to other sites.

www.pcquote.com Digital market data feed with good speed and accuracy. Also offers nice trading platform with charting, technical studies, alerts, news, and more.

www.quote.com Financial and business data on 13,000 U.S. companies and 13,000 global companies.

www.stockmaster.com Shows quotes for stocks and funds and 12-month graphs of daily prices and volumes.

www.stocksmart.com StockSmart is a free, unlimited-usage site for experienced individual and professional investors. Information includes company fundamentals, valuation, and analysis; real-time quotes on stocks, bonds, and mutual funds (the site tracks and analyzes over 5,700 mutual funds from 200 fund families); money markets and options; market news and shareholder information.

www.thestreet.com An online financial publication dedicated to providing investors with timely, insightful, and irreverent reporting.

www.usatoday.com/money/mfront.htm USA Today Money. A comprehensive source of business news and data.

www.wallstreetcity.com Billed as an Internet "supersite," the page is well organized, with best and worst lists, news sections, stock reports, technical breakouts, search engines, and international stock exchanges.

www.yahoo.com Yahoo! Finance. Investments, quotes, real-time quotes, international quotes, financial news, online trading, mutual funds, bonds, futures and options, reference and guides.

www.younginvestor.com Site offers games, advice, and information geared at teaching youngsters about the financial markets.

STOCK QUOTES WEB SITES

www.dbc.com Offers real-time market data to the individual investor.

www.interquote.com One of the Internet's oldest tick-by-tick real-time market quote service; a good source of real-time quotes and graphs.

www.wwquote.com Updated real-time stock quotation system.

SMALL CAP STOCKS

www.financialweb.com Offers information on everything from growth stocks to blue chips, mutual funds, annual reports, stock quotes, and more.

www.stockguide.com   More than 5,000 companies are listed, including ticker, address, phone, industry, and current trading status.

www.stockhouse.com   Maintains a directory of micro- and small-cap companies, as well as daily news releases from the Nasdaq Small-Cap Market, the OTC Bulletin Board, and the Montreal, Toronto, and other Canadian stock exchanges. Several newsletters are also published or reprinted on the site.

www.topstocks.com   Focuses exclusively on the OTC Bulletin Board.

TECHNOLOGY STOCKS

www.troweprice.com   The Silicon Investor is a free service, and a useful resource for clients interested in learning about technology stocks.

MUTUAL FUNDS

www.americancentury.com   American Century Investments is a diversified family of funds.

www.fid-inv.com   Fidelity Investments home page.

www.invesco.com   INVESCO is one of the largest independent global investment management firms.

www.Janus.com   Offers more than 40 pure no-load funds, including the first international mutual fund offered to U.S. investors.

www.mfmag.com   Mutual Fund magazine's home page.

www.montgomery.com   NationsBank Montgomery Securities, Inc.: Montgomery Securities merged with NationsBank Corporation to create a full service investment bank and brokerage firm.

www.rsim.com   Robertson Stephens & Co. provides separate account and mutual fund services.

www.investor.networth.quicken.com. A good interface with a variety of information from Intuit, the makers of Quicken financial software.

www.schwab.com   Charles Schwab: Stocks, mutual funds, stock and index options; and corporate, municipal, and U.S. Government bonds.

www.troweprice.com   The Baltimore-based investment management firm manages $100 billion for 5.5 million individual and institutional accounts.

www.vanguard.com   The Vanguard Group: A comprehensive resource for novice and seasoned fund investors.

www.waterhouse.com   Waterhouse Securities is a discount brokerage firm, the fourth largest nationwide.

BONDS

www.bondmarkets.com   The Bond Market Association's Web site. A bevy of fixed-income information and education: www.bondmarkets.com.

www.investinginbonds.com   Information for the individual investor on bonds.

www.oddlot.com   The Odd-Lot Machine provides an efficient, competitive, and cost-effective method for trading U.S. Treasury securities in amounts under $10 million.

www.salliemae.com   The Student Loan Marketing Association: The nation's largest source of funding for education loans for college. Includes information on planning and paying for college; all types of financial aid and loans; calculators to forecast college costs, loan payments, and more; online account access for borrowers.

www.smartmoney.investing.lycos.com/si/tools/onebond   SmartMoney.com's bond site. Includes information on bond allocation, bond calculator, the living yield curve, and bond funds.

www.vanguard.com/educ/lib/plain/ptlkbnd.html   Vanguard Plain Talk: Bond Fund Investing. Easily understood commentary on bonds and the bond market, from the folks at Vanguard Funds.

OPTIONS

www.cboe.com   Chicago Board Options Exchange, the world's largest options market, trades 95 percent of all index options and 47 percent of all equity options. Lists options on equities, indexes, and interest rates as well as linked notes and warrants.

www.options-iri.com   Investment Research Institute, Inc. (IRI) site has stock and options quotes, investment news, and market research.

www.numa.com   Financial investment Web site of Numa Financial Systems Ltd., which specializes in derivatives.

INTERNATIONAL INVESTING

www.asahi.co.jp   Asahi Broadcasting Corporation: (Site in English and Japanese) Current news from Japan.

www.bolsantiago.cl   Santiago Stock Exchange. (Site in English and Spanish) Information includes a description of the markets in the Exchange, forms of operation and settlement, schedule and cost of transactions, a complete list of brokers, shares listed in the Exchange.

www.borsaitalia.it   Milan Stock Exchange, the Italian Stock Ex-change's Web site, gateway to the Italian stock market, derivatives market, listed companies, and intermediaries. Also daily prices, market data, and links to foreign exchanges.

www.bourse-de-paris.fr   Paris Stock Exchange: (this site is in French only).

www.bovespa.com.br   The Sao Paulo Stock Exchange, the largest in Latin America, lists all of Brazil's stocks (this site is in Spanish only).

www.bradynet.com   A source for Brady bond information on the Internet, specializing in fixed income prices, exotics, market analysis, editorials, and more.

www.economist.com   An authoritative British weekly and news site covering British politics, economics, and international affairs.

www.emgmkts.com   The Emerging Markets Comparison Web site features a convenient window into the emerging economies of Asia, Latin America, Africa, and Eastern Europe. Content contributed by premier market participants and news organizations.

www.euromoney.com   Provides analysis of the world's capital and money markets.

www.financialtimes.com   A global news organization on international business, news analysis, market data, and company information.

www.globalreports.com   Singapore Business Times: Launched at the beginning of 1996, the Global Reports series aims to provide free access to a range of business information and analytical services.

www.hse.fi   The Helsinki Stock Exchange is the market place for Finnish equities in Europe. The HSE produces a range of data concerning stock exchange trading and investment instruments.

www.indoexchange.com   Indonesia NET Exchange, features include: real-time stock quotes, graphs, Asia financial news wire service, dual language search engine for the news, Web pages for all Indonesia listed companies, equity research report, economic research, and more.

www.ise.org   Istanbul Stock Exchange: The ISE is the only securities exchange in Turkey. The ISE provides a transparent and fair trading environment not only for domestic participants, but also for foreign issuers and investors.

www.kse.or.kr   Korea Stock Exchange, the only stock exchange in Korea, is a nonprofit membership organization established by the Securities and Exchange Law (SEL). The KSE provides trading markets for securities and index futures and options, and functions as a self-regulatory body.

www.londonstockexchange.com   Home site of the London Stock Exchange. Features a wealth of economic and investment data for global and local investors.

www.jpmorganchase.com   J.P. Morgan Chase & Co. is a global financial services firm that serves governments, corporations, institutions, and privately held firms with complex financial needs through an integrated range of advisory, financing, trading, investment, and related capabilities.

www.nikkei.co.jp   Nikkei Net: (Site in English and Japanese) Founded in 1876, Nikon Keizai Shimbun, Inc., or Nikkei, serves as the primary business information source for top corporate executives and decision makers in Japan.

www.tse.or.jp   Tokyo Stock Exchange: (Site in English and Japanese) Maintains markets for securities and related futures and options.

www.websontheweb.com   World Benchmark Equity Shares is a new approach to international investing, offering passive index management and facilitating targeted portfolio exposure.

www.yomiuri.co.jp   Yomiuri news organization: (Site in English and Japanese) The Yomiuri Shimbun, the flagship newspaper published by Yomiuri Shimbun-sha, is the largest daily newspaper circulation in the world.

SECURITIES LAW

www.nasdr.com   NASD Regulation provides investor education information and broker disciplinary records. For members, information on continuing education, publications, and news rules.

www.sec.gov   Securities and Exchange Commission site offers news, agency announcements, rule-making actions, searchable archives, and a directory of state securities regulators.

www.seclaw.com   Securities Law Home Page. One of the Web's most popular legal sites, providing comprehensive and timely legal information on the financial markets. Updated monthly.

GOVERNMENTAL

www.cftc.com   The Commodity Futures Trading Commission regulates and provides market oversight of the commodity futures and option markets.

www.edgar-online.com   An EDGAR based interface with free and pay services available.

www.frbchi.org   The Federal Reserve Bank of Chicago is one of the 12 regional Reserve Banks across the United States that, together with the Board of Governors in Washington, D.C., serve as the nation's central bank. Get current and historical data on inflation, interest rates, and currency rates.

www.freeedgar.com   An EDGAR interface with free data and integration with Excel.

www.irs.gov   The Internal Revenue Service's site is a resource for tax information, clarifications, new regulations, and taxpayer appeals.

www.sec.gov   Securities   and   Exchange   Commission. News, agency announcements, rule-making actions, searchable archives, and a directory of state securities regulators.

www.sec.gov/edgarhp.htm   EDGAR, the Electronic Data Gathering, Analysis, and Retrieval system, performs automated collection, validation, indexing, acceptance, and forwarding of submissions by companies and others who are required by law to file forms with the U.S. Securities and Exchange Commission (SEC). Its primary purpose is to increase the efficiency and fairness of the securities market for the benefit of investors, corporations, and the economy by accelerating the receipt, acceptance, dissemination, and analysis of time-sensitive corporate information filed with the agency.

www.ssa.gov   The Official Web Site of the Social Security Admin-
istration, offers information concerning the government and your
money.

BROADCAST NEWS

www.cnbc.com   Research and trading information for investors of
all stripes, from the experts at CNBC. Uses the same hands-on expertise and Wall Street lingo that viewers enjoy so much on television. A good information companion for the tips and news you get
from CNBC's television network.

www.cnn.com   Cable News Network Interactive (CNNin). An online source of information that is current to the programming on
CNN.

www.cnnfn.com   CNNfn.com delivers comprehensive coverage of
world business news and financial markets straight from the
CNNfn newsroom.

www.pointcast.com   The PointCast Network is a leading news
and information service on the Internet for business and colleges.

PUBLICATIONS

www.ap.org   The Associated Press reports on news and business
events in the United States and internationally.

www.barrons.com   Offers market commentary and online investment insight.

www.bloomberg.com   Offers a broad range of features in a single
package, including information and analyses.

www.businessweek.com   *Business Week* magazine online includes
the current issue, archives, and an assortment of worthwhile data.

www.dowjones.com   Dow Jones and Company offers links to many financial and investment related magazines on the Web, such as *The Wall Street Journal, American Demographics, Realty Stock Review,* and *Smart Money.*

www.fortune.com   Offers business and financial information and links like Kiplinger Online.

www.margin.com   *Newsletter Network* is a source for investment news and market analysis.

www.morningstar.net   Includes news and quotes, market commentary and analysis, investment ideas and insights, and portfolio summaries for better investment decisions.

www.nytimes.com   Offers news and analysis of political and economic events.

www.pathfinder.com   Time Warner's Pathfinder Network is an assembly of information-based sites including *Money* magazine, CNNfn, *Time* magazine, and *Fortune* magazine.

www.reuters.com   A business newswire that reports on business, technology, and politics around the world.

www.wsj.com   *The Wall Street Journal* Interactive Edition is updated 24 hours a day.

www.washingtonpost.com   Provides breaking news on politics and policy, including Federal Reserve Board initiatives impacting the stock and bond markets.

MISCELLANEOUS

www.aarp.org   American Association of Retired People: AARP is a nonprofit, nonpartisan organization dedicated to helping older Americans achieve lives of independence, dignity, and purpose.

www.etrade.com   E*TRADE is a Web trading and portfolio management system.

www.futuresource.com   FutureSource is the real-time data vendor for the futures, options, and cash markets, 24 hours a day.

www.hoovers.com   Publishes information about more than 11,000 public and private companies worldwide. Includes capsules and profiles.

www.internet.com   Founded in 1971, Mecklermedia Corporation is a leading provider of Internet news, information, and analysis through its magazines, trade shows and Internet.com, the electronic daily newspaper for Internet information and resources.

www.money.com   Money Online provides news and market information plus interactive tools, in-depth research, and expert advice.

www.openmarket.com   Open Market provides software products that are used to develop infrastructure for Internet commerce. Provides affordable scalability, content flexibility, lower entry and maintenance costs, and enhanced security for businesses of all types.

www.snapshot.com   SnapShot is a financial information and news site providing quotes, portfolio management, alerts, news, and more.

www.stockinfo.standardpoor.com   Standard & Poor's Equity Investor Services Web site offers stock market news, market commentary, S&P 500 Index statistics, company research, and more.

www.wbnet.com   Worldwide Broadcasting Network(™) was founded in 1996, and offers multimedia search and retrieval solutions for corporations and content providers.

www.zacks.com   Quantitative research Web site offering products and information designed to provide institutional money managers with good stock-picking tools.

IN THE KNOW

Knowing where to turn for pertinent information, whether it's news, new listings on stock exchanges, or how much you can expect to receive from the Social Security Trust can save time and make you a better investor. This chapter was designed to put the most valuable resources at your fingertips. Whether you're interested in bond investing, research on Latin American stocks, or some commonsense tips on mutual funds, you'll find the information and Internet resources you need right here. If the early bird gets the worm, the well-read, studious investor builds a successful investment plan. Happy wealth building.

APPENDIX

CNBC AND CNBC.COM RESOURCES

CNBC provides comprehensive business and financial news Monday through Friday from 5:00 A.M. to 8:00 P.M. EST, with real-time market coverage to more than 160 million homes worldwide, including more than 77 million households in the United States and Canada. The network's Business Day programming is produced at CNBC's headquarters in Fort Lee, N.J., with reports from CNBC news bureaus in Midtown Manhattan, the New York Stock Exchange, Washington, D.C., Chicago, Los Angeles, Palo Alto, London, and Singapore.

CNBC Pre-Market (5:00 A.M.–9:30 A.M./EST) programming gives you a head start on the business day, delivering breaking business news from overseas, a look at the day's top stories and a comprehensive rundown of what's in store for the day ahead.

- *Today's Business* (5:00 A.M.–7:00 A.M., Monday–Friday). The breakfast business briefing on important overnight developments such as mergers, earnings, and overseas action with live updates from CNBC's London and Singapore bureaus.

- *Squawk Box* (7:00 A.M.–10:00 A.M., Monday–Friday). The daily word on the street leading up to, and after, the opening bell. Host Mark Haines and CNBC analysts track the strategies of investment professionals, interview prominent business figures, and debate the latest insight from the street.

During Market Hours (9:30 A.M.–4:00 P.M./EST), CNBC is the only place to go for real-time financial news and information and in-depth play-by-play analysis of what's moving the markets and why.

- *Market Watch* (10:00 A.M.–12 Noon, Monday–Friday). Delivers the play-by-play on the daily tug-of-war between buyers and sellers from the worlds of business and finance.

- *Power Lunch* (12 Noon–2:00 P.M., Monday–Friday). An up-close and personal look at the companies, CEOs, and category trends impacting business.

- *Street Signs* (2:00 P.M.–4:00 P.M., Monday–Friday). The suspenseful last two hours of trading. Every twist and turn, winner and loser, is covered, along with the next day's potential. Features live location reports from traders on the floor and industry insiders.

After the Bell (4:00 P.M.–8:00 P.M./EST), CNBC provides a complete wrap-up of the day's events, plus a close look at extended trading hour activity in real time.

- *Market Wrap* (4:00 P.M.–6:00 P.M., Monday–Friday). A comprehensive analysis of the day, covering everything from hot stocks and corporate shake-ups to breaking news after the close. Includes in-studio interviews and extended hours updates.

- *The Edge* (6:00 P.M.–6:30 P.M., Monday–Friday). The first program of CNBC's broadcast day that advises viewers how to adjust their portfolios in anticipation of the next day's opening bell. Emerging trends, cutting-edge products, and extended hours trading are covered while top market analysts and business leaders share their views.

- *Business Center* (6:30 P.M.–8:00 P.M., Monday–Thursday; 6:30 P.M.–7:00 P.M., Friday). Direct from the floor of the New York Stock Exchange, a complete overview of the day's business and financial news.

- *Market Week* (7:30 P.M.–8:00 P.M., Friday). A decisive, reflective wrap-up of the business week in preparation for the next.

Features a wide range of guests, including analysts, traders, and CEOs to give viewers perspective and predictions from the inside.

CNBC.com is a fully integrated interactive Web site that reports original news, provides summaries of on-air news stories and guides to CNBC programming, and contains a full range of investment and personal finance tools including:

- Quotes
- Charts
- Personalized Ticker
- Message Boards
- Company Conference Calls
- Company News and Information
- Analyst Reports
- Insider Trading
- Industry Groups
- Advisor Newsletters
- Personal Resources such as Career Center, Women's Investment Center, Mortgage Center, Auto Loan Center, Home Equity Center, Small Biz Center, Loan Center, and Tax Center.

The CNBC Portfolio Tracker can help you follow your stocks quickly and easily from your computer. Portfolio Tracker can also alert you before the CEO of a company you've invested in appears on CNBC TV. In addition, you can receive real-time quotes (25 a day), a personalized ticker, and the CNBC.com daily newsletter (Money Mail). Portfolio Tracker allows you to keep tabs on all your investments and provides you with current quotes, insider trading information, valuations, and analyst and technical ratings. Called "Best of the Web" by *Money* magazine, Portfolio Tracker monitors market changes and news events related to your stocks, but it also keeps you updated throughout the day via e-mail alerts. And when a guest related to a company in your portfolio appears on CNBC TV, you will be alerted so you can watch firsthand as newsmakers discuss important issues that could affect your picks.

Portfolio Tracker can also send you price breakout alerts. Enter a low or high breakout price for your securities or enter percent price moves, and you'll receive e-mail alerts when a stock in your portfolio reaches the price.

With Portfolio Tracker, you will also have access to Account Tracker, a free service that securely keeps all your personal account balances and activities in one place with one password. And with Stock Screener, you can screen and scan for stocks and mutual funds that meet specific criteria you search on. From projected growth stocks to undervalued stock to stocks with insider buying, you can find the stocks that meet your investment criteria.

annuity   An annuity is a contract between an insurance company and a buyer. The buyer pays a premium, in one or several payments, and the insurance company agrees to pay the buyer a regular return for a specified period of time—usually, the remainder of the buyer's lifetime. The insurance company invests the money to earn interest, receive dividend income, or collect capital gains distributions. The insurance company then pays the buyer an income based on the terms of the contract. Annuities can be variable or fixed, deferred or immediate. A fixed annuity ensures that the insurance company will pay a set principal plus a set interest rate. Returns on a variable annuity, however, fluctuate based on the performance of the investments. With a deferred annuity, the premium gathers tax-free interest for a certain set period of time before payments to the buyer begin. Immediate annuities, on the other hand, establish a return for the buyer based on the buyer's age. Part of this return is considered principal and part of it is considered taxable interest. Thus, age, wealth, and risk tolerance will heavily influence the type of annuity an individual buyer selects.

asset   Assets include any of an individual's possessions that have economic value. The sum of one's assets is considered to be the individual's net worth. Assets include stocks, bonds, cash, real estate, jewelry, investments, and other properties.

asset allocation   Asset allocation refers to the specific distribution of funds among a number of different asset classes within an investment portfolio; it is diversification put into practice. Funds may be distributed among a number of different asset classes, such as stocks, bonds, and cash funds, each of which has unique types of expected risk and return. Within each asset class are several variations of the asset, meaning that there are levels of risk within each asset class. Asset allocation involves determining what percentage of funds will be invested in each asset. Determining how to allocate funds depends on the individual investor. The investor's goals, time frame, and risk tolerance will all affect how an investor wishes to allocate funds based on the investor's desired return and acceptable risk.

back-end load   A back-end load is a sales charge or fee charged when funds are withdrawn from an investment, particularly mutual funds and annuities. In many cases, the fee is reduced over the years of investment, or holding period, and eventually is reduced to zero.

bear   Someone who believes or speculates that a particular security, or the securities in a market, will decline in value is referred to as a bear.

bear market   A bear market is a market in which a group of securities falls in price or loses value over a period of time. A prolonged bear market may result in a decrease of 20 percent or more in market prices. A bear market in stocks may be due to investors' expectations of economic trends; in bonds, a bear market results from rising interest rates.

blue chip   Blue chip refers to companies that have become well established and reliable over time, and have demonstrated sound management and quality products and services. Such companies have shown an ability to function in both good and bad economic times and have usually paid dividends to investors even during lean years.

bond   A bond is essentially a loan made by an investor to a division of the government, a government agency, or a corporation. The bond is a promissory note to repay the loan in full at the end of a fixed time period. The date on which the principal must be repaid is called the *maturity date,* or *maturity*. In addition, the issuer of the bond—that is, the agency or corporation receiving the loan and issuing the promissory note—agrees to make regular payments of interest

at a rate initially stated on the bond. Interest from bonds is taxable, based on the type of bond. Corporate bonds are fully taxable; municipal bonds issued by state or local government agencies are free from federal income tax and usually free from taxes of the issuing jurisdiction; and Treasury bonds are subject to federal taxes but not state and local taxes. Bonds are rated according to many factors, including cost, degree of risk, and rate of income.

bull   Someone who believes that a particular security, or the securities in a market, will increase in value is known as a bull.

bull market   A bull market is a long period of rising prices of securities, usually by 20 percent or more. Bull markets generally involve heavy trading and are marked by a general upward trend in the market, independent of daily fluctuations.

capital gains   A capital gain is appreciation in the value of an asset— that is, when the selling price is greater than the original price at which the security was bought. The tax rate on capital gain depends on how long the security was held.

Certificate of Deposit   A Certificate of Deposit (CD) is a note issued by a bank for a savings deposit that the individual agrees to leave invested in the bank for a certain term. At the end of this term, on the maturity date, the principal may either be repaid to the individual or rolled over into another CD. The bank pays interest to the individual, and interest rates between banks are competitive. Monies deposited into a Certificate of

Deposit are insured by the bank; thus, they are a low-risk investment and a good way of maintaining a principal. Maturities may be as short as a few weeks or as long as several years. Most banks set heavy penalties for premature withdrawal of monies from a Certificate of Deposit.

commission   Commission is a fee charged by an agent who makes transactions of buying or selling securities for another individual. This fee is generally a percentage based on either the number of stocks bought or sold or the value of the stocks bought or sold.

credit risk   Credit risk refers primarily to the risk involved with debt investments, such as bonds. Credit risk is essentially the risk that the principal will not be repaid by the issuer. If the issuer fails to repay the principal, the issuer is said to default.

default   To default is to fail to repay the principal or make timely payments on a bond or other debt investment security issued. Also, a default is a breach of or a failure to fulfill the terms of a note or contract.

diversification   Diversification is the process of optimizing an investment portfolio by allocating funds to a number of different assets. Diversification minimizes risks while maximizing returns by spreading out risk across a number of investments. Different types of assets, such as stocks, bonds, and cash funds, carry different types of risk. For an optimal portfolio, it is important to diversify among assets with dissimilar risk levels. Investing in a number of assets allows for unexpected negative performances to balance out with or be superceded by positive performances.

dividend   A dividend is a payment, made by a company to its shareholders, that is a portion of the profits of the company. The amount to be paid is determined by the board of directors, and dividends may be paid even during a time when the company is not performing profitably. Mutual funds also pay dividends. These monies are paid from the income earned on the investments of the mutual fund. Dividends are paid on a schedule, such as quarterly, semiannually, or annually. Dividends may be paid directly to the investor or reinvested into more shares of the company's stock. Even if dividends are reinvested, the individual is responsible for paying taxes on the dividends. Unfortunately, dividends are not guaranteed and may vary each time they are paid.

Dow Jones Industrial Average   The Dow Jones Industrial Average is an index to which the performance of individual stocks can be compared; it is a means of measuring the change in stock prices. This index is a composite of 30 blue chip companies ranging from AT&T and Hewlett Packard to Kodak and Johnson & Johnson. These 30 companies represent not just the United States; rather, they are involved with commerce on a global scale. The DJIA is computed by adding the prices of these 30 stocks and dividing by an adjusted number that takes into account stock splits and other divisions that would interfere with the average. Stocks represented on the Dow Jones Industrial Average make up between 15 percent and 20 percent of the market.

equity   Equity is the total ownership or partial ownership an individual possesses minus any debts that are owed. Equity is the amount of interest shareholders hold in a company as a part of their rights of partial ownership. Equity is considered synonymous with ownership, a share of ownership, or the rights of ownership.

401(k) plan   A 401(k) plan is a retirement plan sponsored by employers. Employees may choose to have a portion of their salary deferred to any of the 401(k) investment choices selected by the employer. The employer may also contribute to the employees' 401(k) by matching a portion of the investment (for example, $.50 for every $1.00 the employee invests). The investments to which money is deferred may include stocks, bonds, money market funds, and company stocks. Monies deferred into the 401(k) are allowed to grow tax-free, and these monies are subtracted from the employees' taxable income. The maximum amount allowed to be contributed to a 410(k) changes annually. If money is withdrawn from the 401(k) before the employee turns 59 1/2, the individual may have to pay penalties. If the individual changes jobs, the monies in the 401(k) may be rolled over to a 401(k) of the new employer or to an Individual Retirement Account (IRA).

front-end load   A front-end load is a commission or fee that is charged when an investment is initially purchased. Investments that require a front-end load include mutual funds, annuities, and life insurance policies. Typically, the fee amount is a percentage of the net asset value of the investment.

going public   A company that has previously been privately owned is said to be "going public" the first time the company's stock is offered for public sale.

hedge   Hedging is a strategy of reducing risk by offsetting investments with investments of opposite risks. Risks must be negatively correlated in order to hedge each other—for example, an investment with high inflation risk and low immediate returns with investments with low inflation risk and high immediate returns. Long hedges protect against a short-term position, and short hedges protect against a long-term position. Hedging is not the same as diversification; it aims to protect against risk by counterbalancing a specific area of risk.

Individual Retirement Account (IRA)   An Individual Retirement Account allows individuals who are earning income to contribute to a tax-deferred investment fund. An individual can contribute up to $2,000 per year, or $4,000 if married to an unemployed spouse. Contributions to an IRA are tax-deductible, based on the individual's marriage status and income level. Monies contributed to an IRA may be invested in stocks, bonds, mutual funds, annuities, bank savings accounts, Certificates of Deposit, government bonds, and investment trusts, but not more personal and immediate investment such as a home or collectibles. The individual may contribute to the Individual Retirement Account until age 70 1/2, but if money is withdrawn before age 50 1/2, penalties will be incurred.

inflation risk   Inflation risk is the risk that rising prices of goods and services over time—or, generally the cost of living—will decrease the value of the return on investments. Inflation risk is also known as purchasing-power risk because it refers to increased prices of goods and services and a decreased value of cash.

junk bond   Junk bonds are bonds that are considered high yield but also have a high credit risk. They are generally low-rated bonds and are usually bought on speculation. Investors hope for the yield rather than the default. An investor with high risk tolerance may choose to invest in junk bonds.

Keogh Plan   The Keogh Plan is a type of tax-deductible retirement plan, similar to Individual Retirement Accounts, for self-employed individuals. It is also known as a self-employed pension plan. The individual may contribute up to $30,000 or 15 percent of total earned income per year, whichever is less.

liquidity   Liquidity refers to the ease with which investments can be converted to cash at their present market value. Additionally, liquidity is a condition of an investment that shows how greatly the investment price is affected by trading. An investment that is highly liquid is composed of enough units (such as shares) that many transactions can take place without greatly affecting the market price. High liquidity is associated with a high number of buyers and sellers trading investments at a high volume.

market risk   Market risk is the risk that investments will lose money based on the daily fluctuations of the market. Bond market risk results from fluctuations in interest. Stock prices, on the other hand, are influenced by factors ranging from company performance to economic factors to political news and events of national importance. Time is a stabilizing element in the stock market, as returns tend to outweigh risks over long periods of time. Market risk cannot be systematically diversified away.

market value   Market value is the value of an investment if it were to be resold, or the current price of a security being sold on the market.

modern portfolio theory   Aims to minimize the risks of investing while maximizing returns through the diversification of a portfolio. Diversification is the process of allocating funds among a number of different asset classes. Modern portfolio theory looks at three main factors in determining appropriate investments for an investor's portfolio: (1) the investor's goals and objectives for investing, (2) the time frame of investment, and (3) the investor's risk tolerance, or how comfortable the investor is with taking certain risks. Optimizing a portfolio according to modern portfolio theory involves matching the statistics of expected risk and return for a number of different assets with the individual's terms of investment.

mutual fund   Mutual funds are investment companies whose job it is to handle their investors' money by reinvesting it into stocks, bonds, or a combination of both. Because mutual funds are divided into shares and can be bought much like stocks, they have high liquidity. Mutual funds are convenient, particularly for small investors, because they diversify an individual's monies among a number of investments. Investors share in the profits of a mutual fund, and mutual fund shares can be sold back to the company on any business day at the net asset value price. Mutual funds may or may not have a load, or fee; however, funds with a load will provide advice from a specialist, which may help the investor in choosing a mutual fund.

NASD (National Association of Securities Dealers)   The National Association of Securities Dealers is an organization of broker/dealers who trade over-the-counter securities. The NASD is self-regulated. The largest self-regulated securities organization, this organization operates and regulates both the Nasdaq and over-the-counter markets, ensuring that securities are traded fairly and ethically.

Nasdaq (National Association of Securities Dealers Automated Quotation)   The National Association of Securities Dealers Automated Quotation is a global automated computer system that provides up-to-the-minute information on approximately 5,500 over-the-counter stocks. Whereas on the New York Stock Exchange (NYSE) securities are bought and sold on the trading floor, securities on the Nasdaq are traded via computer.

NAV (net asset value)   Net asset value is the price of a share in a mutual fund or investment company. This price is calculated once or twice daily. Net asset value is the amount by which the assets' value exceeds the company's liabilities. It is calculated by adding up the market value of all securities owned by the company, subtracting the company's liabilities, and dividing this value by the number of shares of the company outstanding. Thus, the NAV indicates the current buying or selling price of a share in an investment company.

NYSE (New York Stock Exchange)   Established in 1792, the New York Stock Exchange is the largest securities exchange in the United States. Securities are traded by brokers and dealers for customers on the trading floor at 11 Wall Street in New York City. The exchange is headed by a board of directors that includes a chairman and 20 representatives who represent both the public and the members of the exchange. This board approves applicants as new NYSE dealers, sets policies for the exchange, oversees the exchange, regulates members' activities, and lists securities.

option   An option is a security that can be bought as a contract to fix the price on another, underlying security. The buyer can pay the issuer of the option a premium that fixes the price on particular investments, including stocks, bonds, real estate, and others, for a specified period of time. The holder of the option can choose to buy or sell the underlying security at the fixed price during this time period; however, the holder is under no obligation to buy. For example, if the holder purchases an option to buy a stock at $30, the individual may not wish to buy the stock during the time period of the option if the shares are being sold for $27. However, if the shares are being sold for $33, the holder will save $3 per share with the option. Thus, options may or may not prove advantageous to the holder.

price–earnings ratio   The price-earnings ratio is a measure of how much buyers are willing to pay for shares in a company, based on that company's earnings. The price-earnings ratio is calculated by dividing the current price of a share in a company by the most recent year's earnings per share of the company. This ratio is a useful way of comparing the value of stocks and helps to indicate expectations for the company's growth in earnings. It is important, however, to compare the P/E ratios of companies in similar industries. The price-earnings ratio is sometimes also called the "multiple."

quotation   A quotation, or quote, refers to the current price of a security, be it either the highest bid price for that security or the lowest ask price.

real rate of return   The real rate of return refers to the annual return on an investment after being adjusted for inflation and taxes.

reinvest   Reinvestment is the use of capital gains, including interest, dividends, or profit, to buy more of the same investment. For example, the dividends received from stock holdings may be reinvested by buying more shares of the same stock.

SEC (Securities and Exchange Commission)   The Securities and Exchange Commission is a federal government agency comprised of five commissioners appointed by the President and approved by the Senate. The SEC was established to protect individual investors from fraud and malpractice in the marketplace. The Commission oversees and regulates the activities of registered investment advisors, stock and bond markets, broker/dealers, and mutual funds.

security   A security is any investment purchased with the expectation of making a profit. Securities include total or partial ownership of an asset, rights to ownership of an asset, and certificates of debt from an institution. Examples of securities include stocks, bonds, certificates of deposit, and options.

S&P (Standard & Poor's) 500 Index   The Standard & Poor's 500 Index is a market index of 500 of the top-performing U.S. corporations. This index, a broader measure of the domestic market than the Dow Jones Industrial Average, indicates broad market changes. The S&P 500 Index includes 400 industrial firms, 20 transportation firms, 40 utilities, and 40 financial firms.

split   A split occurs when a company's board of directors and shareholders agree to increase the number of shares outstanding. The shareholders' equity does not change; instead, the number of shares increases while the value of each share decreases proportionally. For example, in a 2-for-1 split, a shareholder with 100 shares prior to the split would now own 200 shares. The price of the shares, however, would be cut in half; shares that cost $40 before the split would be worth $20 after the split.

ticker   The ticker displays information on a movable tape or, in modern times, as a scrolling electronic display on a screen. The symbols and numbers shown on the ticker indicate the security being traded, the latest sale price of the security, and the volume of the most recent transaction.

underwriter   An underwriter is an individual who distributes securities as an intermediary between the issuer and the buyer of the securities. For example, an underwriter may be the agent selling insurance policies or the person distributing shares of a mutual fund to broker/dealers or investors. Generally, the underwriter agrees to purchase the remaining units of the security, such as remaining shares of stocks or bonds, from the issuer if the public does not buy all specified units.

An underwriter may also be a company that backs the issue of a contract by agreeing to accept responsibility for fulfilling the contract in return for a premium.

volatility   Volatility is an indicator of expected risk. It demonstrates the degree to which the market price of an asset, rate, or index fluctuates from the average. Volatility is calculated by finding the standard deviation from the mean, or average, return.

warrant   A warrant is similar to an option. It gives the holder the right to purchase securities at a set price for a specific period of time. Warrant certificates last longer than options, typically holding value for a few years or indefinitely. Warrants are often traded as securities at a price that reflects the underlying security.

yield   Yield is the return, or profit, on an investment. Yield refers to the interest gained on a bond or the rate of return on an investment, such as dividends paid on a mutual fund. Yield does not include capital gains.

INDEX